IMAGES of America

HILL COUNTY

I0806292

On the Cover: A parade commemorated the Fourth of July in 1914. The Lou Lucke Company was one of several businesses that entered a float in the parade. Behind the vehicle is the Mathews home, located at 124 Third Street. John Mathews was a bookkeeper for Board of Trade Saloon owner Pat Yeon. The home is among the oldest in Havre. (Courtesy of the Clack Museum.)

IMAGES
of America

HILL COUNTY

Emily Ann Mayer and the Clack Museum

ARCADIA
PUBLISHING

ISBN 978-0-7385-6933-8

Published by Arcadia Publishing
Charleston SC, Chicago IL, Portsmouth NH, San Francisco CA

Printed in the United States of America

Library of Congress Control Number: 2008940177

For all general information contact Arcadia Publishing at:
Telephone 843-853-2070
Fax 843-853-0044
E-mail sales@arcadiapublishing.com
For customer service and orders:
Toll-Free 1-888-313-2665

Visit us on the Internet at www.arcadiapublishing.com

This book is dedicated to my parents, Mark and Darleen Mayer; all photographers past, present, and future; and Lou Lucke, whose help is greatly appreciated.

Contents

ACKNOWLEDGMENTS

Special thanks go to the following for allowing the use of photographs and providing information, guidance, and encouragement for this publication: MSU-Northern Archives/Al Lucke Collection; Emily Mayer Photograph Collection; Montana Historical Society; Clack Museum/Wahkpa Chu'gn Buffalo Jump, especially John and Cheryl Gilbert; Havre Beneath the Streets; Frank DeRosa Memorial Railroad Museum; Fort Assinniboine Preservation Association; Rudyard Historical Society, especially Martha Jurenka, Bonnie Terry, Cliff Ulmen, and Bud Een; Gary Wilson; Ruth Morse; Palace Bar/Jupe Compton; Floyd Whaley; Elinor Clack; Toni Hagener; Arnold Peterson; Paula Kase; Eunice DeRosa; Jim Yeon; *Havre Daily News*; Havre/Hill County Library; Jim Faber; Havre Elks; Dorothy Cady; Lilas McCormick; Arvid Kristoffersen; Susie Leonard; and Floyd Witt. Thanks to Virginia Naber, who suggested to Arcadia that I might be interested in writing this book; to the IGA Photo Department crew for processing my film; to Lou Lucke for all his help scanning (and sometimes re-scanning!) photographs, providing information, and offering encouragement when I needed it the most; and to my editors, John Poultney and Hannah Carney, for their patience and expertise.

INTRODUCTION

Hill County, Montana, was formed on February 28, 1912, as a result of an election; however, its start began millions of years ago. The area was once underwater and also hosted a tropical climate. Aquatic and land dinosaurs roamed the land and sea, and rare fossil samples can be found in Hill County. The Rudyard area in particular yields fantastic specimens, and some are housed in the Rudyard Depot Museum's dinosaur building. Jack Horner, a dinosaur expert from Montana State University–Bozeman's Museum of the Rockies and of *Jurassic Park* fame, assisted in developing the exhibits and preservation of these precious finds.

Ancient peoples occupied Hill County long before Caucasians arrived. As testament, Wahkpa Chu'gn Buffalo Jump, the first site in Hill County to be placed on the National Register of Historic Places, literally shows the layers of history of the people who used the site to process buffalo for food, clothing, and shelter. Many Native American tribes such as the Blackfeet, Assinniboine, Gros Ventre, Chippewa, and Cree hunted buffalo and other wildlife, fished the streams, and lived off the land.

Fort Assinniboine was established after the Battle of the Little Big Horn near Hardin, Montana, and the Battle of the Bear Paws, 16 miles south of Chinook, Montana, about 20 miles to the east of Havre. The fort was constructed so fast that Native American tribes described it as "rising from the earth." There were no major Native American battles fought at the fort; the biggest enemy was boredom. The arrival of the railroad made going absent without leave much easier.

When Fort Assinniboine was being built, there were already a few Caucasian settlers in the area. Fort Assinniboine brought more Caucasians, as well as the Buffalo Soldiers, African American troops of the U.S. Army. When the St. Paul, Minneapolis, and Manitoba Railroad arrived in September 1887, Japanese and some Chinese were employed to help build the rails. With the railroad came more settlers seeking land, business opportunities, and the hope of a prosperous life. With all of the cultures already living here and those that arrived later, Hill County can aptly be described as a melting pot of cultures, for better or worse.

Havre's beginnings were modest, with tents being used for both businesses and housing. Later wood-frame buildings were constructed. The Great Fire of 1904 changed the business district's building practices to those of concrete, brick, or stone as main building materials, as passed by city ordinance. As incomes increased, beautiful homes were built to show progress and the good fortunes of the successful ones. Modest homes of workers were nestled among the grander homes, proof that it takes people from all walks of life to create a community. Furthermore, vice establishments such as brothels and illegal gambling halls were within a stone's throw of respectable, legitimate businesses. What little law enforcement existed was ineffective during Havre's early days. With the advent of Prohibition and Hill County's proximity to Canada, adventurous entrepreneurs willing to take a chance ran illegal booze from our northern neighbors into Hill County. From there, speakeasies were able to quench the thirst of willing patrons.

The Homestead Act brought many people seeking a "free farm from Uncle Sam." Population increased, and towns such as Kremlin, Gildford, Hingham, Rudyard, Simpson, Cottonwood, Goldstone, and Lilacs were created, among many others. Some towns consisted of at least a post office, a school nearby, and perhaps a general store. Over the years, these little towns consolidated with others or ceased all together.

Hill County can be a land of extremes: hot, cold, precipitation (too much rain, hail, or snow or none at all), wind, long distances between places, feast, famine. Floods from the Milk River and its tributaries were major occurrences and sometimes deadly. Winds have been known to blow over brick buildings. A trip to town could take days by horse-drawn wagon. There is nothing fun about 100-degree-plus temperatures in the summer and 40 below zero in the winter. The ever-present gentle Montana breezes that can reach hurricane force make it worse. Because of the economic, social, and weather-related hardships, the people of Hill County, especially its longtime residents, are a hardy breed who, through it all, choose to stay.

Life in Hill County has progressed, but the old-fashioned values and lessons in life are carried on by those who hold them dear. It isn't all work; Hill County residents are known to join church and civic organizations to perform various charitable contributions and public service projects to better the community. Hill County has a wealth of cultural, educational, recreational, and entertainment opportunities: the annual Rocky Boy Pow-Wow on nearby Rocky Boy Reservation is held every August, and the Chippewa-Cree tribe is gracious in teaching others about their traditions; programs available at the Havre/Hill County Library, Montana State University–Northern, Stone Child College, public schools, and museums entice residents to increase their knowledge on a myriad of subjects; and there are performing arts concerts and plays to attend. Sports are very popular in Hill County. From middle school to high school, college, and leagues, there is something for everyone to participate in and have fun. Beaver Creek Park, the largest county park in the United States, is located only a few short miles from Havre and offers fishing, hiking, biking, and camping opportunities. Fresno Reservoir, located east of Havre, also offers fishing and various choices of water sports. Winter does not hamper Hill County residents; ice fishing, ice skating, and hockey are popular, as are skiing and snowboarding at the Bear Paw Ski Bowl on Rocky Boy Reservation. In addition, a lot of local artistic talent can be seen throughout the community.

Hill County might be small in population—only about 17,000 according to the 2000 census—but we tend to keep busy with family, church, and social activities. There is always something to do here, and we take immense pride in our heritage and invite others to at least visit and maybe even stay if you find it to your liking.

One

Hill County

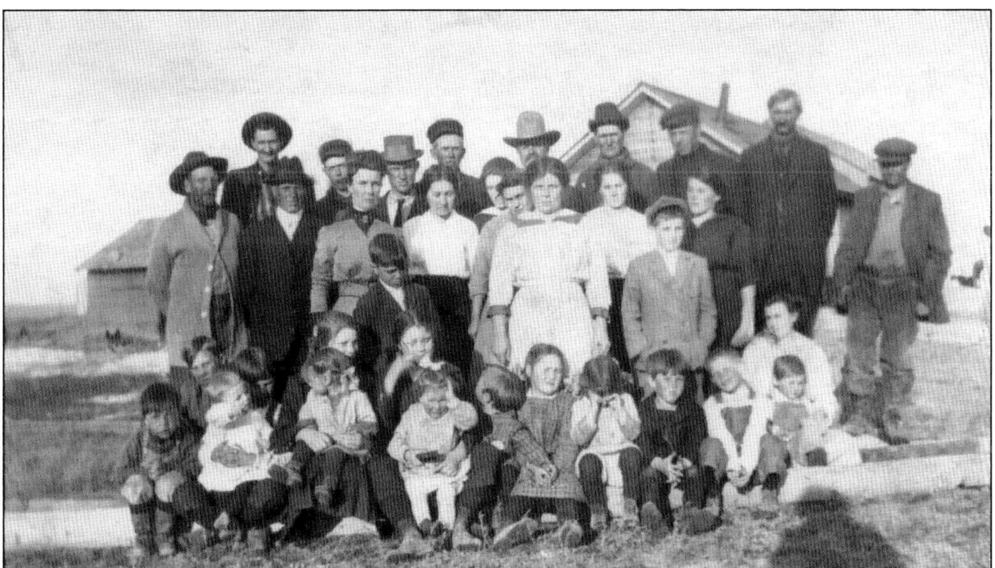

Farming in the early 1900s was no easy task, but the Simpson community found time to celebrate Easter in 1917 at the Joe Cable homestead. Pictured are those who attended the festivities, including the Bunton, Whaley, Brower, Pailthorp, Stuwe, McDougal, and Penrod families. The day must have been very sunny, based on the children squinting and shielding their eyes from the bright light. (Courtesy of Emily Mayer.)

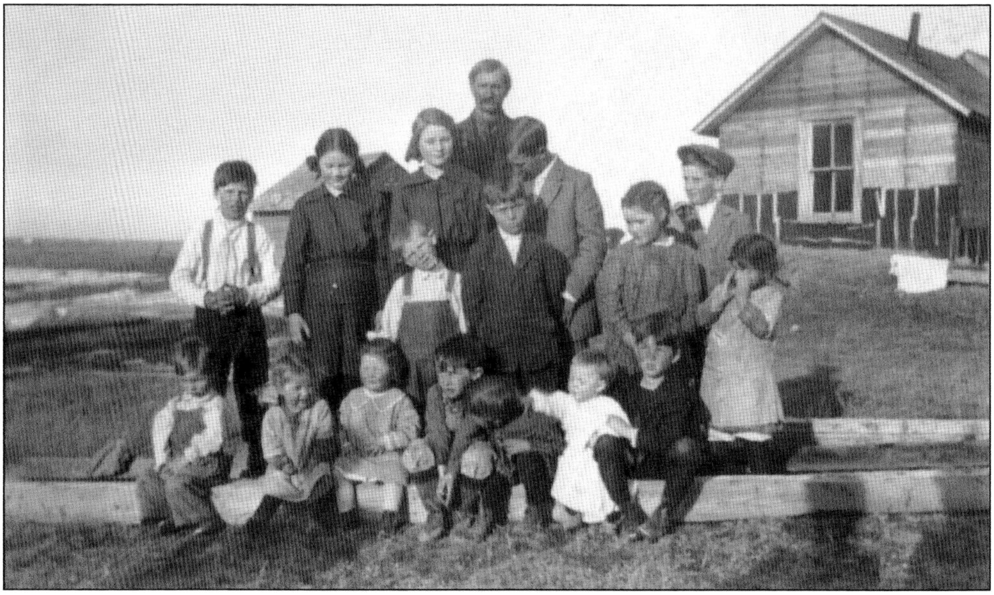

The children of Simpson dressed in their Easter Sunday best. Shown are, from left to right, (first row) Wesley Whaley, Violet Bunton, unidentified, Lester Stuwe, two unidentified, and A. J. Bunton; (second row) Floyd Whaley, Harold "Fat" Bunton, and two unidentified; (third row) a Brower boy, Vera Bunton, Freda Bunton, Joe Cable (centered in the back), unidentified, and Ross Pailthorp. (Courtesy of Emily Mayer.)

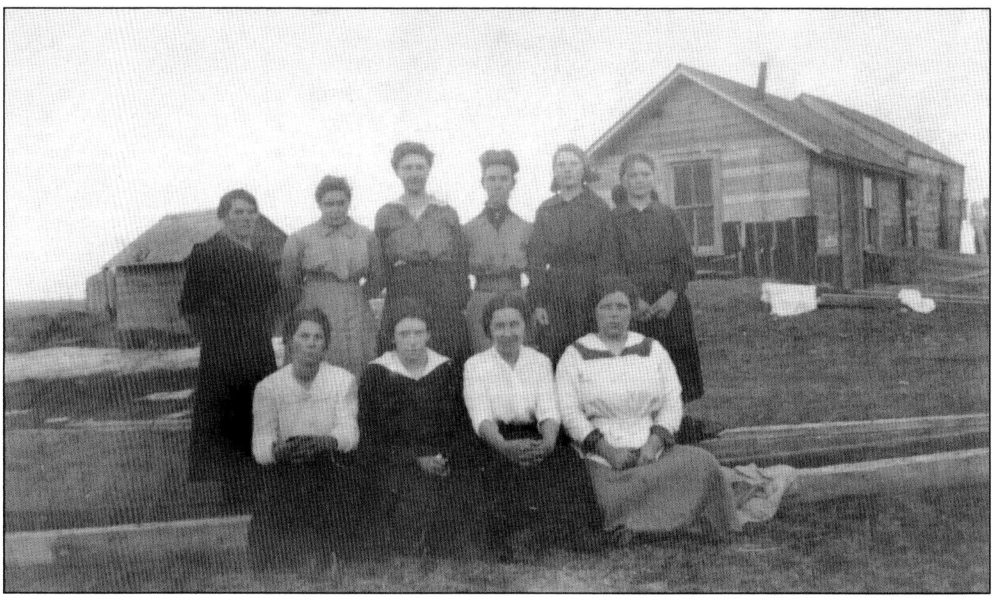

The women of Simpson, who probably worked very hard all day to prepare the Easter feast, included, from left to right, (first row) Clara Stuwe, Nellie Brower, ? Penrod, and Myrtle Bunton; (second row) unidentified, ? McDougal, unidentified, ? Brower, Freda Bunton, and Vera Bunton. The Cable homestead stands in the background, complete with tar paper and shiplap siding. (Courtesy of Emily Mayer.)

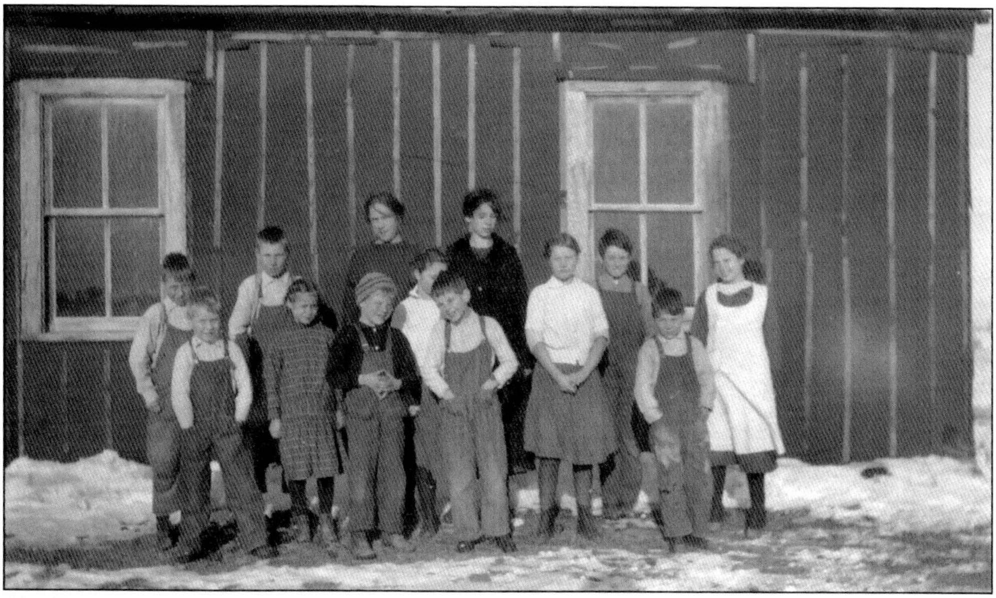

The First Spring Coulee School was located near Simpson, about 36 miles north of Havre. The school was originally the John Bentz house and was refurbished to serve as the school. Over time, the tar paper was replaced by clapboard siding. The school was last updated in 1955. After the school closed, it remained vacant until 1997, when it was moved west of Havre, where it still stands today. (Courtesy of Ruth Morse.)

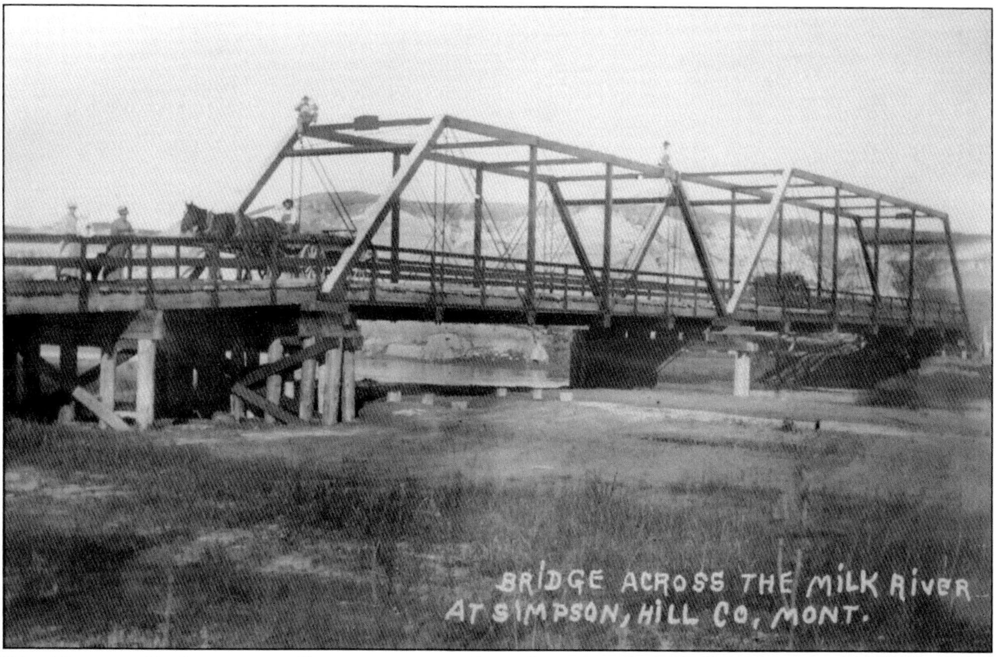

The Simpson Bridge was vitally important to those living in the area for commerce, for delivering mail, and holding celebrations. When the bridge was out of service, it disrupted the lives of many people. It was so important when it burned in 1928 that several people recalled how it affected them nearly 40 years later in a community memoir, *In Days Gone By*. (Courtesy of the Rudyard Historical Society.)

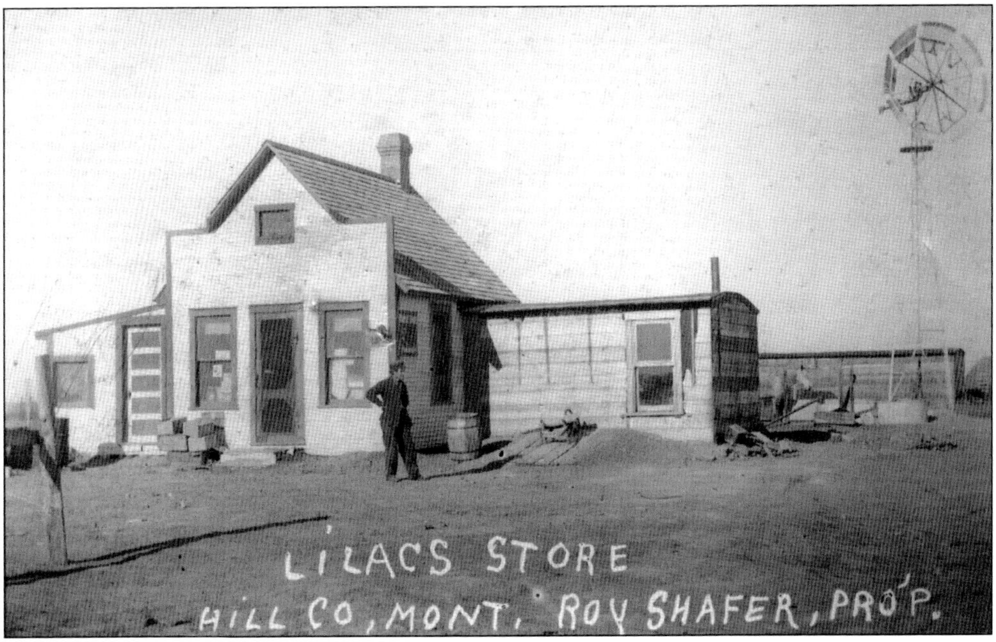

Lilacs was a homestead community located north of Gildford. The Lilacs Store, pictured here, also served as a post office from 1911 to 1914, with Mabel Claviter as postmaster. After the Lilacs Post Office closed, mail was delivered to Fairchild, about 6 miles north of Lilacs. The shack to the right was a later addition to the building. Pictured is Roy Shafer, owner of the Lilacs Store. (Courtesy of the Rudyard Historical Society.)

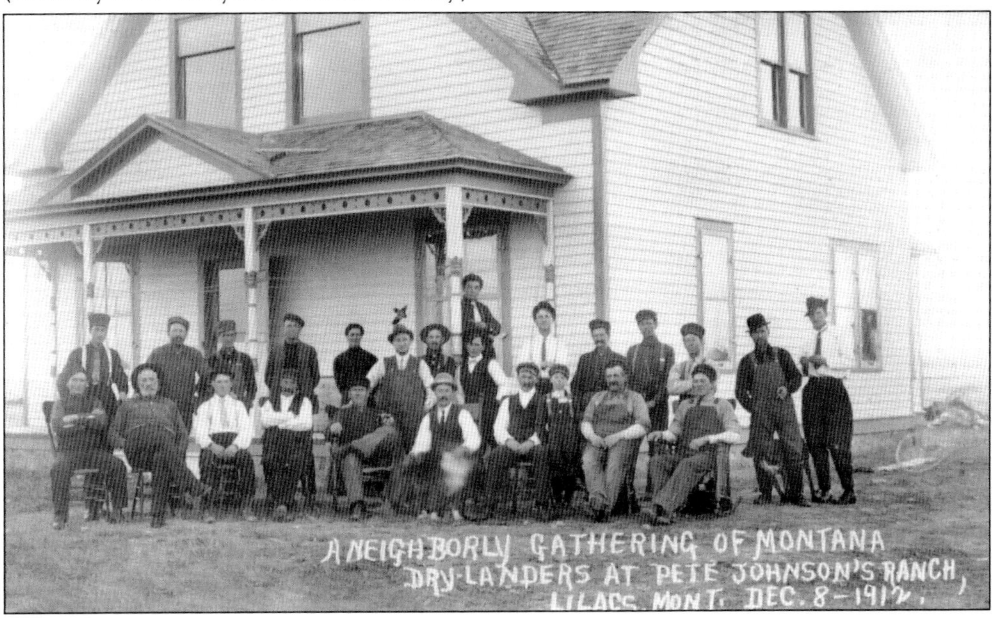

"A Neighborly Gathering of Montana Dry-Landers at Pete Johnson's Ranch, Lilacs, Montana, December 8, 1912" indicates an "open winter," or perhaps a chinook, with no snow pictured and men wearing light jackets. Out of all the men photographed, only two have been identified: Lars Kapperud is standing on the porch near the pillar, and sitting in the first row, second from left, is ranch owner Pete Johnson. (Courtesy of the Rudyard Historical Society.)

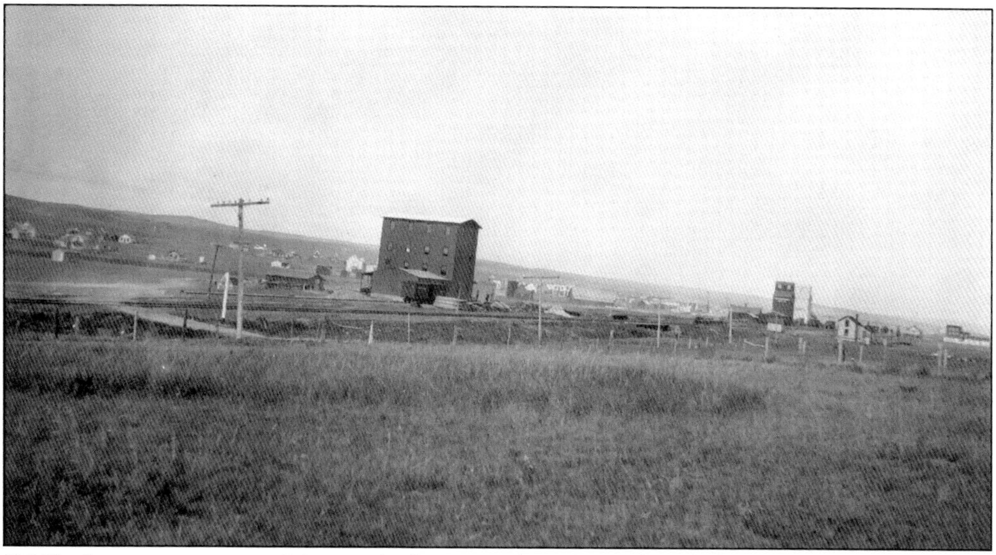

Gildford was a town created during the homestead era. It was founded in 1910 and over time had at least seven lumberyards, two hotels, three saloons, four livery stables, two banks, a newspaper, general stores, and grain elevators. The first school opened in 1911, and 1915 saw the completion of a church. (Courtesy of MSU-Northern, Al Lucke Collection.)

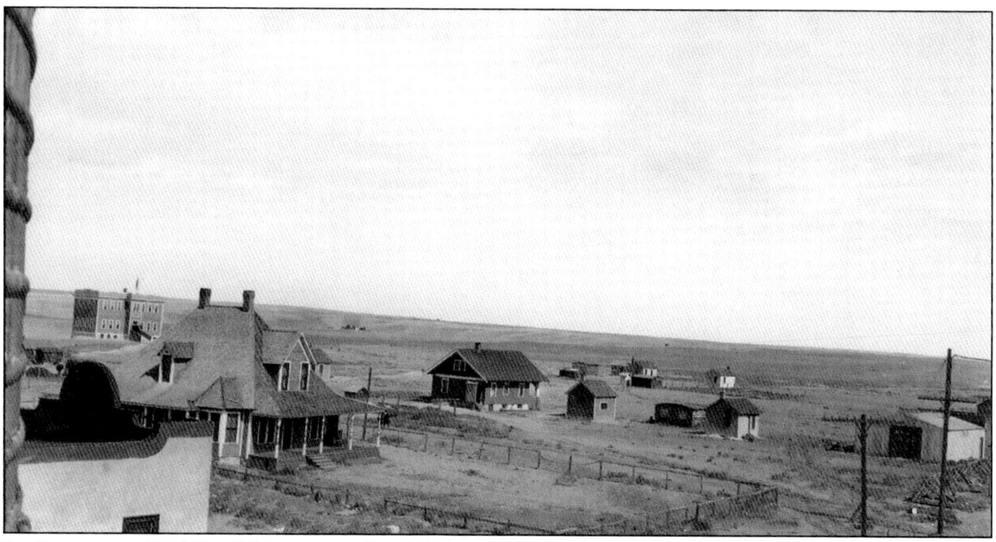

In this view of Gildford, Montana, the Schwartz House can be seen on the left of the photograph. It was the first home constructed in Gildford and was built in 1904. The Schwartz family came to the area some time in the 1890s and lived in Dayton. It was located only a mile west of present-day Gildford. Mrs. H. F. Schwartz served as Dayton's postmaster. Just up from the Schwartz House is the Gildford School, constructed in 1912. (Courtesy of MSU-Northern, Al Lucke Collection.)

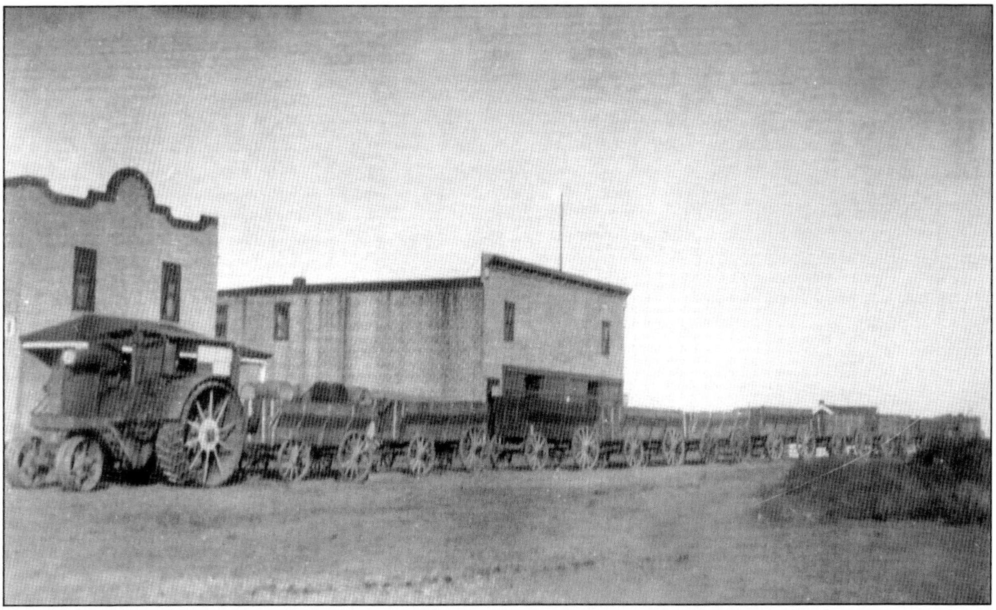

Freighting was no easy task in Gildford, Montana, or anywhere else. The Gildford Hotel is located on the left of the photograph and is north of the railroad tracks. The Gildford Hotel is in a modified mission style. This style of architecture was popular in California and is defined by curvaceous parapets, or walls that rise above the roofline. While the building does not have all mission elements, the intent is clear with its false front. (Courtesy of the Rudyard Historical Society.)

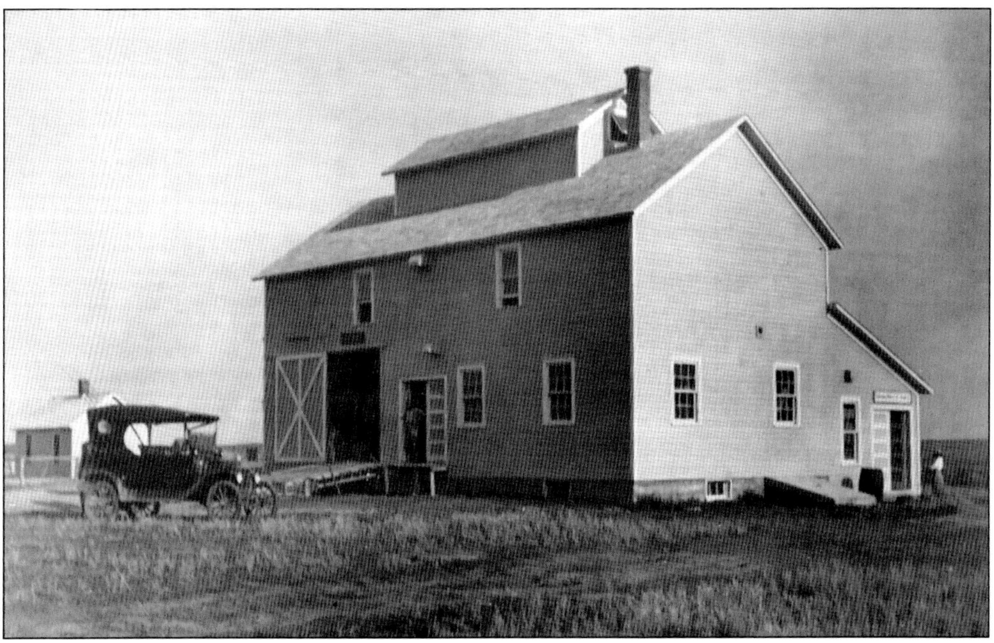

The Gildford Roller Mill was owned by Fred Mundy. It was built in 1915 and started its operation on Labor Day of that year. People would bring in their wheat to be made into the flour so necessary for survival in Hill County. By all accounts, Mundy was a fair man in his business. The Gildford Roller Mill operated until 1951. Mundy served as a senator in the Montana Legislature in later years. (Courtesy of the Rudyard Historical Society.)

Two men show the sizes of flour offered by the Gildford Roller Mill. Flour sacks played a quiet but useful role in the lives of many housewives. Some mills offered patterned flour sacks, which were collected by thrifty housewives and in turn were used to make clothing, quilts, and other items. Those who have used authentic flour sacks to dry dishes will testify, "They don't make them like they used to!" (Courtesy of the Rudyard Historical Society.)

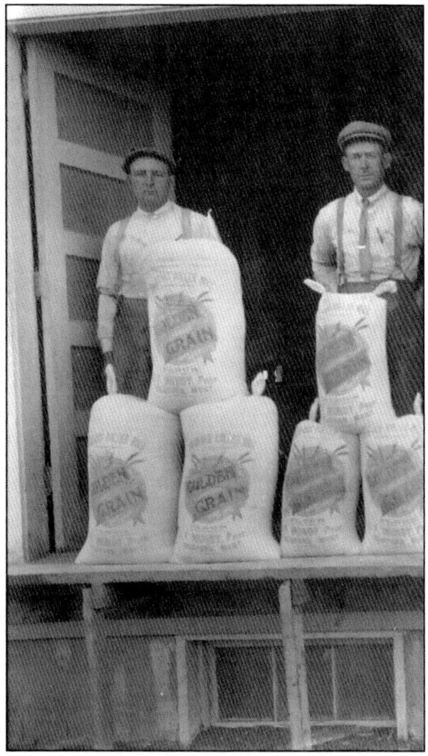

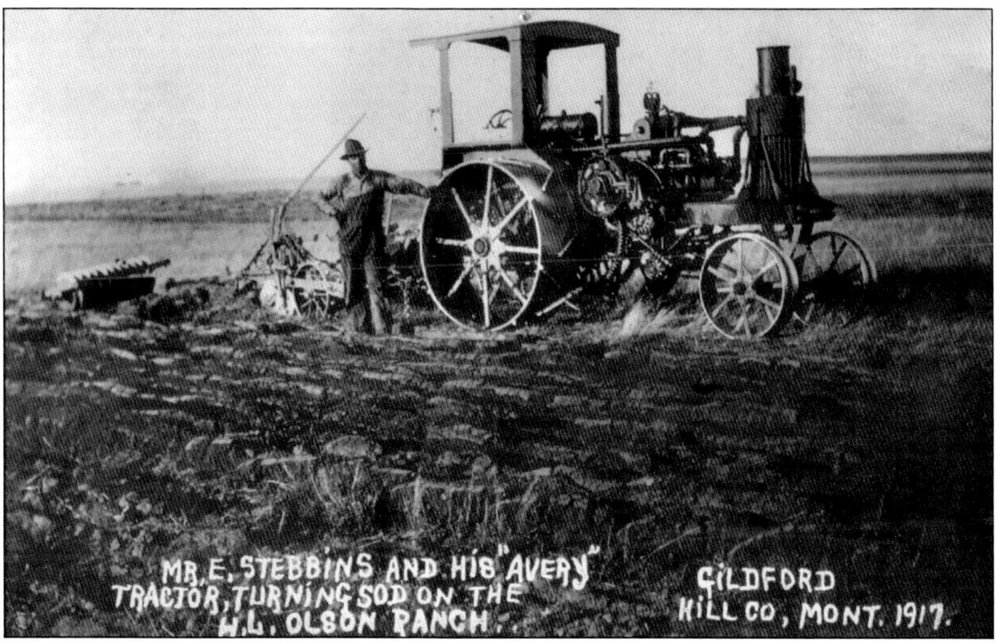

E. Stebbins and his Avery tractor turn sod on the H. L. Olson Ranch near Gildford. Gas-powered tractors replaced horse-drawn plows and made the job of turning sod much easier and faster for the farmer. Subsequently, crops were planted, mostly wheat, and barring unforeseen circumstances such as no rain, hot weather, hail, and/or grasshoppers, a successful harvest could be almost expected. (Courtesy of the Rudyard Historical Society.)

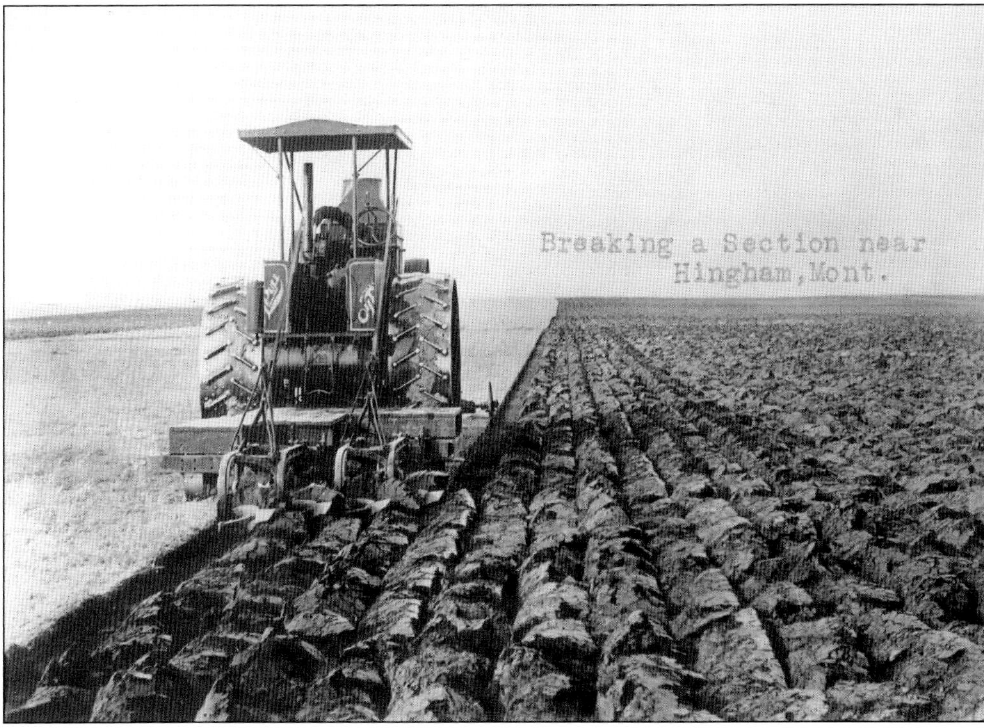

This image shows men breaking sod near Hingham, Montana. Hingham was another Hill County town founded by homesteaders in the area. It was founded in 1910. Over Hingham's history have been hotels, a newspaper, harness shop, livery stables, general stores, a blacksmith shop, lumberyards, implement stores, and two hospitals. In September, Hingham hosted the Hi-Line Fair, which gave farmers and ranchers the opportunity to showcase their crops and livestock. (Courtesy of MSU-Northern, Al Lucke Collection.)

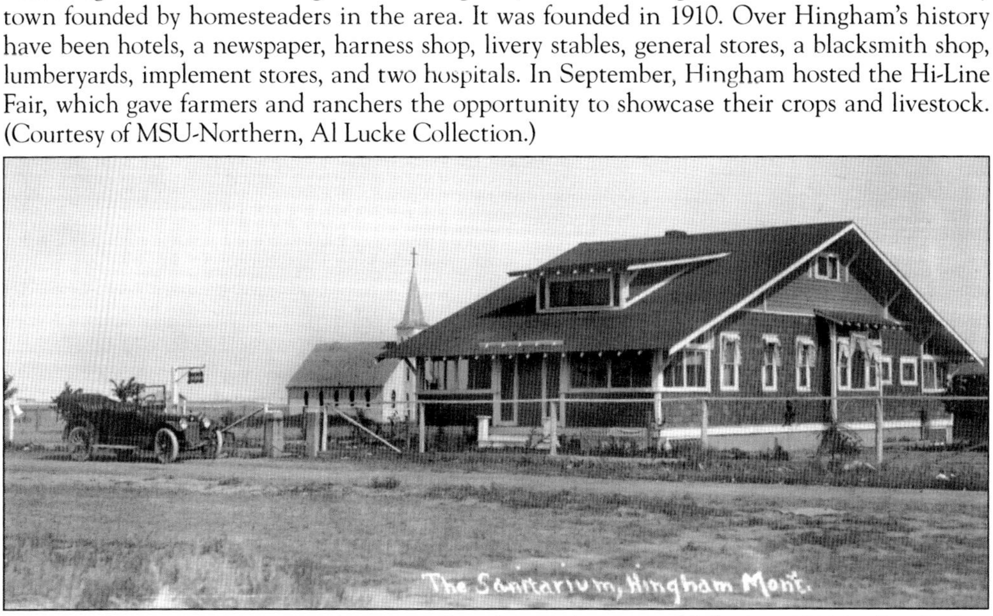

The Hingham Sanitarium, another name for a hospital, was established in 1913 by Dr. Arthur Husser. He arrived in Hingham a year earlier at the request of the Hingham Commercial Club. Nurses and aides assisted in the operation. It was considered to be a modern facility and an asset to the area. In December 1919, a fire resulting from an overheated furnace destroyed the sanitarium. Patients were moved to nearby homes. (Courtesy of the Rudyard Historical Society and Eunice DeRosa.)

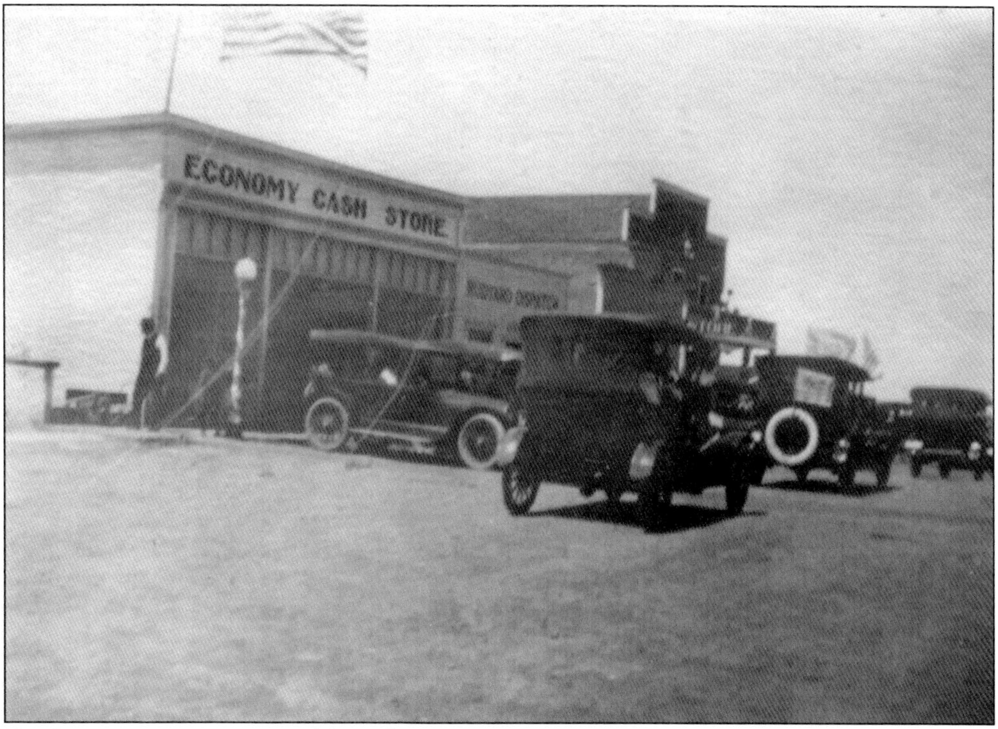

Flag Day, June 14, 1918, was celebrated with gatherings and other activities in Rudyard, along with proud, prominent displays of the flag. Pictured are the Economy Cash Store, *Rudyard Dispatch* (its first newspaper), and a couple of other stores in downtown Rudyard. (Courtesy of the Rudyard Historical Society.)

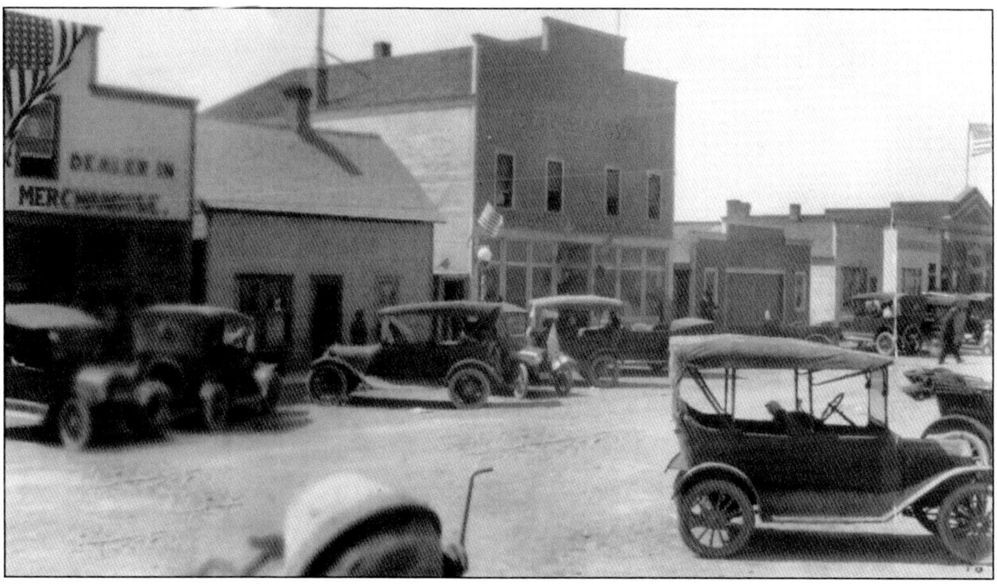

The General Store and Kimpel-Jenson Implement and Hardware Store are pictured in downtown Rudyard on Flag Day 1918. On the right of the photograph are the Farmer's State Bank and Rudyard's second bank. The day appears to be very windy, something most residents of Hill County know well and come to expect. (Courtesy of the Rudyard Historical Society.)

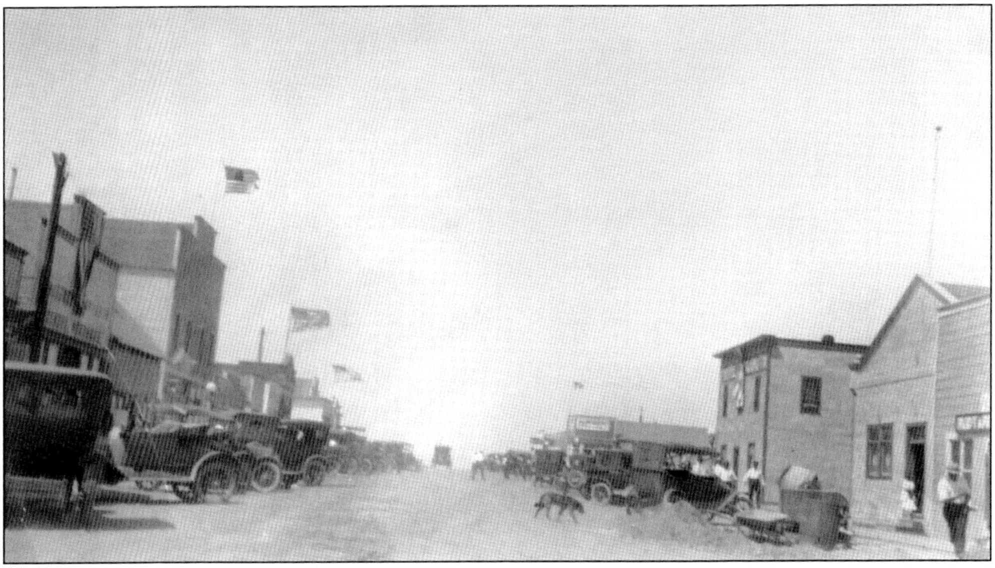

A view of downtown Rudyard faces north on Flag Day 1918. The Hotel Spannuth is the third building from the right, and the second building from left is a general store. The brick bank building can be seen a short distance from the store. (Courtesy of the Rudyard Historical Society.)

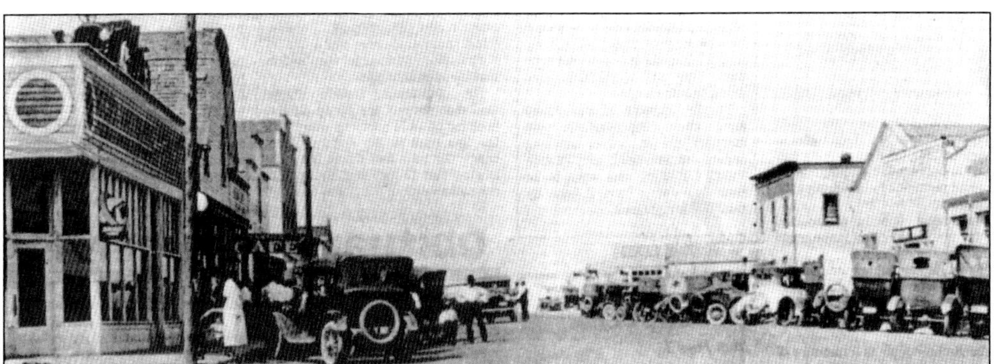

This photograph of early downtown Rudyard shows a vibrant, active area of commerce. The residents of Rudyard, like many in rural America, were quick to adopt the automobile as a form of transportation. The arrival of the automobile made travel much easier, especially for those who lived many miles from the nearest town. (Courtesy of the Rudyard Historical Society.)

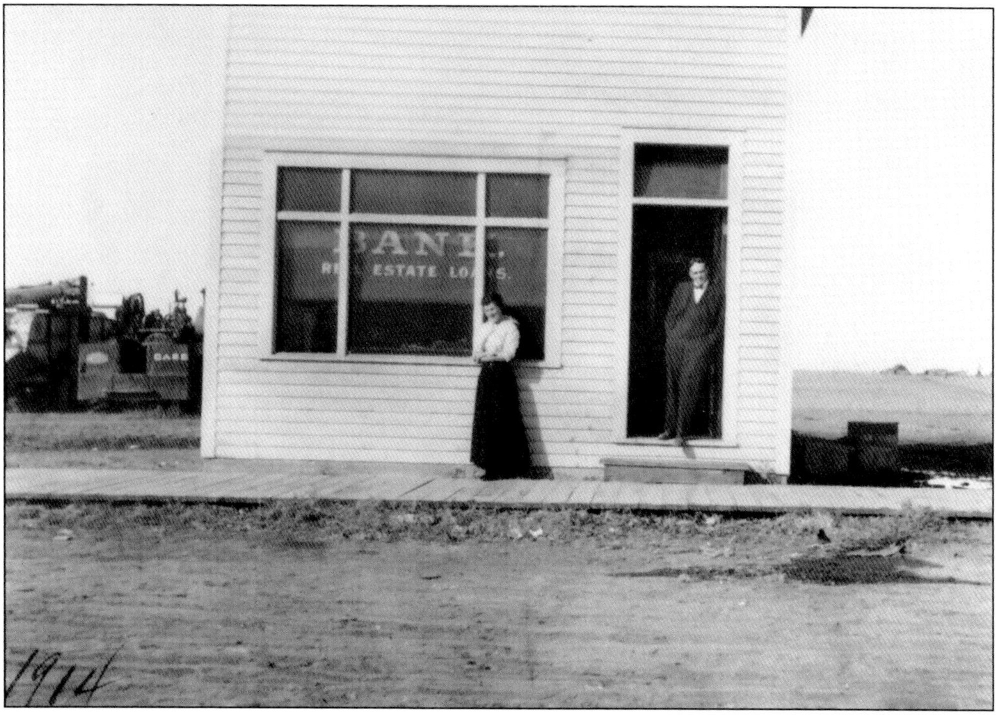

Rudyard's first bank was the Farmer's State Bank, a branch of a Hingham bank. It opened in 1914 with O. B. Wellan, Otto M. Rigg, and E. Koefod as directors. Koefod also served as cashier. The Rudyard Farmer's State Bank was capitalized at $20,000. (Courtesy of the Rudyard Historical Society.)

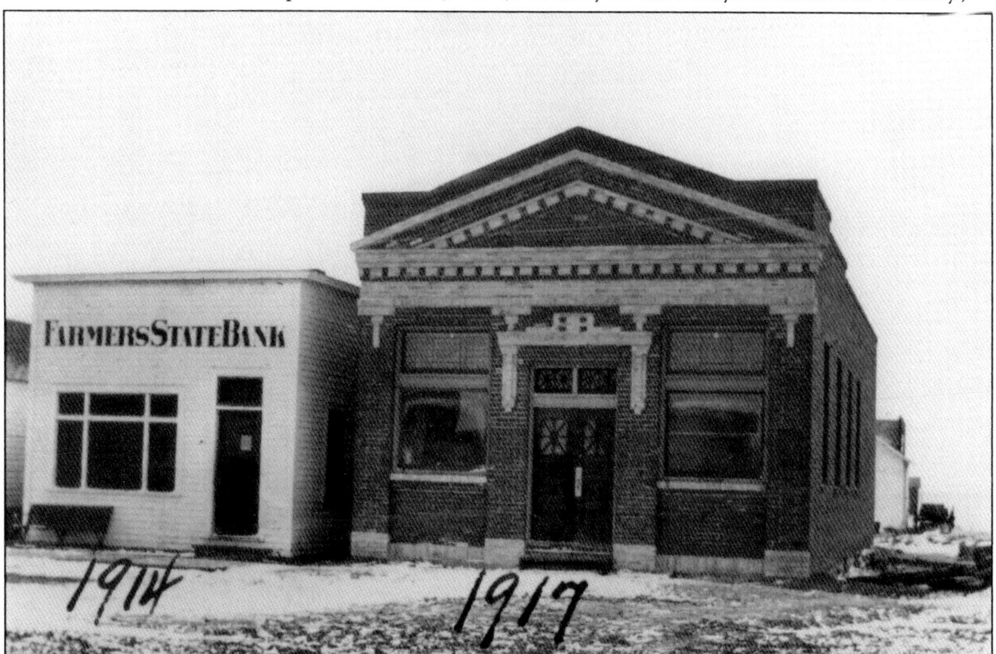

A few years later, a second bank in Rudyard opened right next door. The second bank, a brick building, later became the Bank Bar. (Courtesy of the Rudyard Historical Society.)

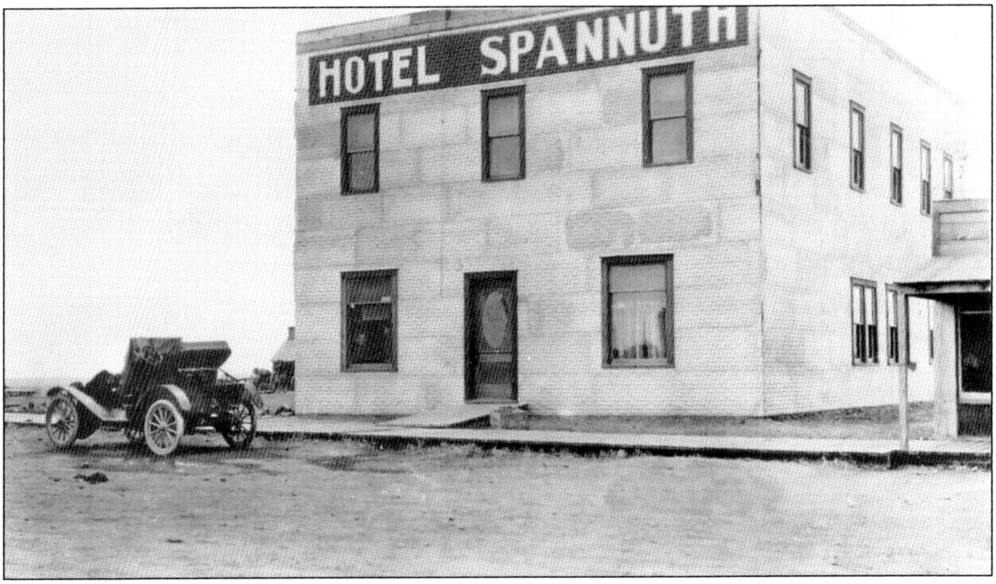

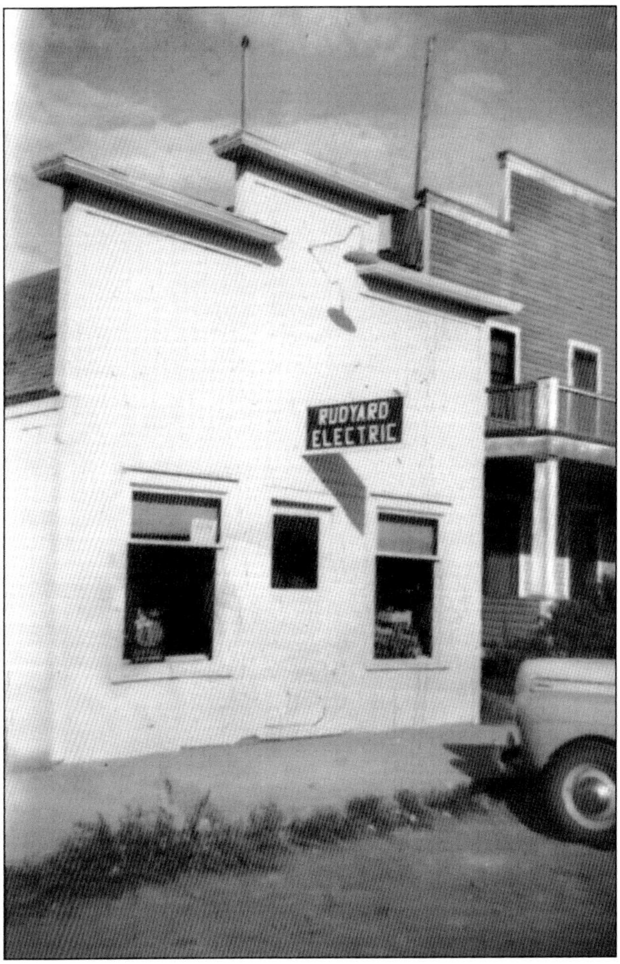

The Hotel Spannuth was constructed around 1910–1912. It had 10 rooms, a large lobby, and dining room. Br. Walter Van Orsdel is said to have preached in the lobby some time prior to 1914. The hotel quickly became the center of social functions. Fred Spannuth owned an auto livery, delivering Great Northern Railroad passengers and light freight within the city limits. (Courtesy of the Rudyard Historical Society.)

The Rudyard Electric Company was owned by Bud Een and Cliff Ulmen from 1946 to 1947. Een learned the electrical trade while serving in the army. The Rudyard Electric Company served the local area and was sold to Chuck Cross. The building was located between a hotel and a beauty parlor. It was later torn down. (Courtesy of the Rudyard Historical Society.)

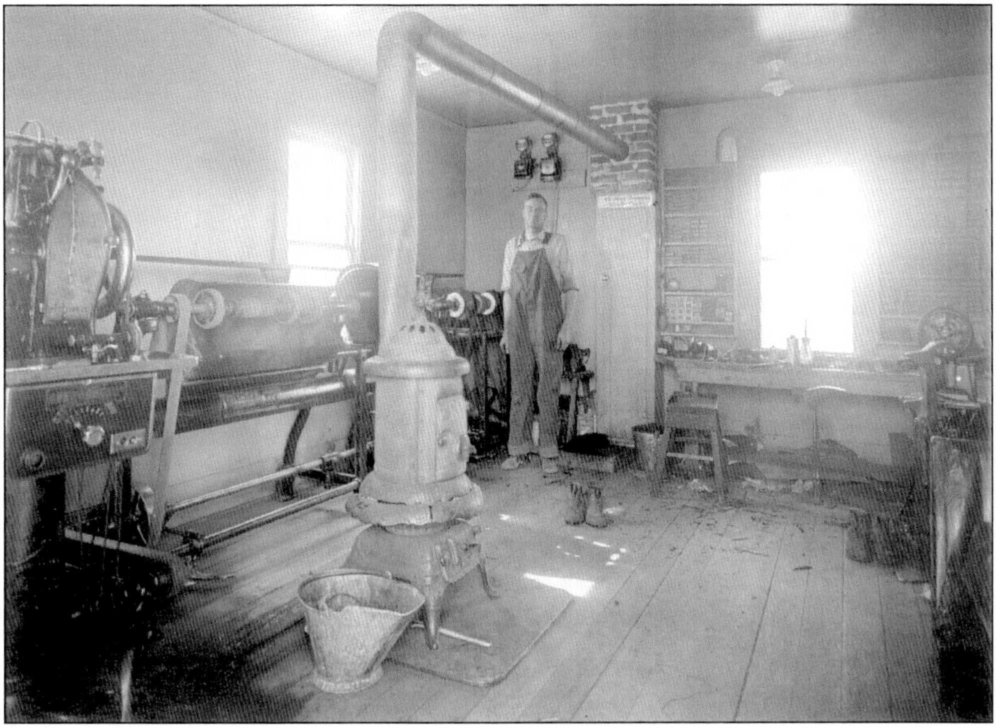

Albert Berge owned the Shoe Hospital in Rudyard. Cobblers were vitally important to frontier towns, as they not only repaired shoes, they also custom made them for their clients. Some cobblers had established shops for customers to patronize; others traveled the countryside offering their services to homesteaders and other residents of rural America. (Courtesy of the Rudyard Historical Society.)

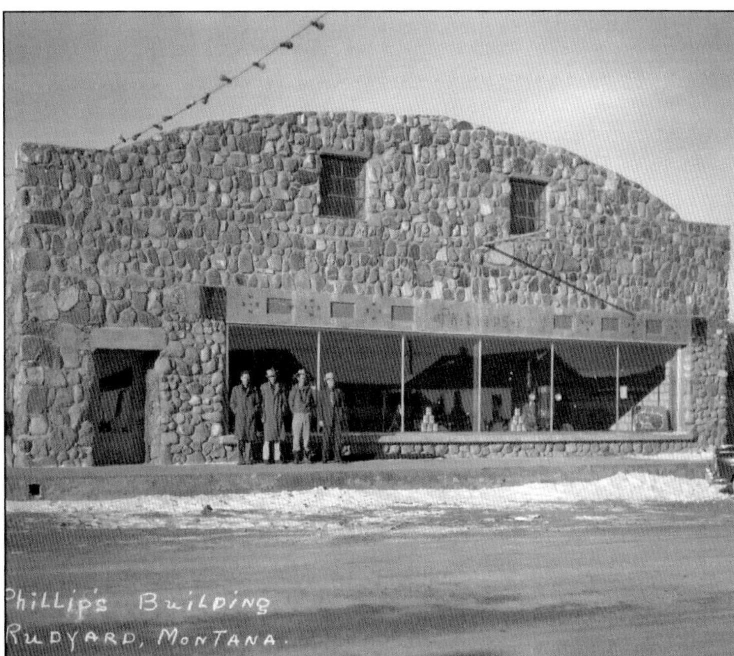

The Phillips Implement Company was constructed in 1947 and featured local fieldstone on the exterior surface. It sold International farm implements to local farmers. It was in operation for several years before closing. The building had been vacant for quite some time until 2007, when it became the Hi-Line Vintage Motor Museum. (Courtesy of the Rudyard Historical Society.)

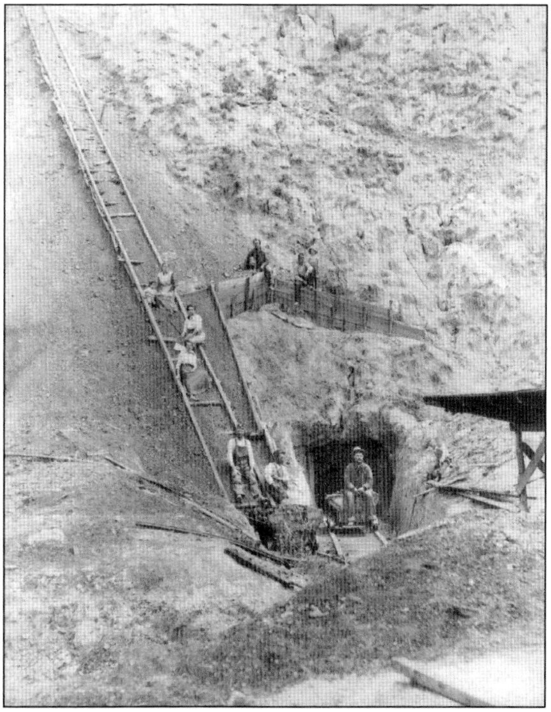

While Hill County is not known for large tracts of wooded areas except the Bear Paw Mountains, it is rich in coal deposits. Several coal mines once dotted the prairie, where families would come and purchase coal to heat their homes and cook meals. The coal mine featured is near Rudyard. Everyone pitched in to gather coal, including women and children. (Courtesy of the Rudyard Historical Society.)

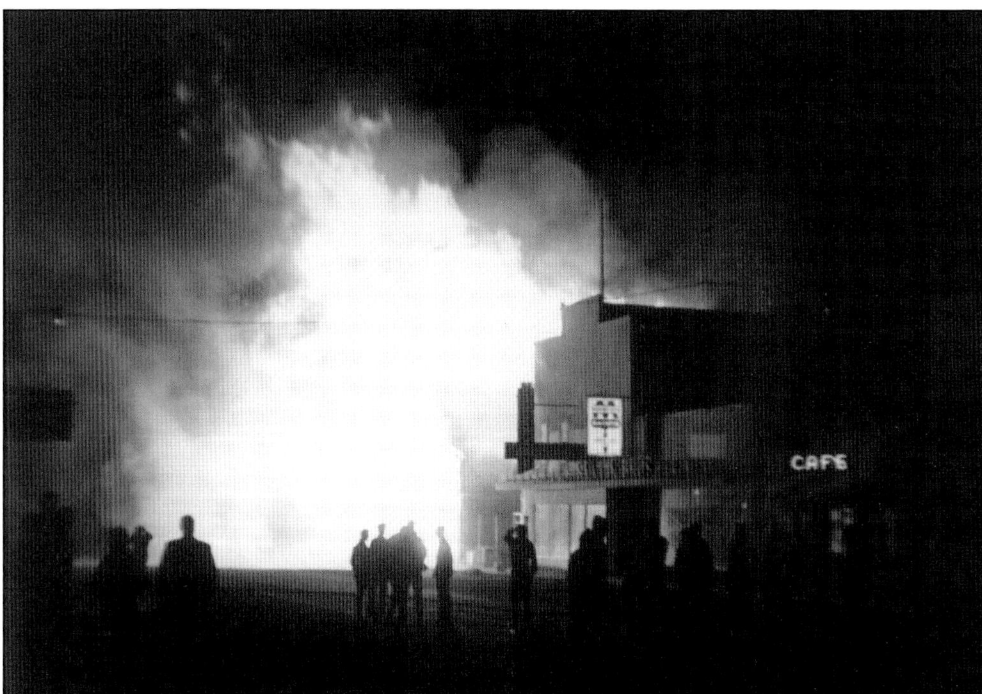

In November 1963, on Thanksgiving Day, a fire ripped through the International Building in downtown Rudyard. In addition, the neighboring Farmer's Union Oil Company building was burned. Local residents and volunteer fire departments fought the blaze, as did the Havre Fire Department. The loss was estimated to be over $200,000. (Courtesy of the Rudyard Historical Society.)

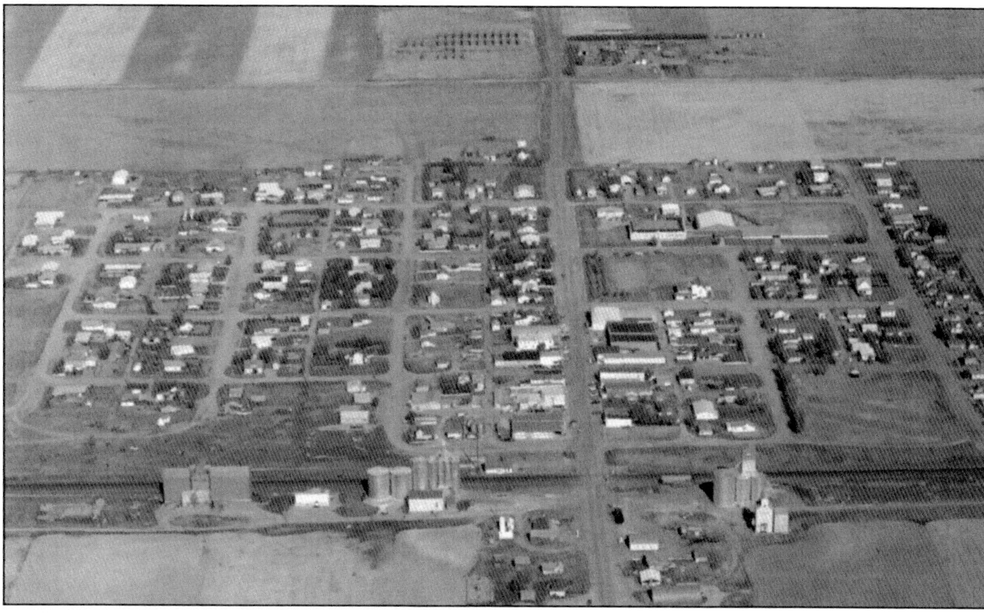

In this c. 1970 aerial view of Rudyard, the Rudyard Train Depot can be seen to the right of the middle grain elevator. It was moved to its current location and found adaptive reuse as a museum featuring artifacts of Hill County from Kremlin to Inverness as well as communities found in northern Hill County. The farm at the top of the photograph is the Wendland family homestead and, like many, is still operated by the original homesteader's descendants. (Courtesy of the Rudyard Historical Society.)

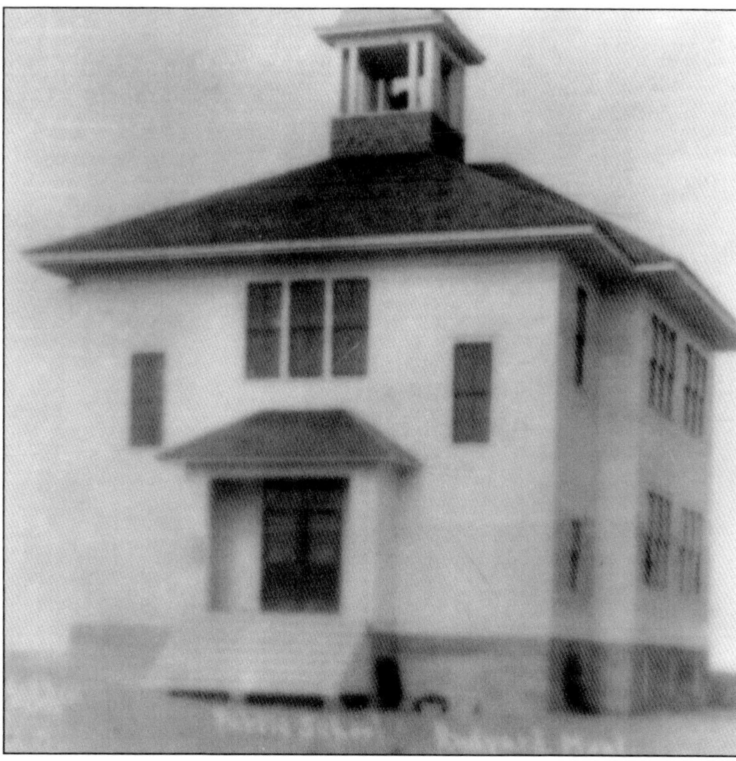

The original Rudyard School was built in 1914 for both elementary and high school. It was destroyed by fire on May 3, 1928. Nothing was salvageable from the fire. There were three weeks remaining in the school year, and the Rudyard Hall and the Farmer's State Bank were used for classes. A new school was built using insurance money from the fire and $35,000 in bonds. (Courtesy of the Rudyard Historical Society.)

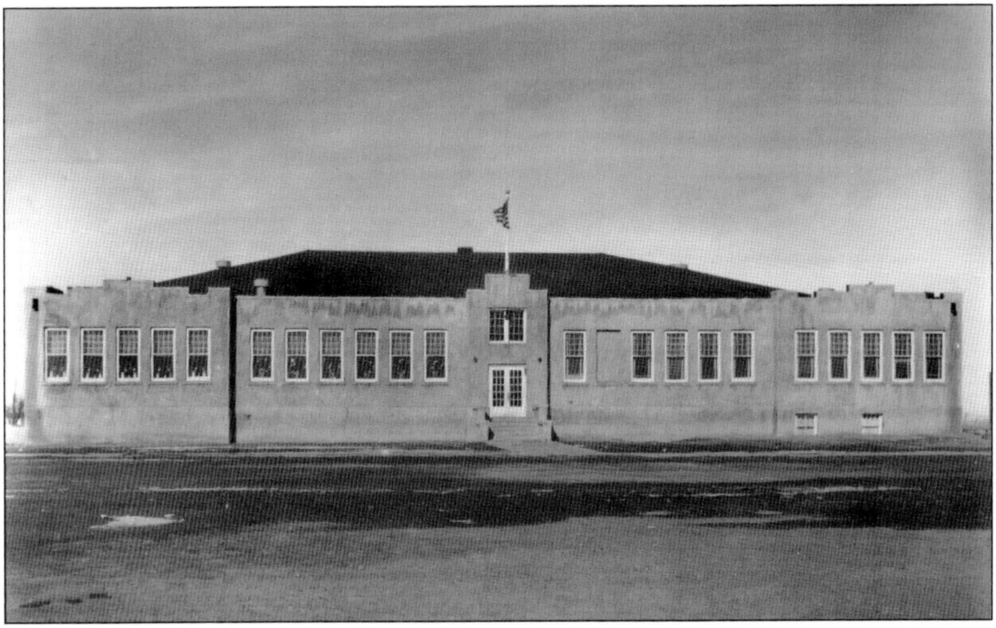

The Rudyard School appears here several years after its construction and before the addition. In March 1954, an election was held to sell $90,000 in bonds to build a new elementary school, leaving the current school to be used as a high school. In 1955, the Rudyard Elementary School opened for classes. (Courtesy of the Rudyard Historical Society.)

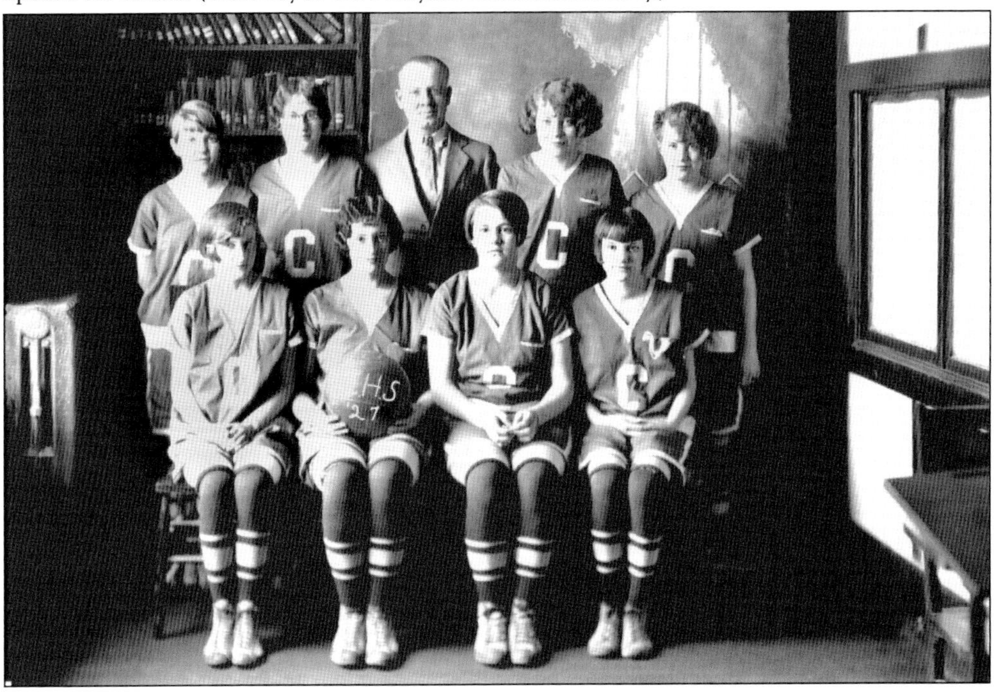

Girls were allowed to play school sports, too, and this photograph shows the girls' basketball team from Rudyard in 1927. Girls' sports were popular in the 1920s, but during the Depression and World War II, interest in girls' sports waned. These activities did not become popular again until the 1960s, and they remain popular today. (Courtesy of MSU-Northern, Al Lucke Collection.)

Mr. and Mrs. Louis Brandel were the first couple to marry in the Rudyard area. They were married in the home of the bride's parents by Reverend Grant, a friend of the groom. Their son, Harold F. Brandel, was the first child born in the Rudyard area. He was born September 9, 1912. Dr. Arthur Husser was the attending physician. (Courtesy of the Clack Museum.)

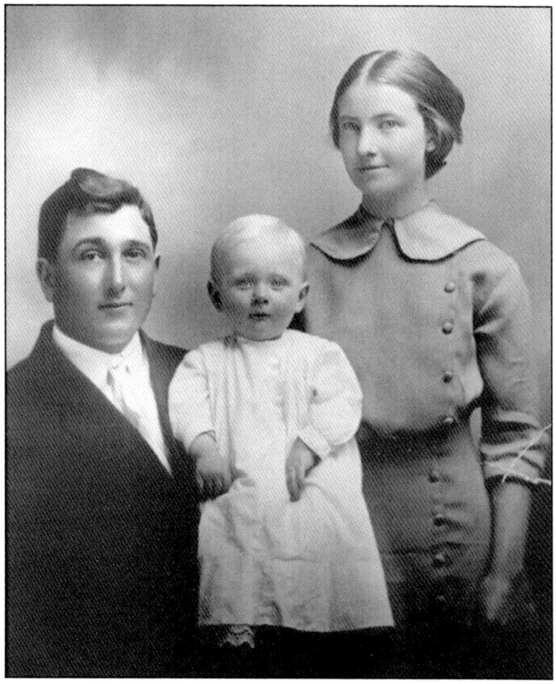

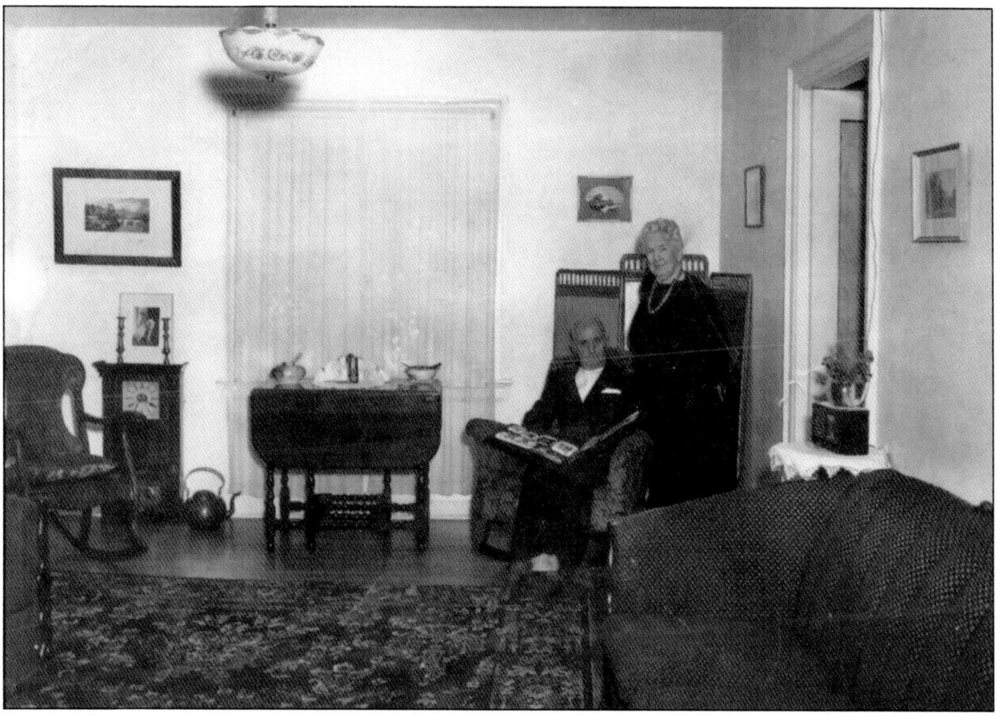

Dr. Augustus and Margaret Curtis lived in the Rudyard area for approximately 20 years before retiring in the mid-1940s to Canada. He was a very well-respected doctor, tending to the medical needs of the community. They are photographed here in their home. Upon retirement, Dr. and Mrs. Curtis were presented with a photograph album organized by his patients. (Courtesy of the Rudyard Historical Society.)

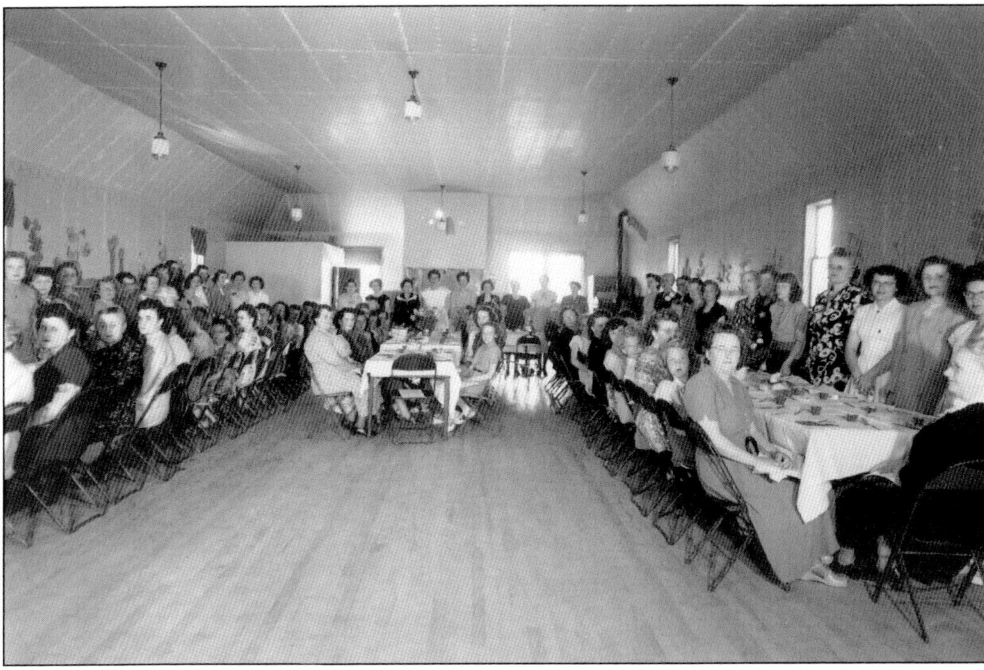

A mother-daughter banquet was held in Rudyard on Mother's Day, May 7, 1949. Events such as these were important to rural communities, as they offered the chance for people to get together, visit, and catch up on news from their neighbors. Adults and children mingled, making these multi-generational gatherings even more significant to the community's history. (Courtesy of the Rudyard Historical Society.)

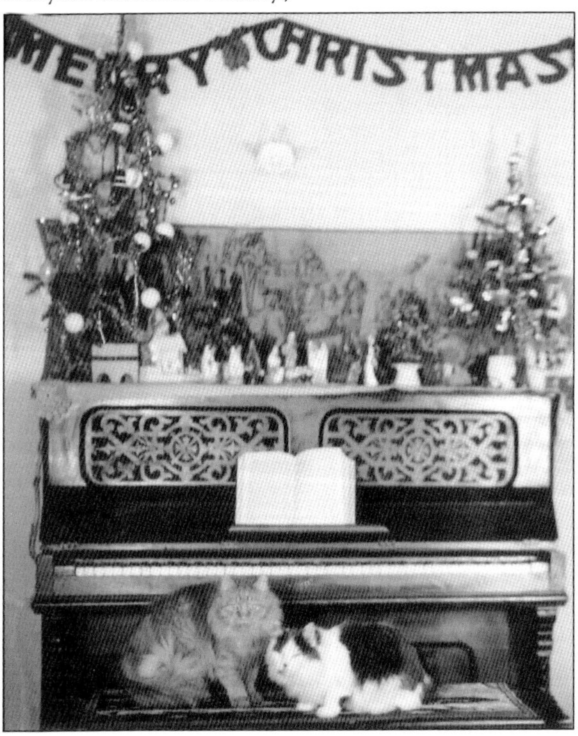

Early settlers in Hill County loved their pets as much as we do today. At an unidentified home in the Rudyard area, two cats are featured along with Christmas decorations on an old pump-style organ. This photograph would have been taken in the late 1930s or the early 1940s, as evidenced by the ball-style ornaments on the tree, developed by Corning Glass Company in 1939, and the bubble lights, which made their debut in the 1930s. (Courtesy of the Rudyard Historical Society.)

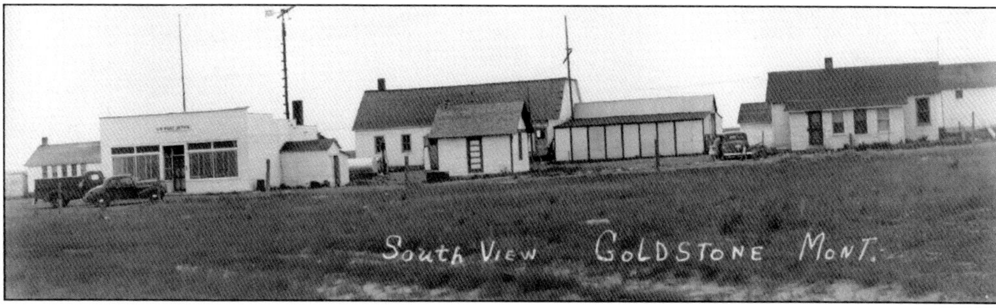

Goldstone, Montana, got its name when Frank Novak, its first postmaster, picked up a stone that looked like gold. Novak also owned a general store. Goldstone once had several businesses, such as an implement building, a blacksmith shop, a community hall, a restaurant, a meat market, and a school. Goldstone is pictured here from the south in 1948. (Courtesy of the Rudyard Historical Society.)

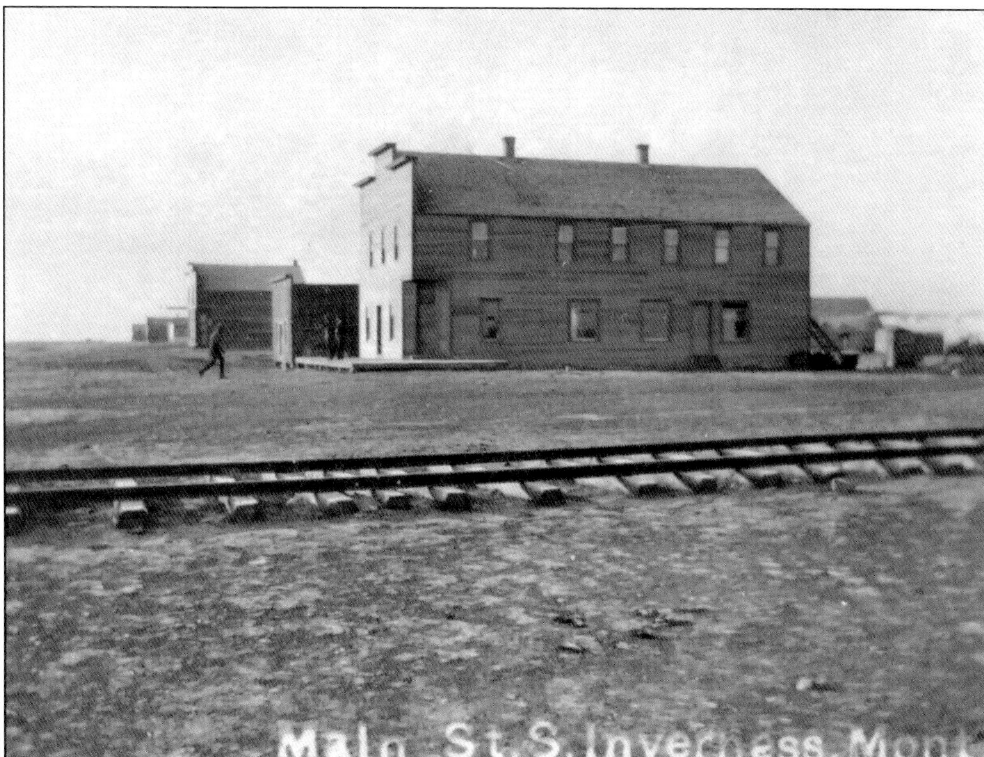

This is a view of Inverness south of the railroad tracks. The Inverness Hotel is the two-story building. It was built around 1914. In 1931, Claude Meyers purchased the hotel, which included a bar in the building. It was operated by the Meyers family until the early 1960s, when it was sold to Dalton Daheke. The building is still in Inverness and is a bar and restaurant. (Courtesy of the Rudyard Historical Society.)

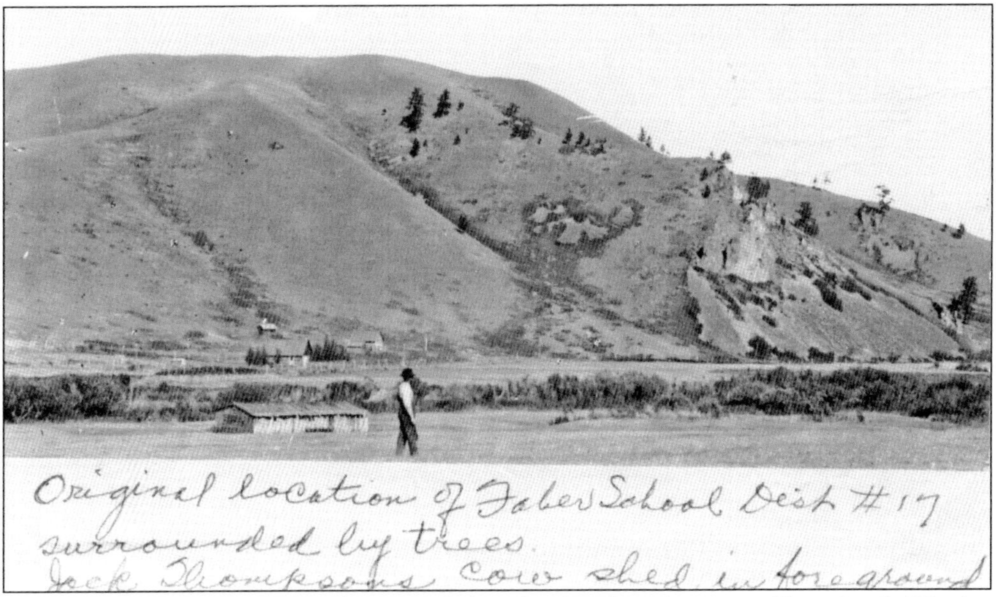

This view is of the Faber Schoolhouse and the schoolteacher's home on Clear Creek. The log schoolhouse, established in 1915, was in use for many years until replaced in the 1950s by a more modern structure. The original schoolhouse was then moved to the Clack Museum, where it stands today as a reminder of school days past. (Courtesy of the Clack Museum.)

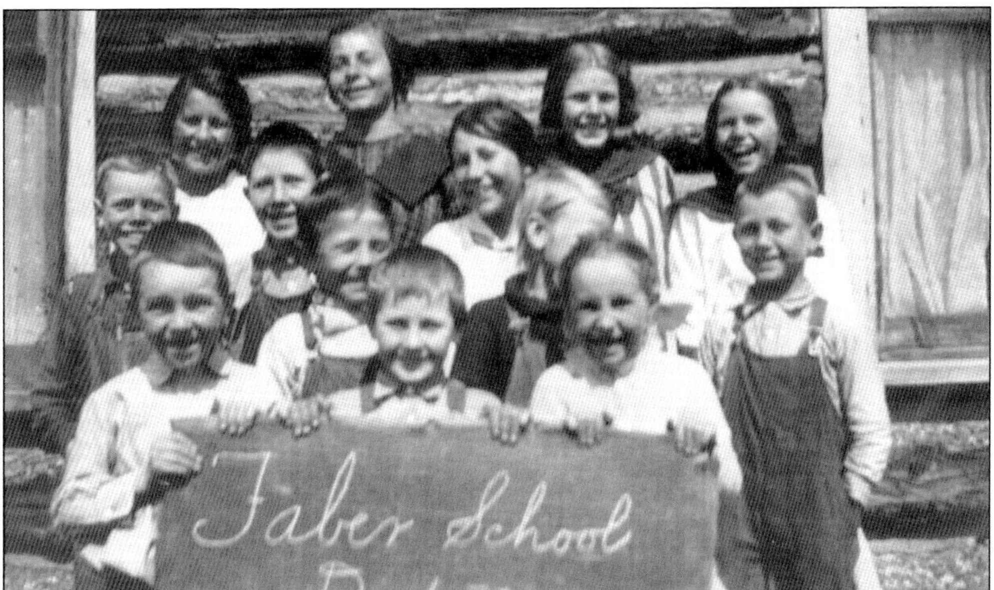

Students of the original Faber Schoolhouse in the Bear Paw Mountains gather for their class photograph. Pictured are, from left to right, (first row) Bourke Kinsella, Leonard Faber, and Rosemary Kinsella; (second row) Bill Morrell, Joe Faber, Pat LaSalle, Fritz Morrell, and Paul Faber; (third row) Georgana LaSalle, Ann Morrell, Dorothy LaSalle, Grace Morrell, and Virginia Morrell. (Courtesy of the Clack Museum.)

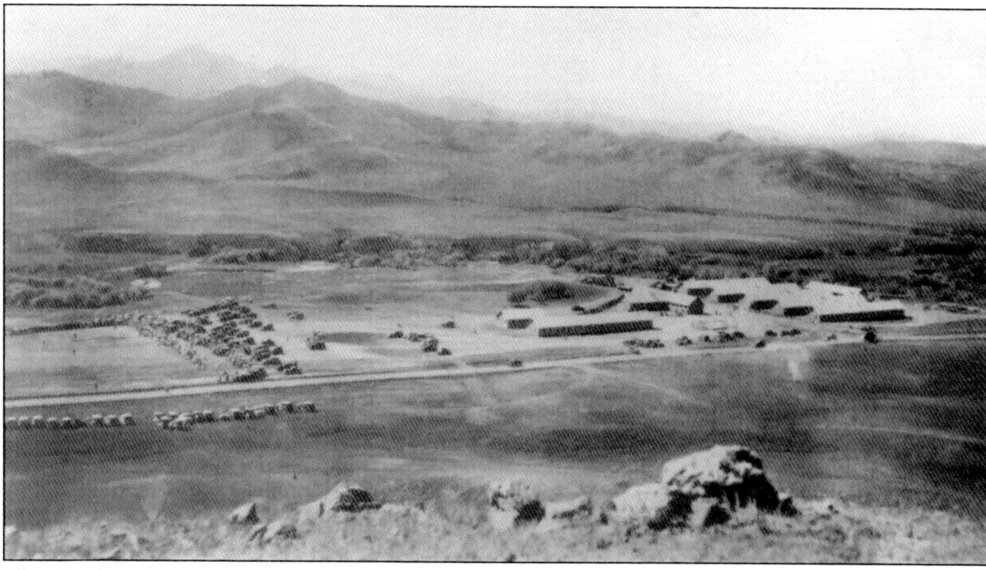

The Civilian Conservation Corps camp was located in the Bear Paw Mountains. Those serving in the Civilian Conservation Corps were young men from all walks of life. Among them was Whitey Ophus, who had a Ph.D. in business but ran a "Cat skinner," a Caterpillar with a blade in front for moving dirt. All that remains at the camp are a couple of log buildings and stone walls from the fish hatchery. (Courtesy of MSU-Northern, Al Lucke Collection.)

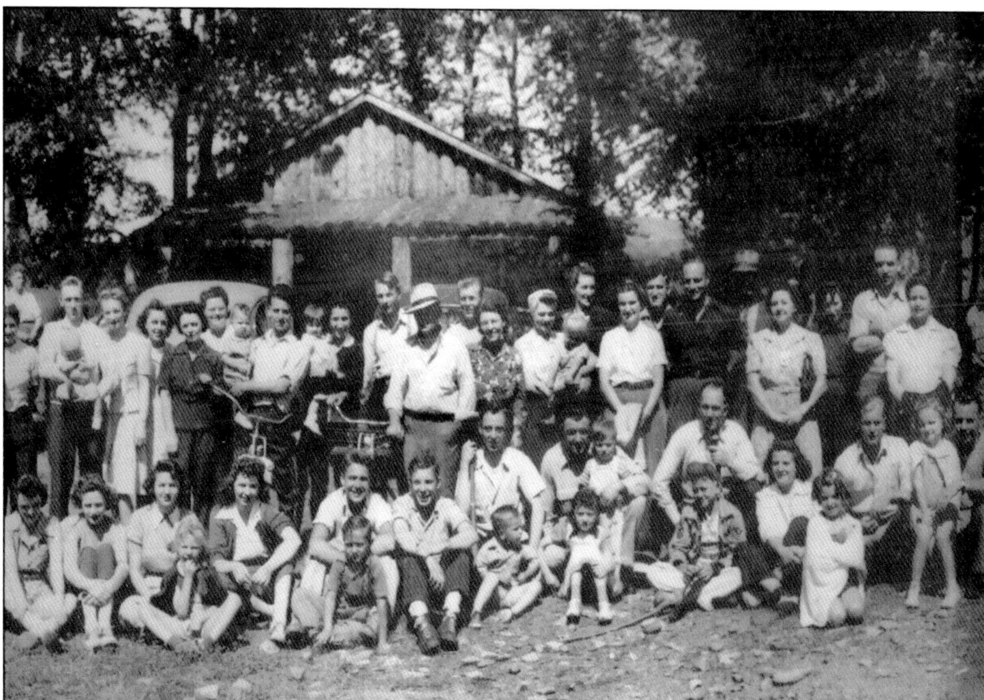

Members of the Buttrey Reylon Club gather in front of the chapel at Camp Kiwanis in the Bear Paw Mountains on July 11, 1943. The chapel was constructed in the 1930s and was used by several denominations for services. The Reylon Club consisted of Buttrey's employees, who held meetings and organized picnics, dances, and other social gatherings. (Courtesy of Havre Beneath the Streets.)

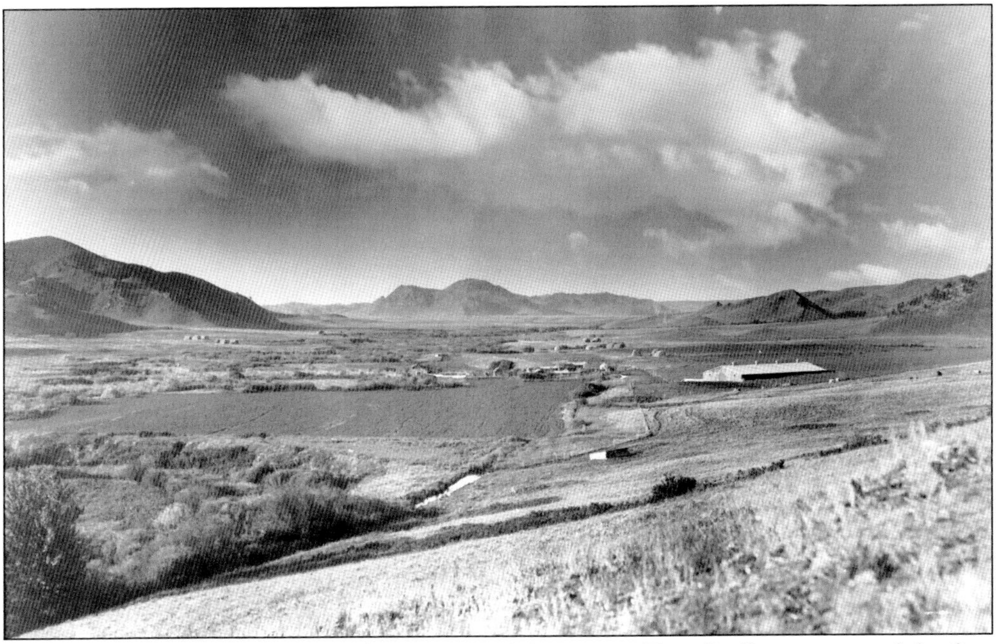

The Griffin Ranch is located in the Bear Paw Mountains. Tom Griffin was one of the first to homestead in the Bear Paws and had established his ranch long before others created their ranches. Ranching in the Bear Paws occurred mostly on the mountain range's east side, and initially sheep outnumbered cattle because of the fact there was more money in sheep. Eventually, cattle became the predominant livestock and remain so today. (Courtesy of MSU-Northern, Al Lucke Collection.)

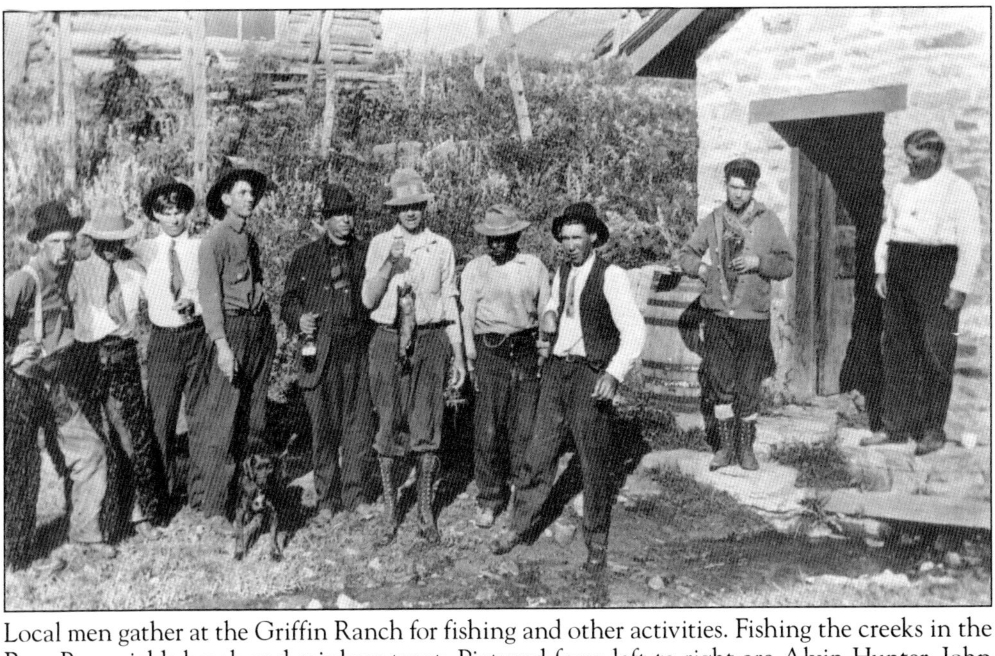

Local men gather at the Griffin Ranch for fishing and other activities. Fishing the creeks in the Bear Paws yields brook and rainbow trout. Pictured from left to right are Alvin Hunter, John Griffith, Frank Griffin, George DeMars, Ned Kinsella, Silas Jones, Tom Griffin, unidentified, and Lou Lucke. (Courtesy of MSU-Northern, Al Lucke Collection.)

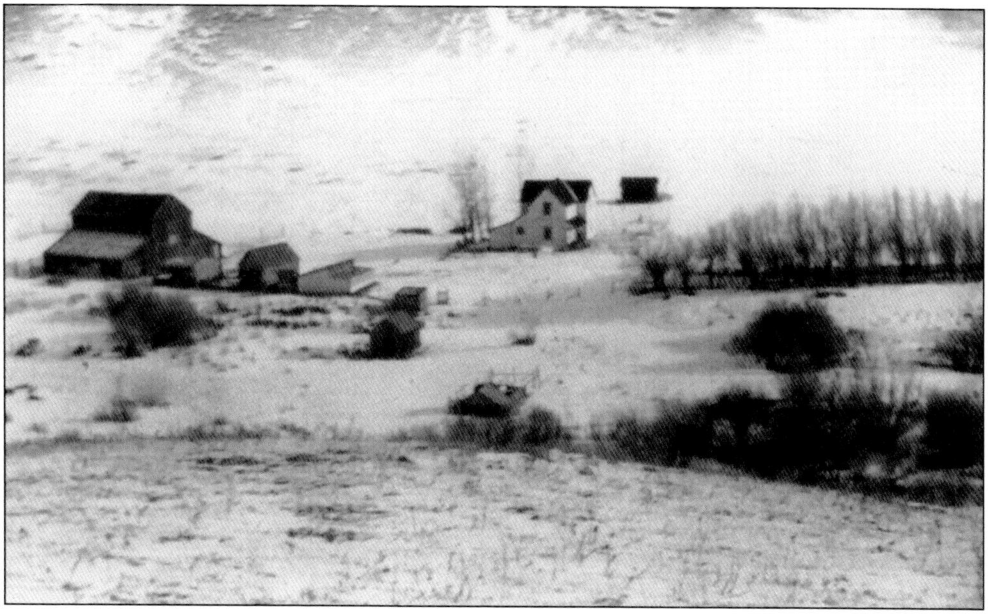

The Faber Ranch is one of the oldest in the Bear Paws and is pictured here about 1915. The picture shows the house, the old barn (later replaced), and other outbuildings necessary to operate a ranch. The neat and orderly arrangement of the buildings assisted in helping the ranch run smoothly. (Courtesy of Jim Faber.)

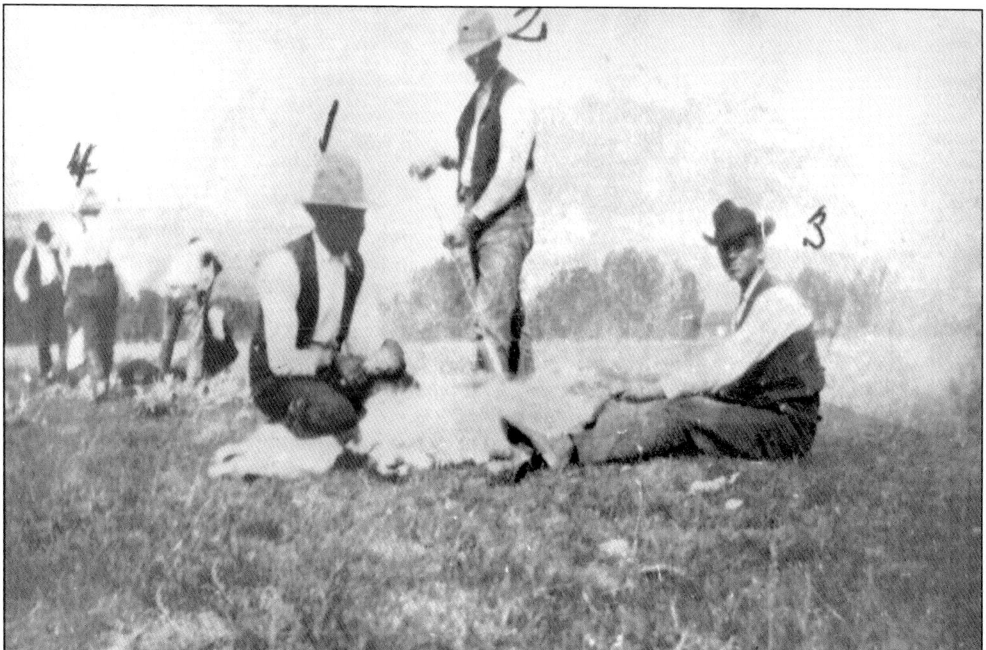

Branding cattle is a necessary activity in ranching in order to prove ownership and is popular in the springtime after the calves are born. Neighboring ranchers organize brandings and help each other out during the process, which includes vaccination and dehorning. The ranch women are responsible for preparing and bringing food, as well as taking care of the children. (Courtesy of MSU-Northern, Al Lucke Collection.)

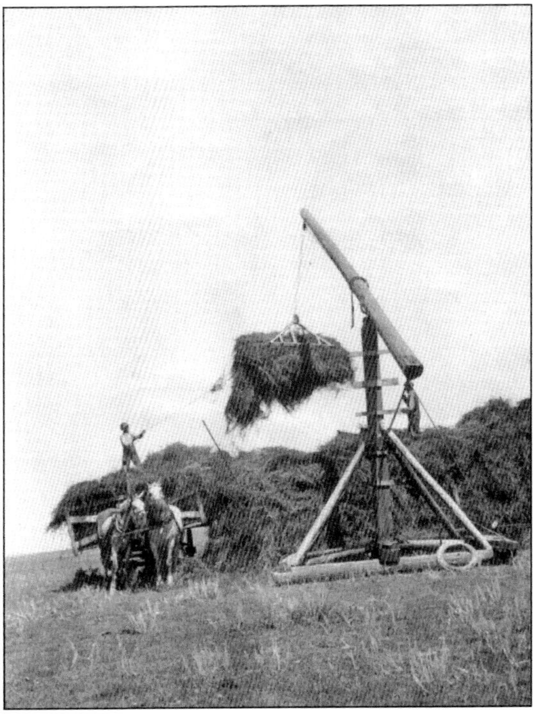

"Making hay while the sun still shone" was important for ranchers in order to have enough feed to last the long, hard winters; otherwise livestock might not make it to spring. One method of baling hay was by using a beaver slide. Weaver Clack, a brother to H. Earl Clack, used the one pictured. (Courtesy of Elinor Clack.)

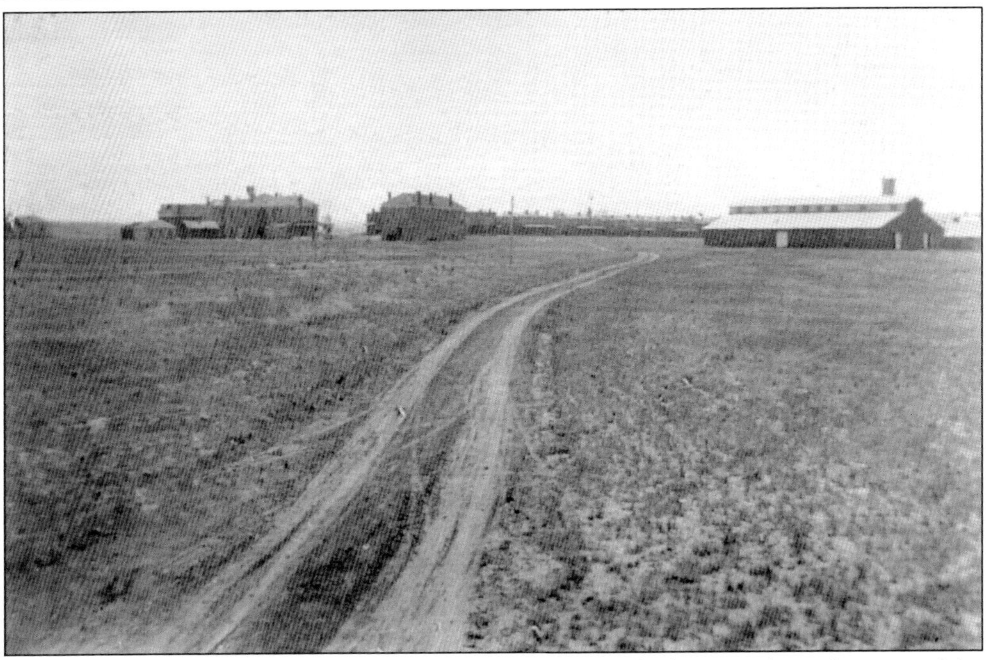

Fort Assinniboine, located 6 miles south of Havre, was once the largest military fort west of the Mississippi River. Constructed in 1879–1880, Fort Assinniboine at its peak had 108 buildings. In 1911, due to military downsizing, Fort Assinniboine was decommissioned and abandoned. Most of the buildings were demolished and the bricks reused for other buildings in Havre. The fort is now home to the Northern Montana Agricultural Experiment Station, a part of Montana State University. (Courtesy of the Clack Museum.)

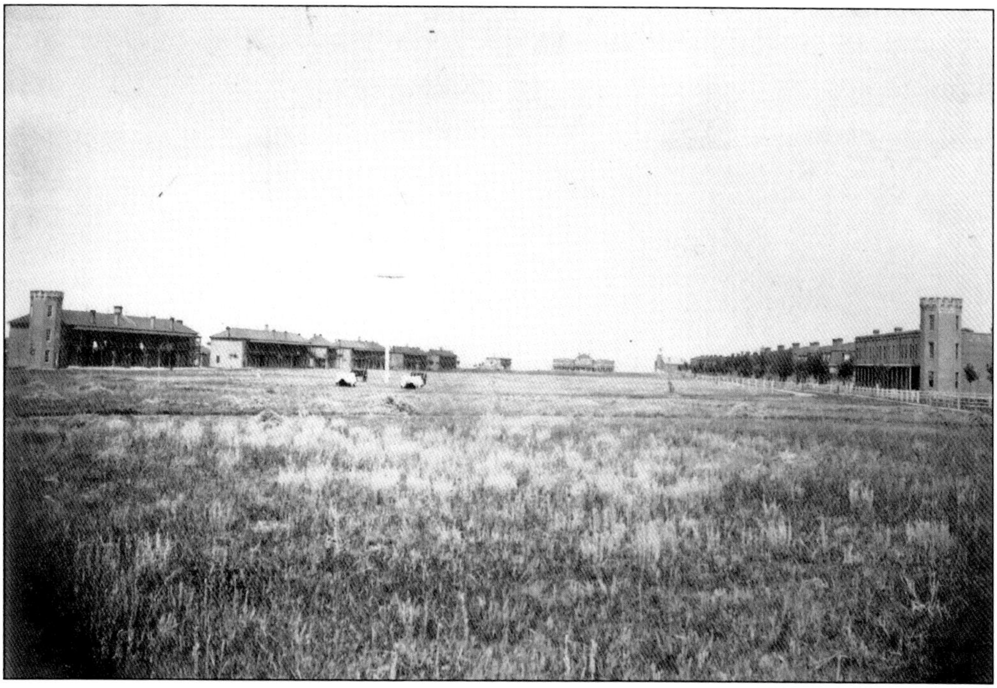

The enlisted men's barracks are to the left in this photograph of Fort Assinniboine, with "Officer's Row" to the right, separated by a parade ground that measured 425 feet between the rows and 2,011 feet from the original flagpole to the post hospital. At the end of the parade ground were the Enlisted Men's Amusement Hall and Band Headquarters, the post hospital, and the chapel. (Courtesy of the Montana Historical Society.)

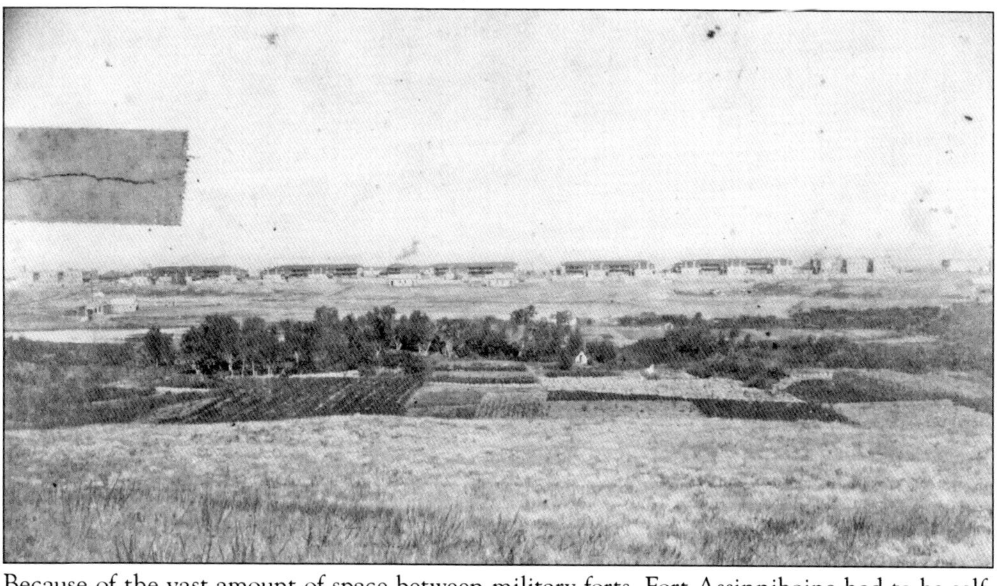

Because of the vast amount of space between military forts, Fort Assinniboine had to be self-sustaining. Large 50-acre vegetable gardens, seen at center, were grown and harvested. In 1902, three commissary root cellars were constructed to store the food grown in the gardens. Each root cellar had 52,000 cubic feet of storage capability. (Courtesy of the Fort Assinniboine Preservation Association.)

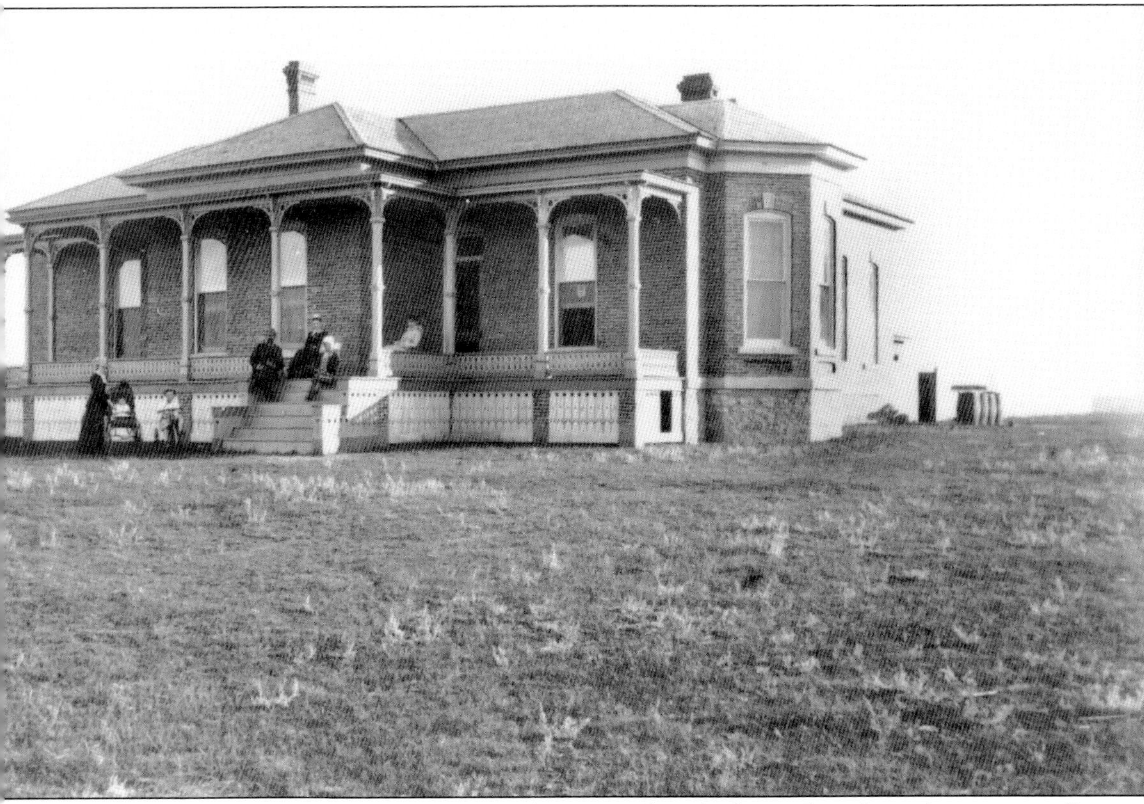

The Post Trader's Residence at Fort Assinniboine was described as "a showplace of a vast region." The post trader's building was located a short distance away. It was the oldest structure on the fort, built in 1879. It had a hotel, general store, barbershop, post office, photography shop, restaurant, and several warehouses of merchandise and officer's clubrooms. Only a small portion of this beautiful home remains; it is part of a vehicle storage building. (Courtesy of the Montana Historical Society.)

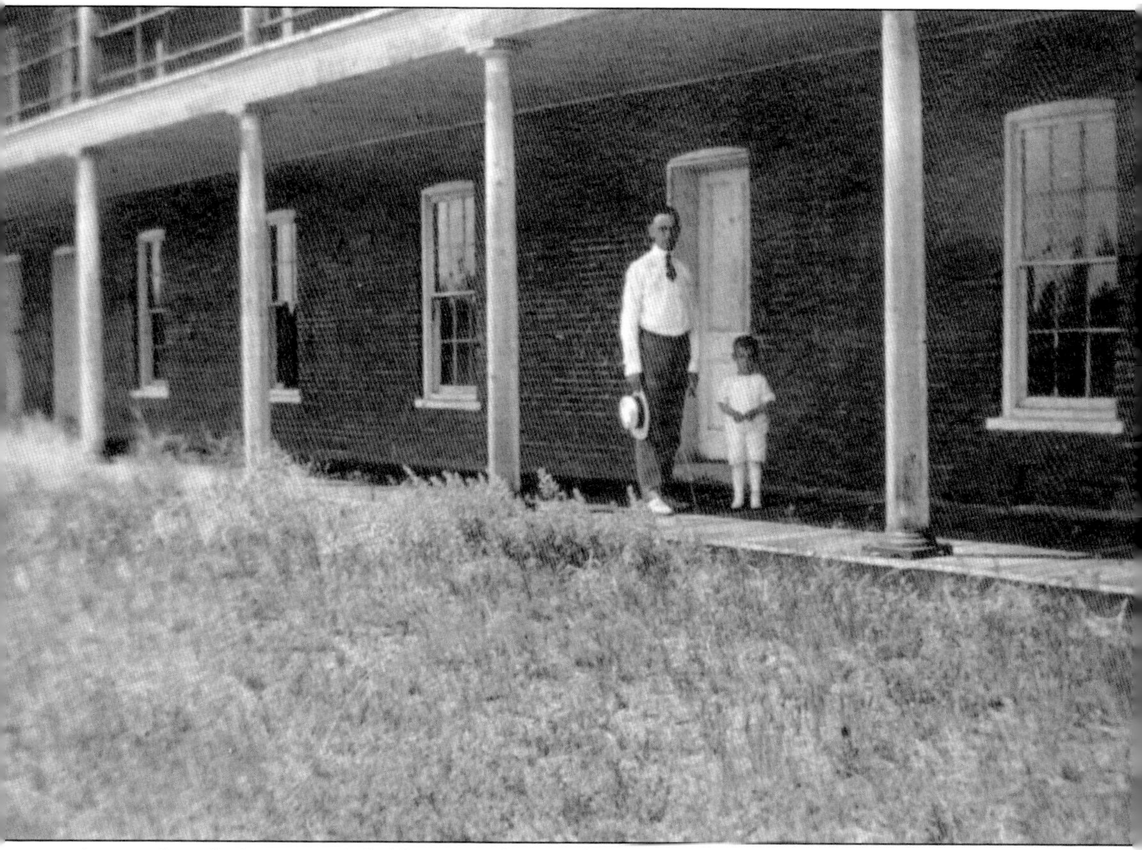

An unidentified man and child are on the porch of the barracks at Fort Assinniboine some time after its decommission. The brick barracks buildings with second-floor balconies facing the parade grounds were self-contained with their own office, store, supply rooms, kitchen, mess hall, and sergeants' quarters below. The enlisted men lived on the second floor. One of the barracks was retained and was used by various groups for camps and other gatherings. It burned in 1954. (Courtesy of the Clack Museum.)

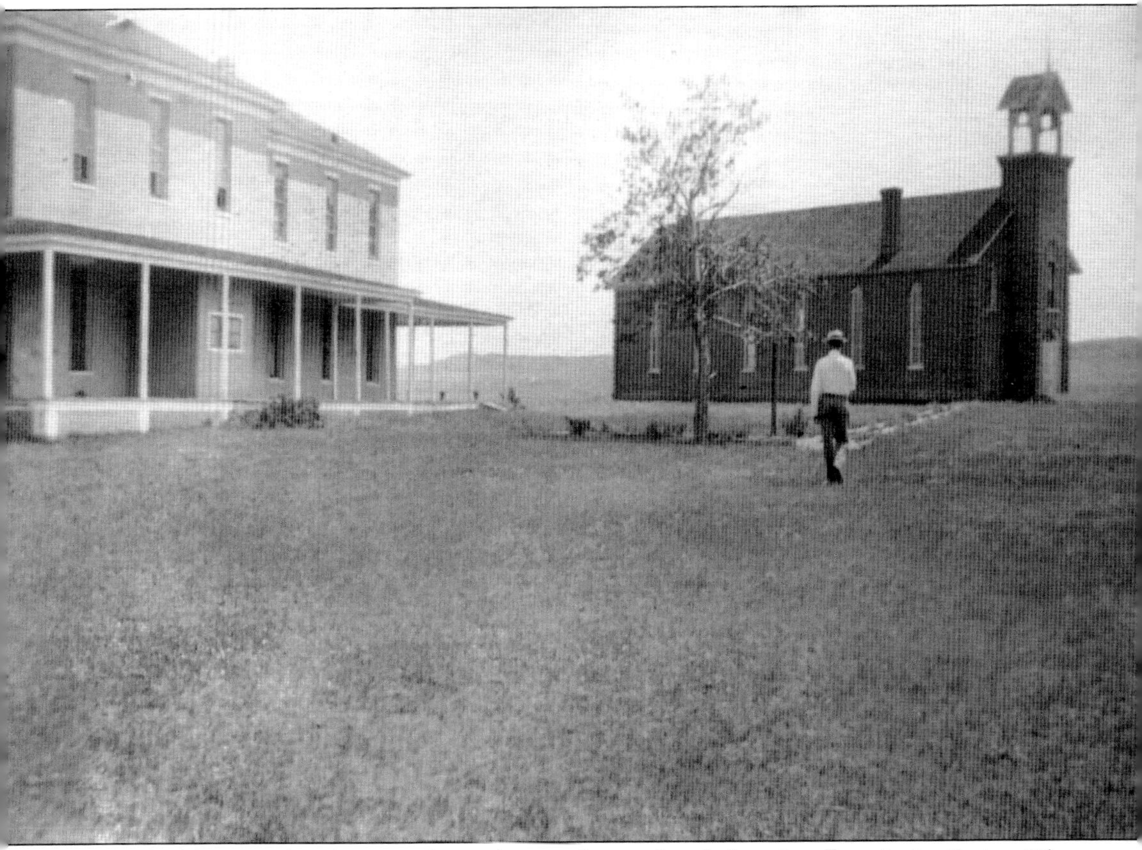

The buildings in the photograph are the post hospital and chapel at Fort Assinniboine. The hospital had 12 rooms and was constructed from 1879 to 1882. The chapel also served as a school for children on the fort as well as neighboring communities. It was constructed in 1881 and had an elaborate bell tower. Both buildings were demolished after the fort was decommissioned. (Courtesy of the Clack Museum.)

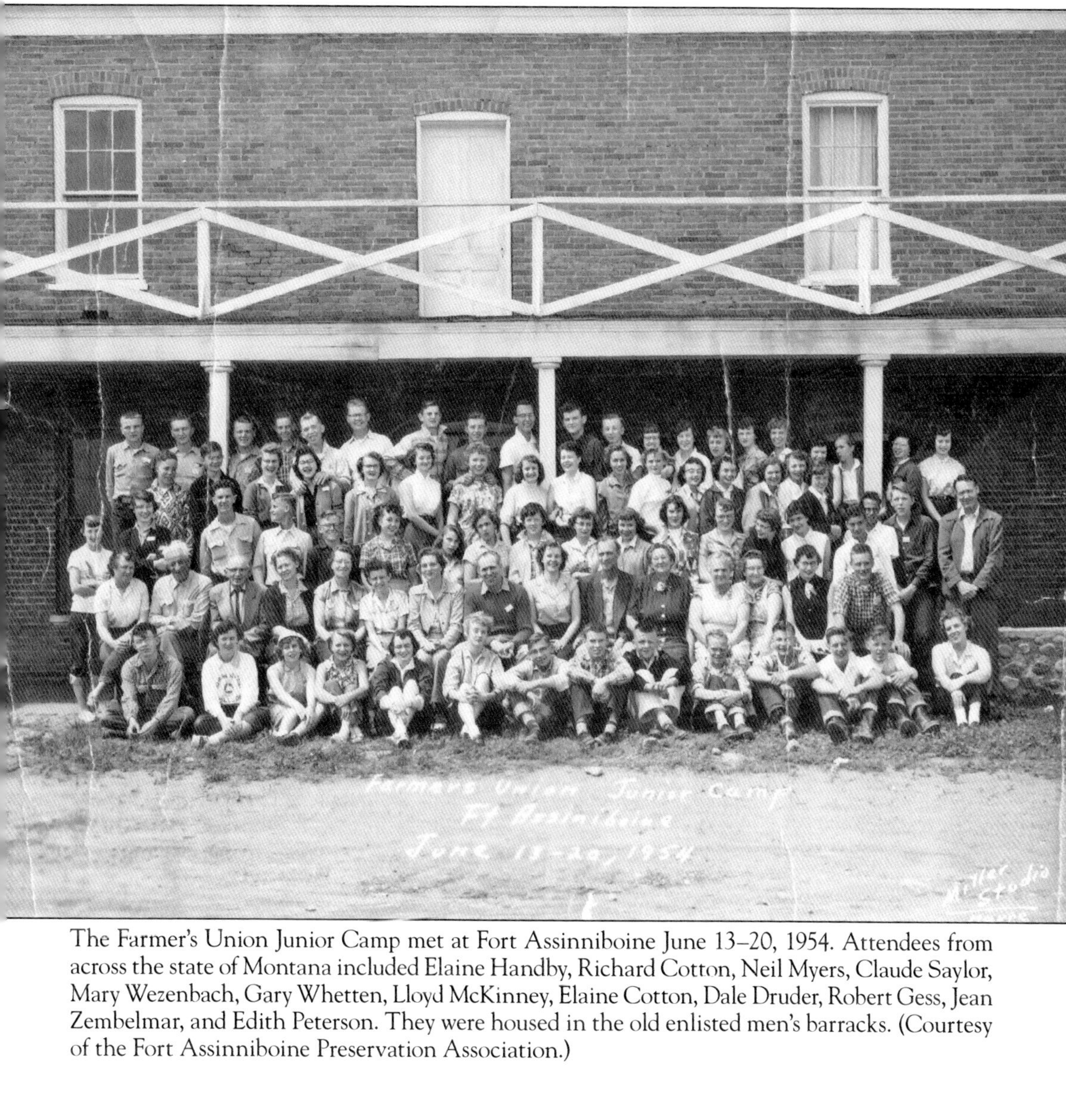

The Farmer's Union Junior Camp met at Fort Assinniboine June 13–20, 1954. Attendees from across the state of Montana included Elaine Handby, Richard Cotton, Neil Myers, Claude Saylor, Mary Wezenbach, Gary Whetten, Lloyd McKinney, Elaine Cotton, Dale Druder, Robert Gess, Jean Zembelmar, and Edith Peterson. They were housed in the old enlisted men's barracks. (Courtesy of the Fort Assinniboine Preservation Association.)

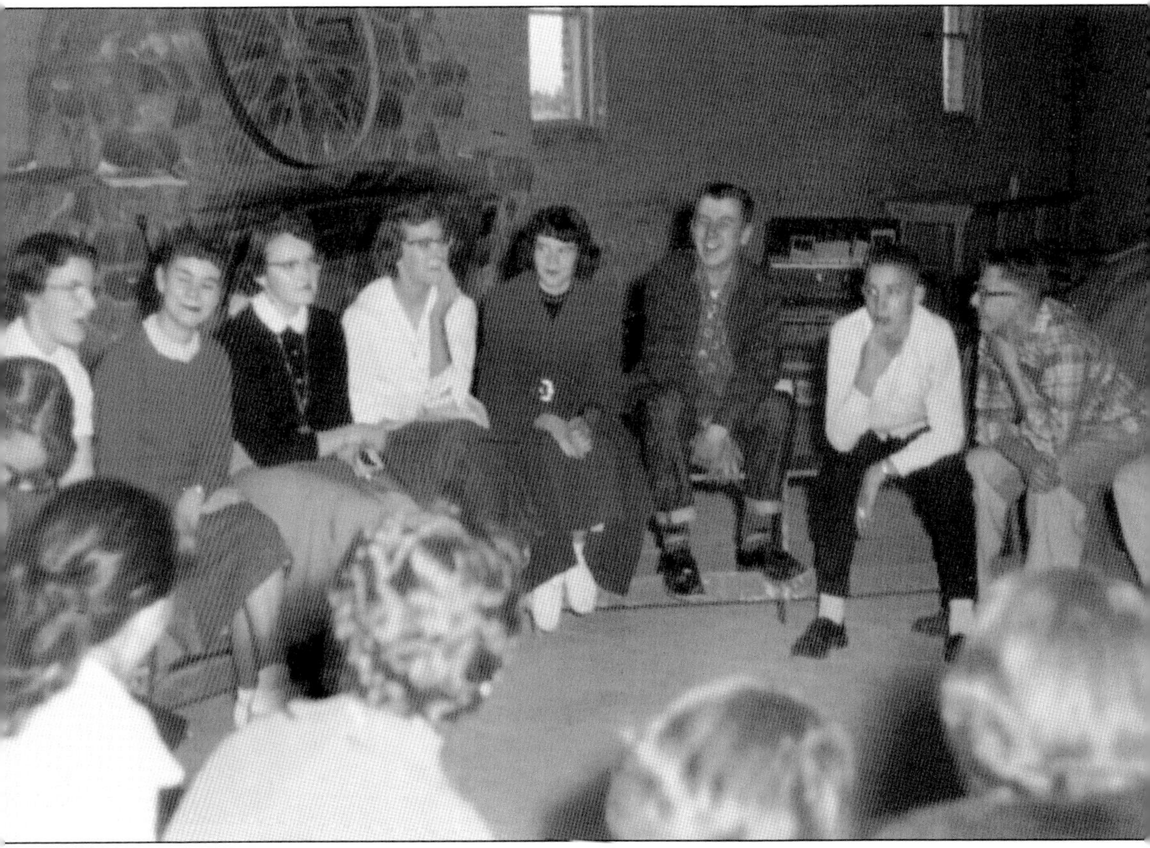

The only remaining stable at Fort Assinniboine was remodeled to serve as a meeting place for community groups. There were up to six stables at Fort Assinniboine during its operation. Here an unidentified group is conducting a meeting in the fall of 1956 inside the updated stable, complete with a stage and a fireplace made of local fieldstone. (Courtesy of Emily Mayer.)

Two

HAVRE

The Hill County Courthouse was designed by Havre architect Frank Bossuot in the Beaux Arts style. The style contains many classical features, such as the fluted half-columns in the Corinthian order. Construction started in 1915, and by February 1916, the building was occupied with various Hill County offices. This undated photograph shows the old steps with their ornate light fixtures and one-door entry. (Courtesy of MSU-Northern, Al Lucke Collection.)

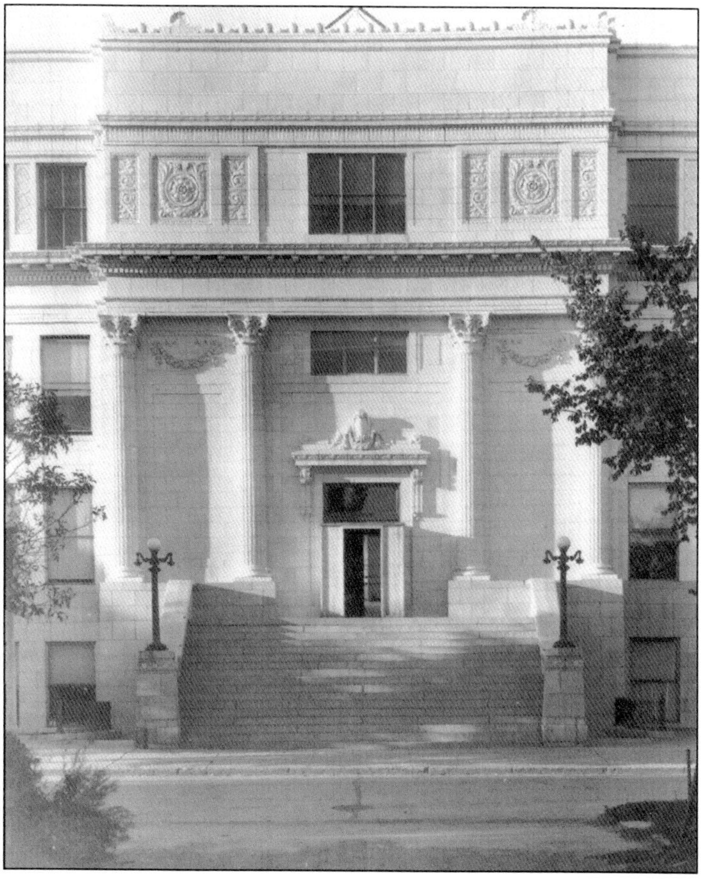

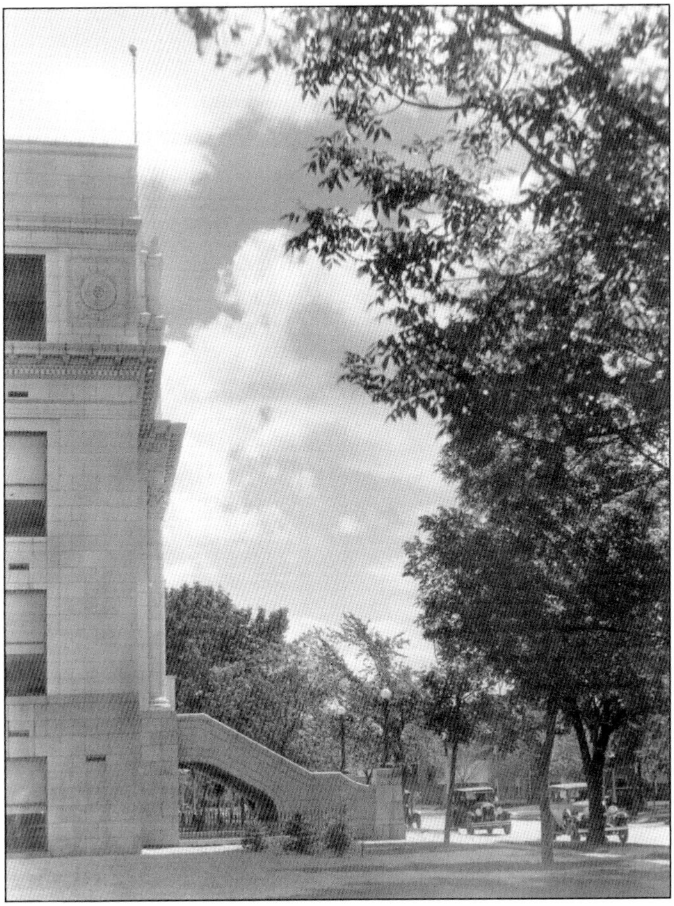

The Hill County Courthouse was built with an open, arched staircase. Access to the basement of the courthouse was by another set of stairs flanking the main staircase that led down to another doorway. This photograph of the courthouse's early days shows the open staircase perfectly, along with a wrought-iron fence bordering the west staircase, which led down to the basement level. (Courtesy of MSU-Northern, Al Lucke Collection.)

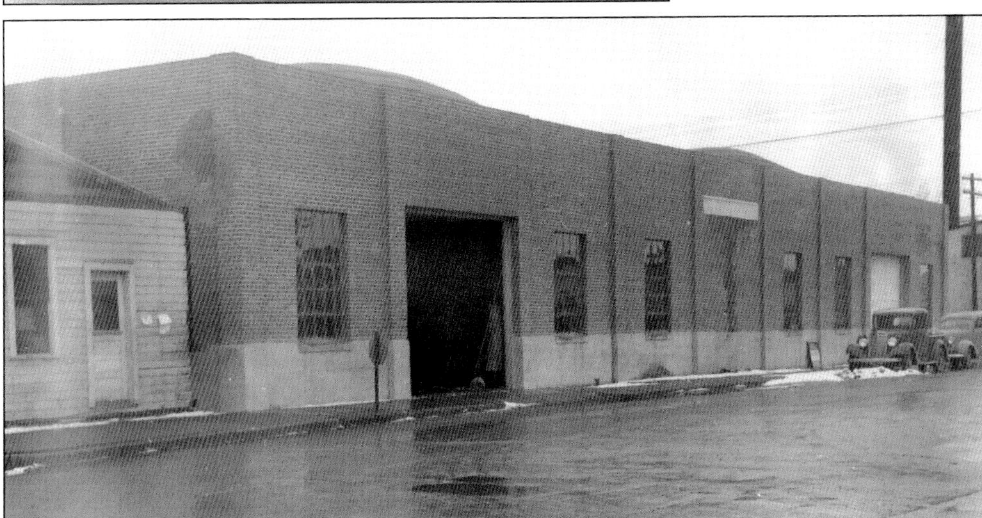

The old Hill County Shop building was located on the corner of First Avenue and Second Street. It was constructed in 1936–1937 by Fuglevand and Sundberg as a Works Progress Administration project. It served as the county shop until 1991. In the mid-1990s, the building suffered severe roof damage. It was razed on March 26, 1997. (Courtesy of the Clack Museum.)

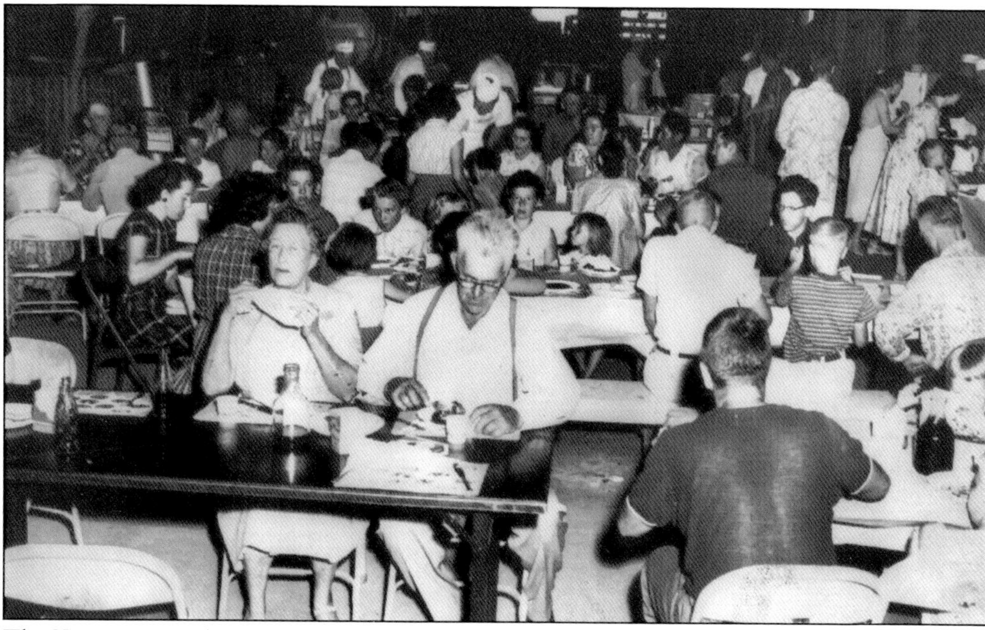

The Kiwanis Pancake Breakfast has long been a welcome tradition in Havre. For many years, the Kiwanis hosted their annual event at the Hill County Shop, located at the corner of First Avenue and Second Street. After the roof collapsed in the mid-1990s, in 1996, the Pancake Breakfast was held at the National Guard Armory. It has since moved to the Vet's Club. (Courtesy of the *Havre Daily News*.)

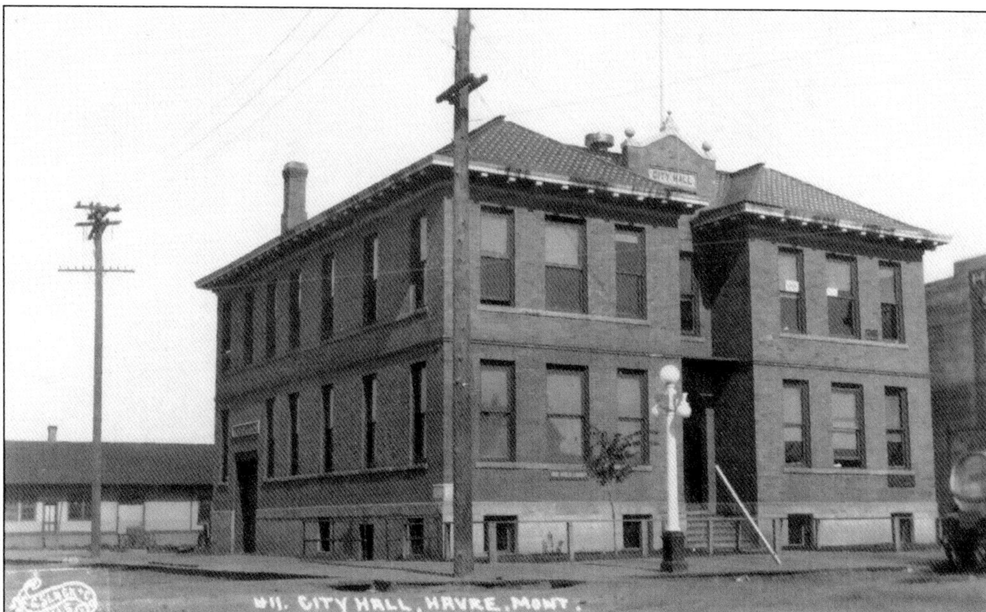

The Havre City Hall was located on Fourth Avenue between Main and First Streets. The brick structure was built in 1908 and contained the fire department, a library, the police department, the jail, a courtroom, and city offices. It was designed by Havre architect F. F. Bossuot, and city businesses were conducted here. By 1971, the offices were moved to the current city hall. The old city hall was demolished in 1971. (Courtesy of the Clack Museum.)

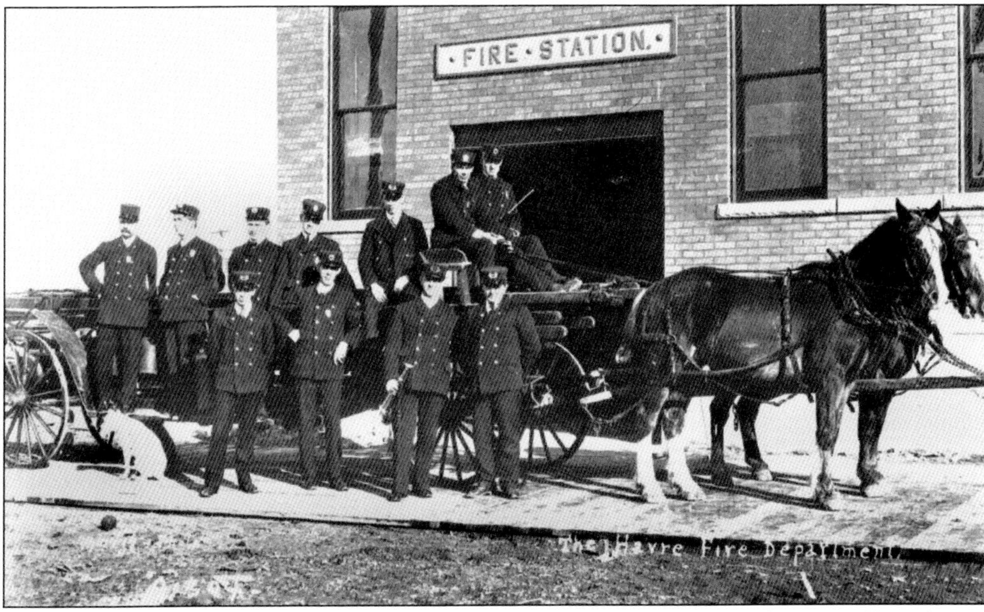

The Havre Fire Department was originally staffed with volunteers. After the Great Fire of 1904, the following year saw the creation of a formal fire department. Its first fire truck was man powered. After a few years, major upgrades were brought to the fire department by purchasing equipment driven by horsepower. (Courtesy of MSU-Northern, Al Lucke Collection.)

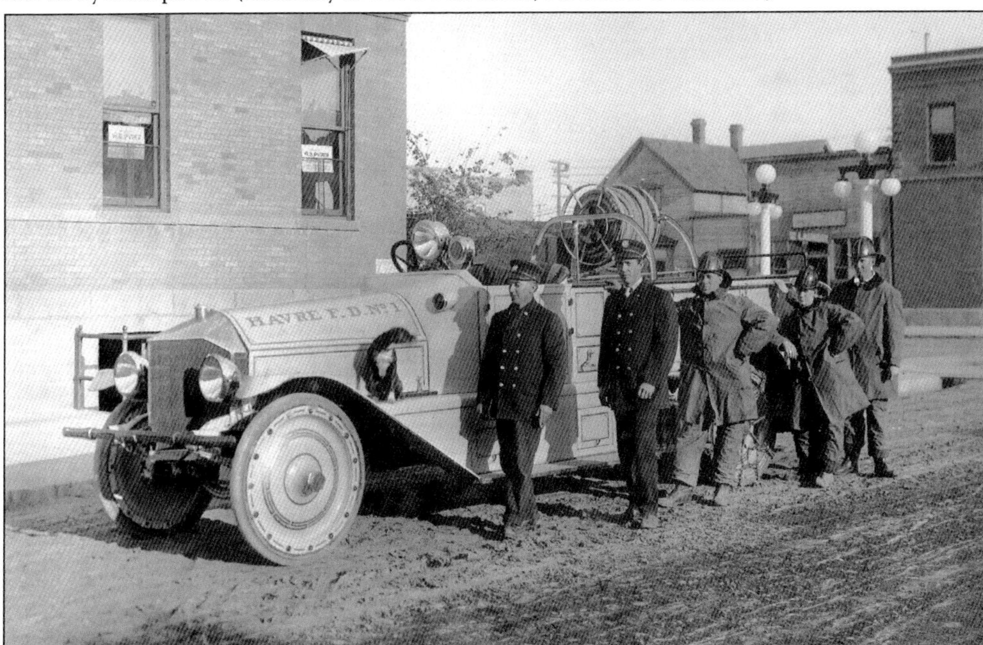

By 1918, the Havre Fire Department had purchased a 1918 LaFrance fire engine. The photograph was taken just outside the office of Judge William Pyper, one of the area's most respected citizens and judges. Among the cases Judge Pyper presided over was "Long" George Francis's infamous trial in which the defendant was found guilty of horse theft. Across the street between the two light poles is Sing Kee Laundry. (Courtesy of MSU-Northern, Al Lucke Collection.)

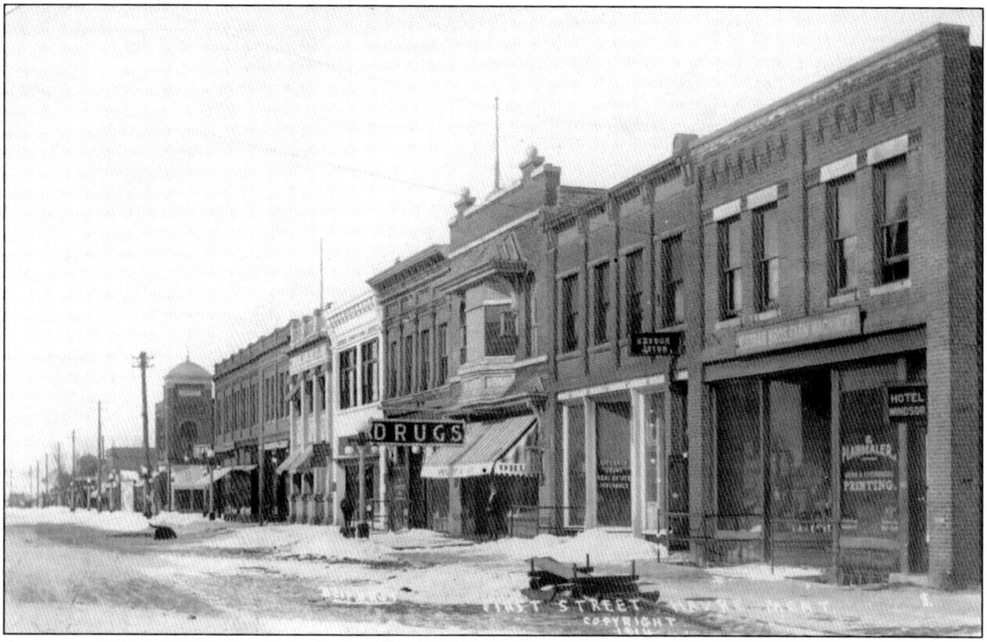

A view of First Street in 1914 shows the buildings as relatively new. At the end of the block is a bar and pool hall, followed by law offices, Owl Drug with Drs. Duncan S. MacKenzie's and John Duncan's offices above, a real estate office, Hotels Hoover and Windsor, and the *Plaindealer*, an early Havre newspaper. Entrances to businesses underground can clearly be seen. (Courtesy of the Clack Museum.)

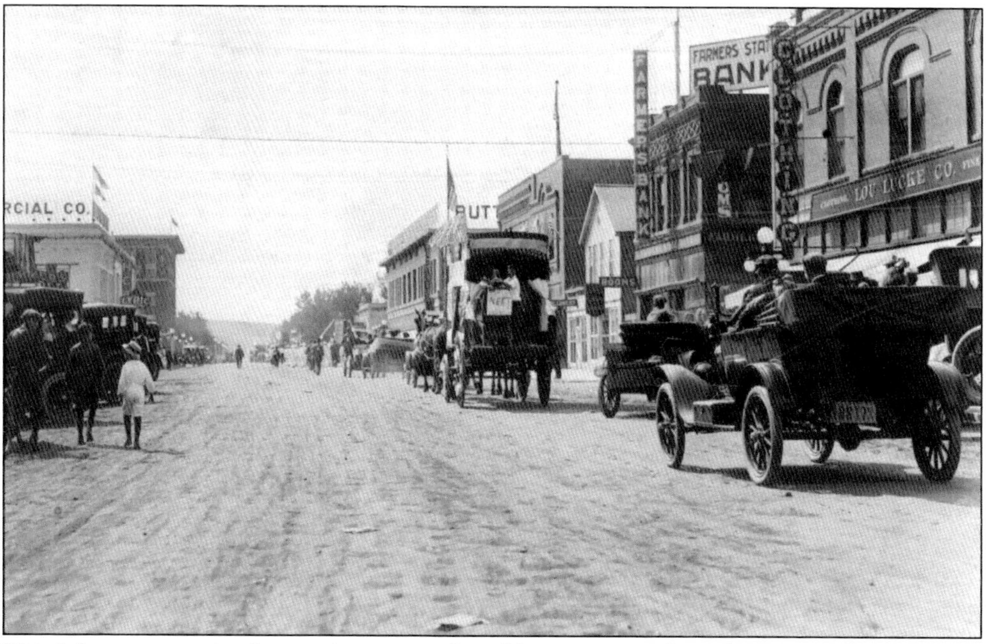

Third Avenue contained many long-remembered businesses, such as the Lou Lucke Company, Farmer's State Bank, Buttrey's Department Store, Havre Commercial Company, the Lyric Theatre, and the Masonic Temple. Many of these buildings proudly displayed the American flag from poles erected on the buildings' roofs. (Courtesy of the Clack Museum.)

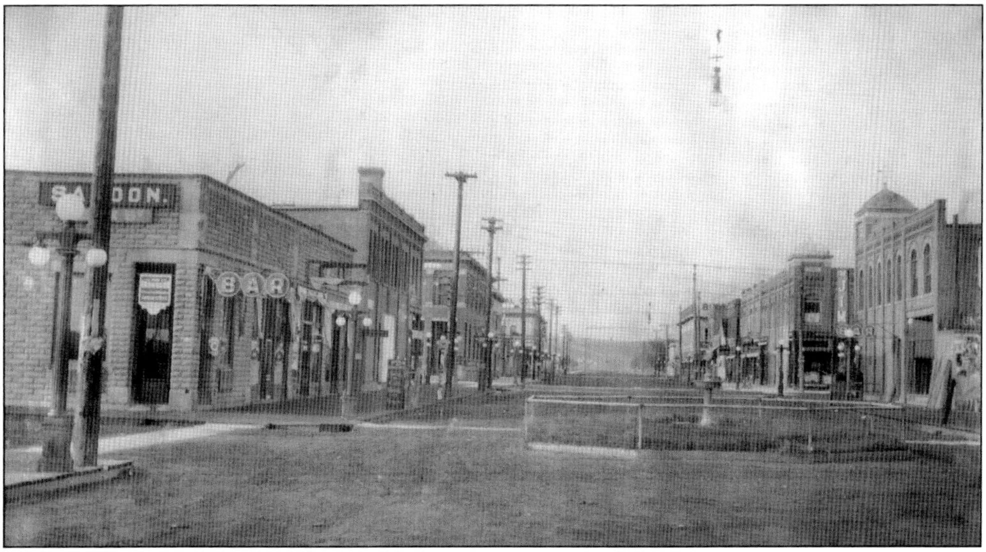

The original fountain can be seen in the middle of the street in Havre at Main Street and Third Avenue. One could purchase a beer for 5¢ at the bar at the left of the photograph. Just up the block, one could order noodles and chop suey at all hours of the day at the Chicago Café. Across Third Avenue was the Jim Bar. (Courtesy of the Clack Museum.)

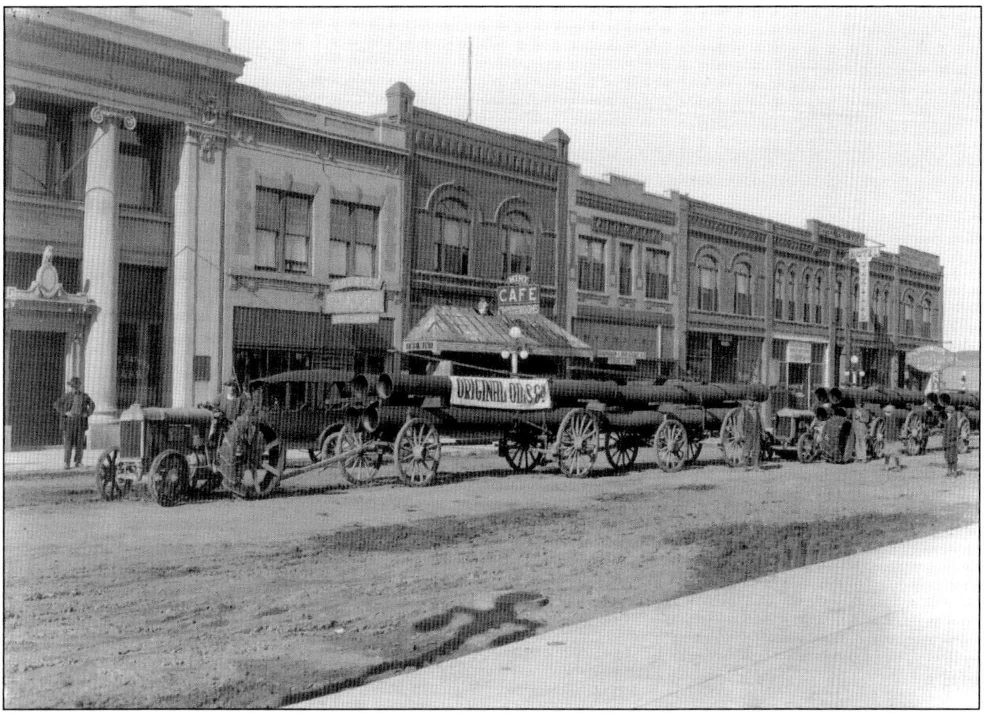

The oil business has long been in Hill County. Here freight for the Original Oils Company is being hauled down First Street in 1921. In the background are the Havre National Bank, Gourley Brother's Bakery, the Mint Café, Pioneer Meat Market, and the Hotel Oakland. (Courtesy of the Clack Museum.)

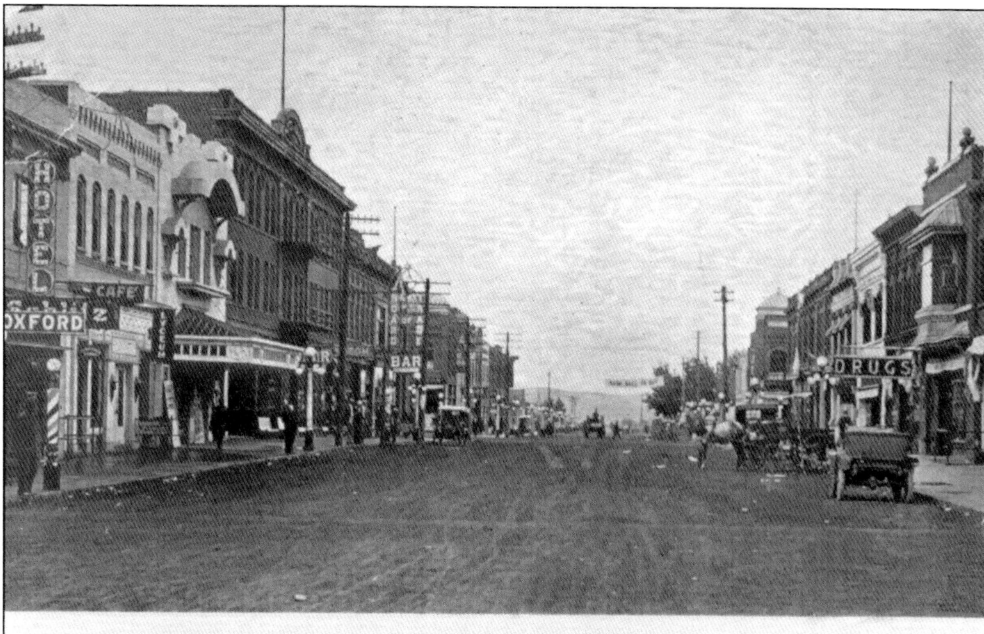

First Street Looking West, Havre, Mont.

Here is another view of First Street. Havre was quick to embrace electricity, and the maze of electrical lines was quite prominent along the streetscape. In later years, the lines were moved to alleys to service the businesses. The Board of Trade Saloon, toward the middle of the left side of the photograph, was once owned by Pat Yeon. Among his claims to fame were live dancing bears. (Courtesy of the Clack Museum.)

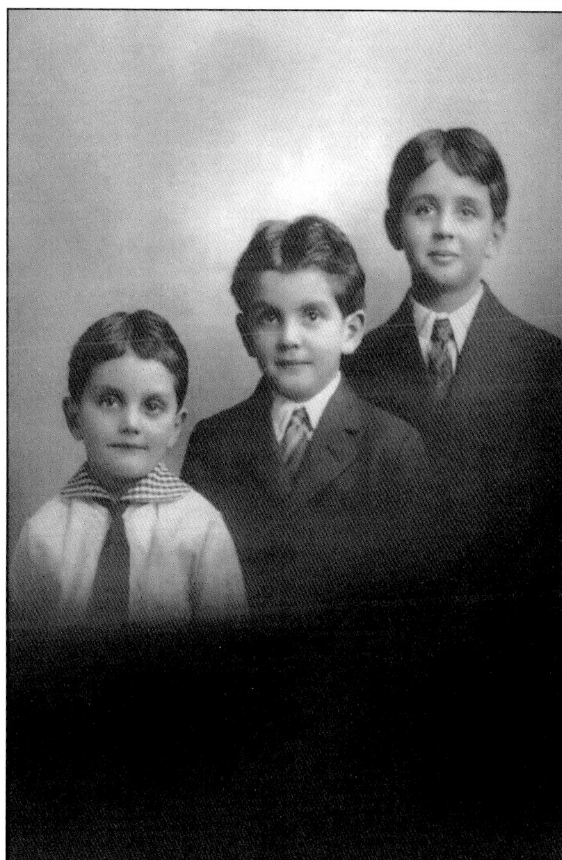

These three boys are the sons of Pat and Virginia Yeon. From left to right are Lee, age 7; Wray, age 10; and "Little" Pat, age 12. John Patrick Yeon came to Havre from Canada, and Virginia came from Missouri. Pat was a well-respected businessman, and he and Virginia hosted many parties in their home. The Virginia Apartments on the corner of Sixth Avenue and Second Street were named after Virginia Yeon. (Courtesy of Havre Beneath the Streets.)

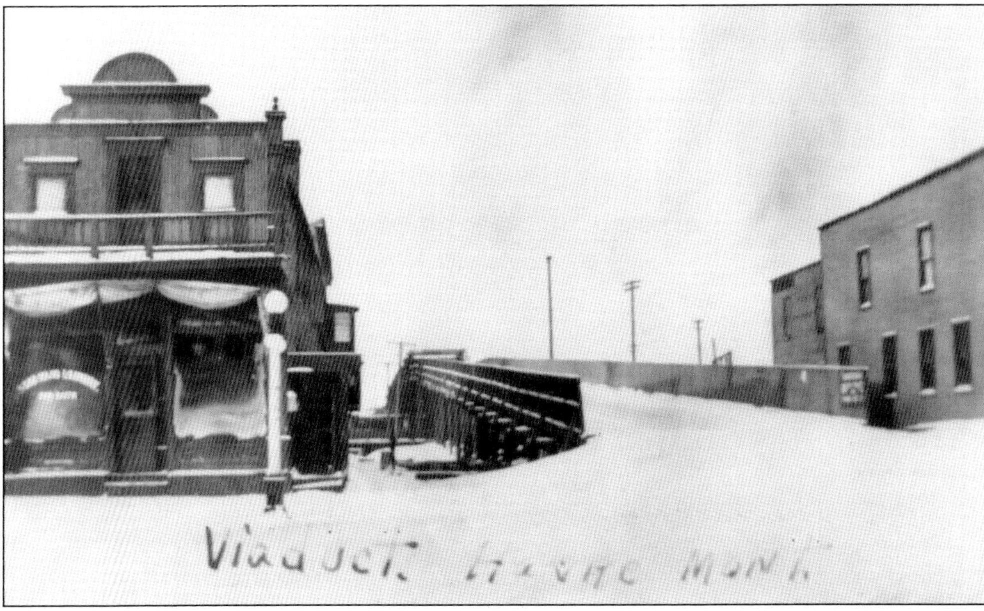

Havre's viaduct provides a much-needed bridge between north Havre and the city's business district. Other access routes can oftentimes make crossing a lengthy wait, thanks to trains arriving and departing. To the left is a laundry and bathhouse. This building, as well as others, was later demolished. Boxcar's Restaurant and Bar is now in this location. (Courtesy of the Clack Museum.)

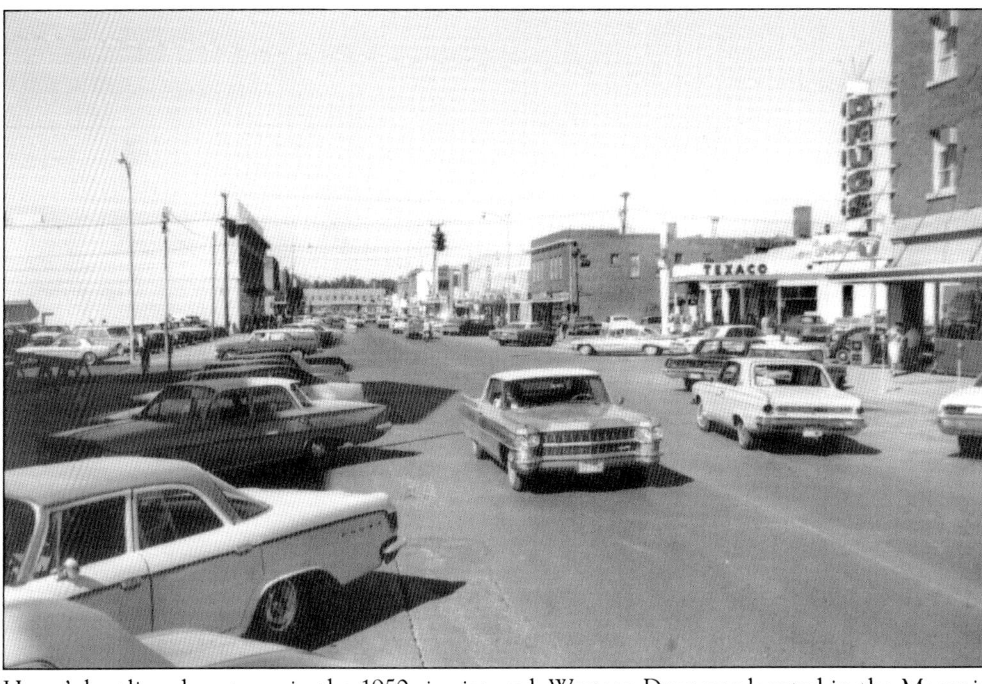

Havre's bustling downtown in the 1950s is pictured. Western Drug was located in the Masonic Temple for many years and was owned by Don Vaupel. A Texaco station, owned by Hjalmer Larson, was located where Koefod Agency is currently. The Koefod Agency building was formerly Don's Medical Pharmacy, also owned by Don Vaupel. (Courtesy of the Clack Museum.)

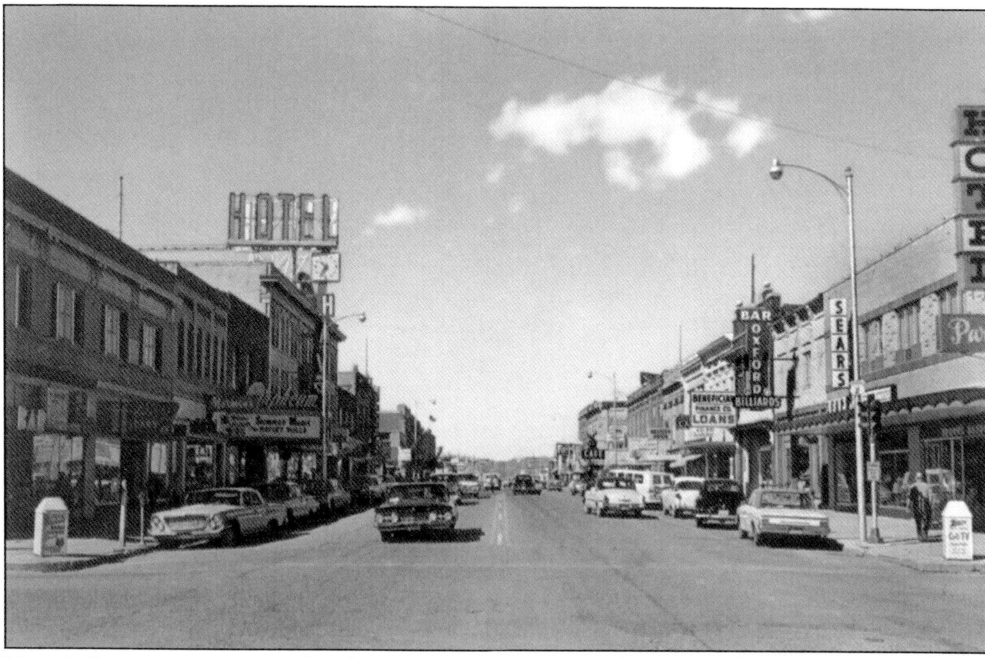

Havre's downtown was once a bustling scene of commerce and activity. This *c.* 1964 postcard shows the 300 block of First Street looking west. Downtown had everything: retail shopping, restaurants, banks, hotels, and bars. Much has changed, as the entire blocks where the Havre Hotel and the Dutch Shop Café are here were razed many years ago. (Courtesy of Emily Mayer.)

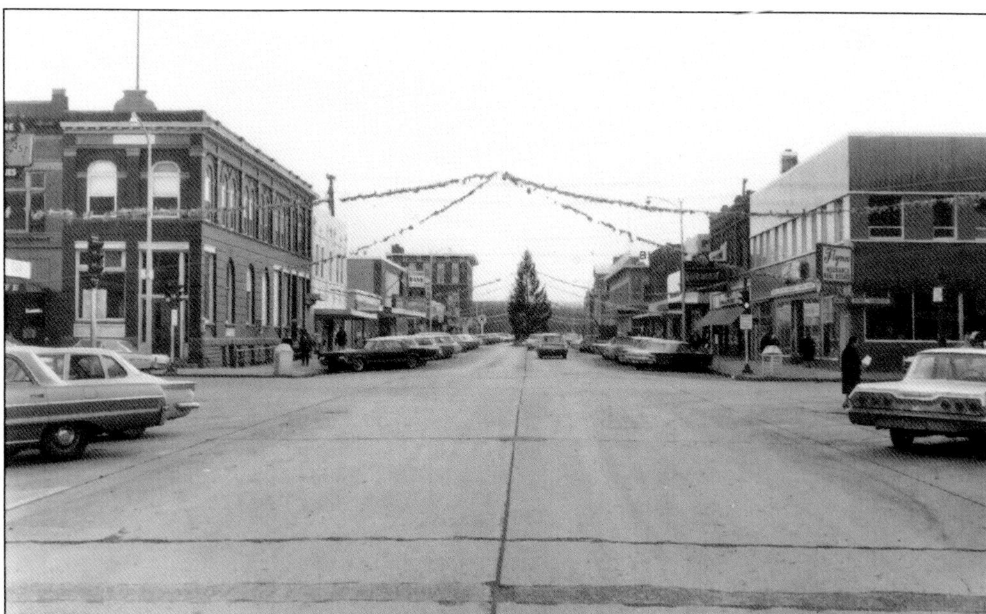
Christmas on Third Avenue in the late 1960s was celebrated with garlands and a tree in the intersection of Third and Second Street. To the right of the bank building on the left side of the photograph, one can see access to the businesses located underground. (Courtesy of the Clack Museum.)

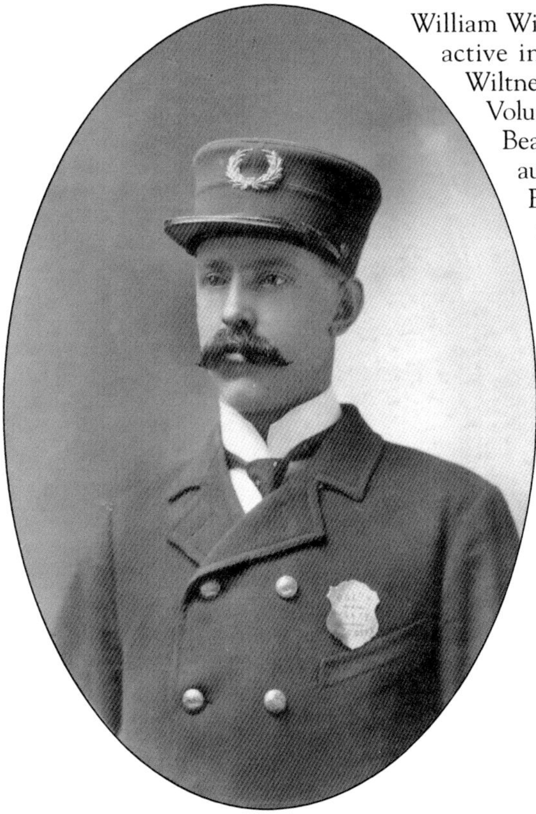

William Wiltner came to Havre in 1895 and was very active in the community. In addition to owning Wiltner's Market, he served as chief of the Havre Volunteer Fire Department, owned a farm along Beaver Creek, and was considered to be a local authority on Havre's early days. In 1969, Earl Bronson interviewed Wiltner, who recalled a rowdy and raucous town when he first arrived. (Courtesy of the Clack Museum.)

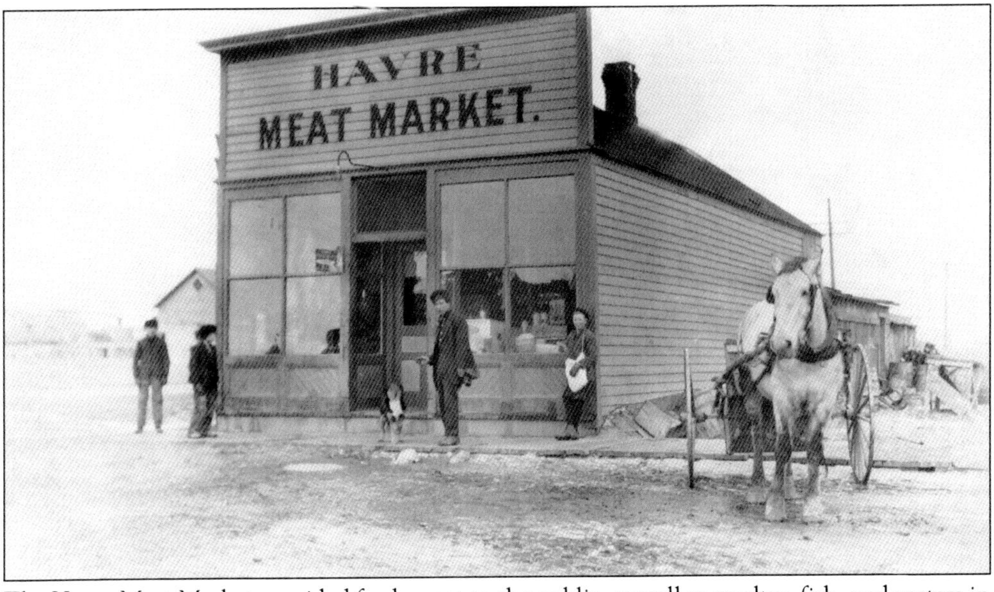

The Havre Meat Market provided fresh meat to the public, as well as poultry, fish, and oysters in season. The building was located on the south side of the 300 block of Second Street and later became Wiltner's Meat and Grocery Store. The false front and recessed doorway are typical of downtown structures during that era. The chimney is of an interesting style, rather than being straight and plain. (Courtesy of the Clack Museum.)

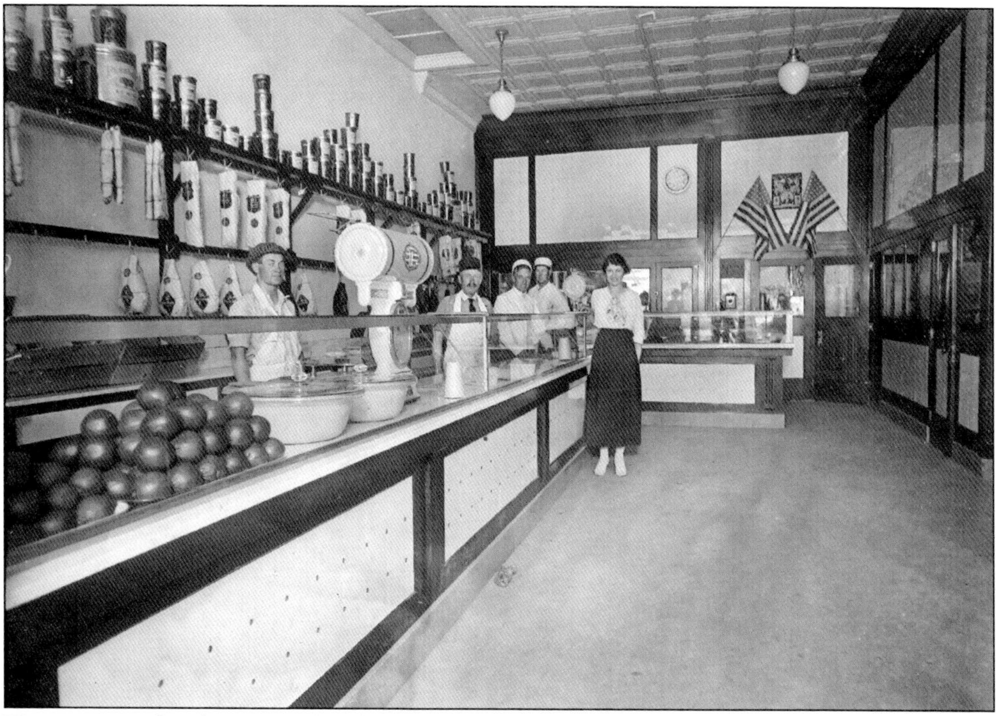

The interior of Wiltner's Market shows a clean and orderly operation. Wiltner's Market offered many choices of meats, including ham, sausages, and several brands of lard. Wiltner's Market was located on Second Street. The building was later Anthony's Clothing Store. (Courtesy of MSU-Northern, Al Lucke Collection.)

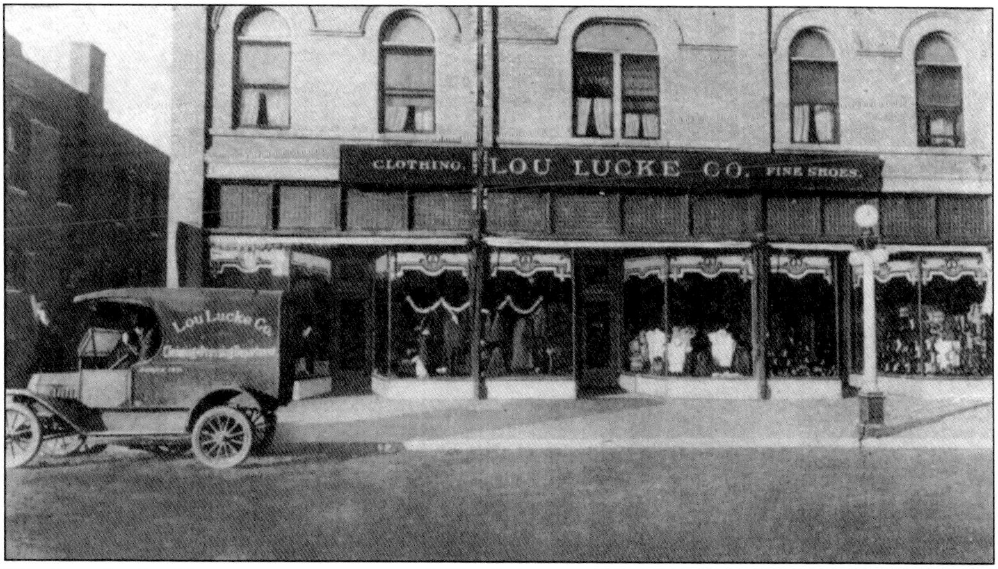

The Lou Lucke Company was an icon of Third Avenue for many years. Catering to "Clothing for Men, Shoes for Everyone," it sold products including Florsheim shoes for the men, Peacock shoes for the ladies, Hart Schaeffner suits, Stetson hats, Samsonite luggage, and Pendleton shirts and blankets. It operated at its location at 321 Third Avenue from 1911 to 1962, and the phone number was 151. (Courtesy of the Clack Museum.)

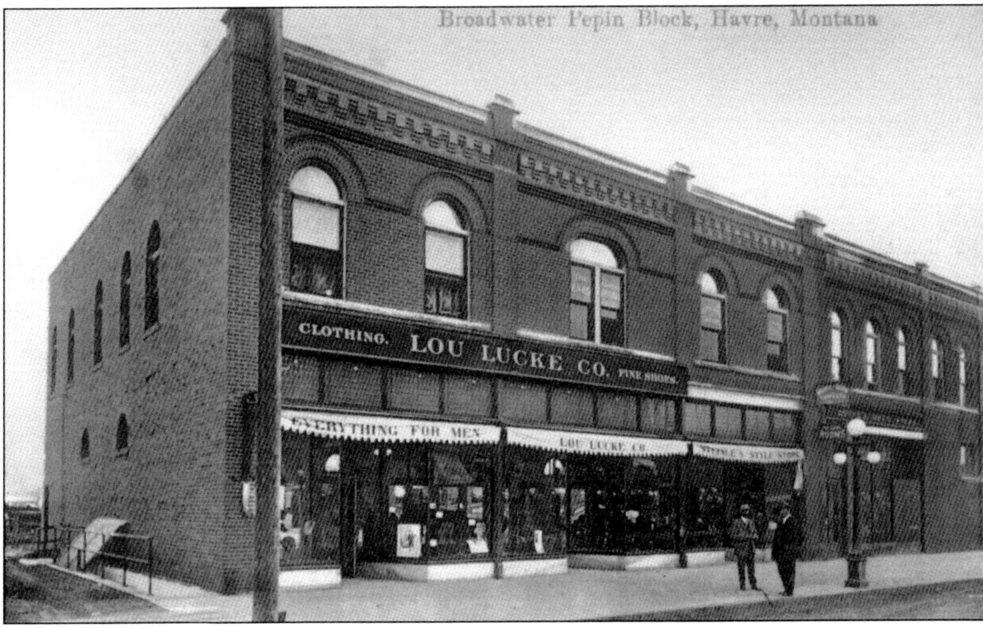

This postcard shows the exterior of the Lou Lucke store and Boone's Drug Store around 1917. Rooms on the second floor were offered for rent until 1958. Boone's Drug Store had several locations in Havre over time. It offered prescriptions and medicines for humans, vaccines and medicines for animals, and a soda fountain. (Courtesy of MSU-Northern, Al Lucke Collection.)

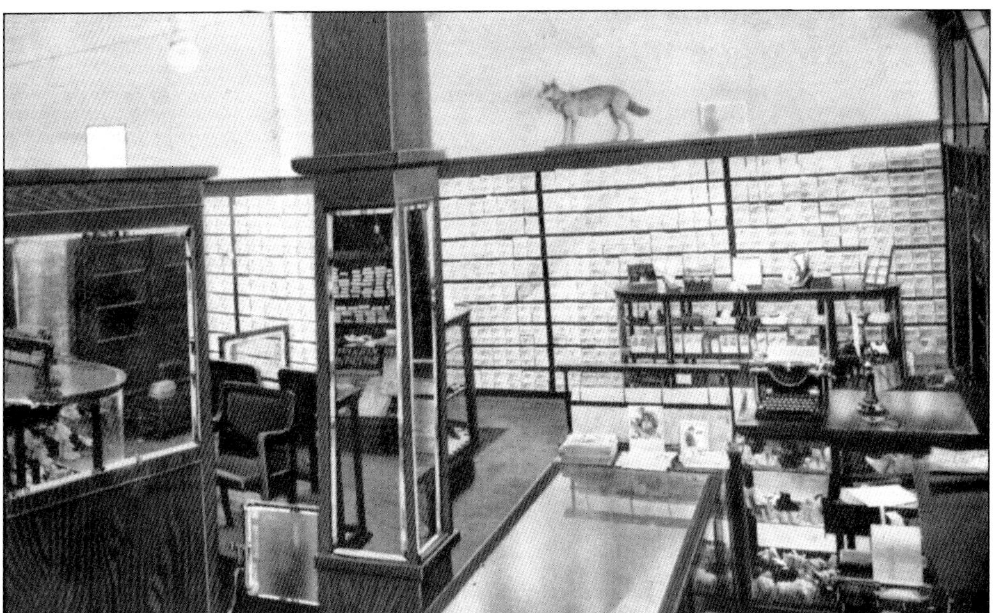

The interior of the Lou Lucke Company shows rows of shoes and a stuffed coyote on the top shelf. The Lou Lucke Company was noted not only for its good selection of shoes and clothing, but also for the stuffed animals that could be found throughout the store. The coyote can be seen at the Clack Museum. (Courtesy of MSU-Northern, Al Lucke Collection.)

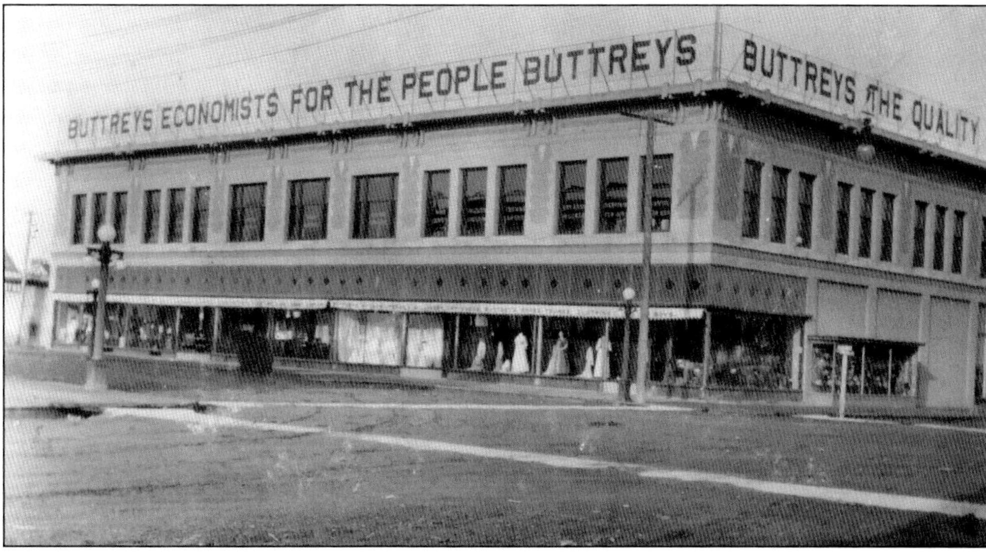

The Buttrey Department Store, located where the Atrium Mall is currently, sold everything from clothing to furnishings. Montana's first radio station, KFBB, was also headquartered here. In addition, a restaurant was located in the basement under the sidewalk. Many people recall the restaurant, which could be very cold in the winter and very warm in the summer. By all accounts, the food was good, so the varying temperatures did not keep customers away. (Courtesy of MSU-Northern, Al Lucke Collection.)

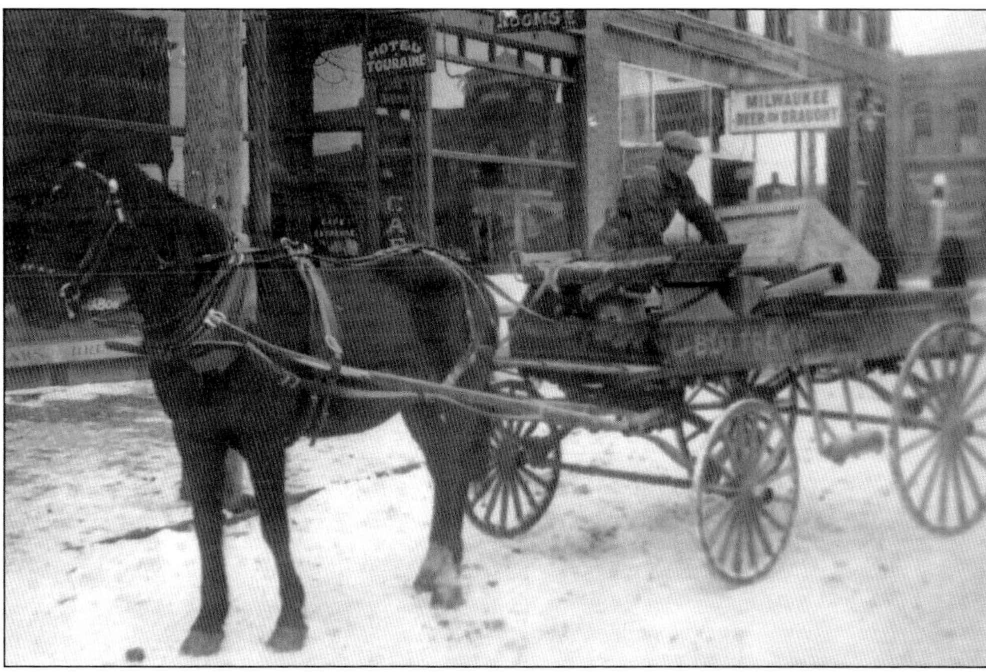

Buttrey's offered its customers delivery service by horse-drawn wagon during its early days. A delivery is being made along First Street about 1912. The following year, Buttrey's was the first to offer delivery via automobile in the state of Montana. A Verrac delivery truck was purchased to make the convenient delivery to those who requested it. (Courtesy of MSU-Northern, Al Lucke Collection.)

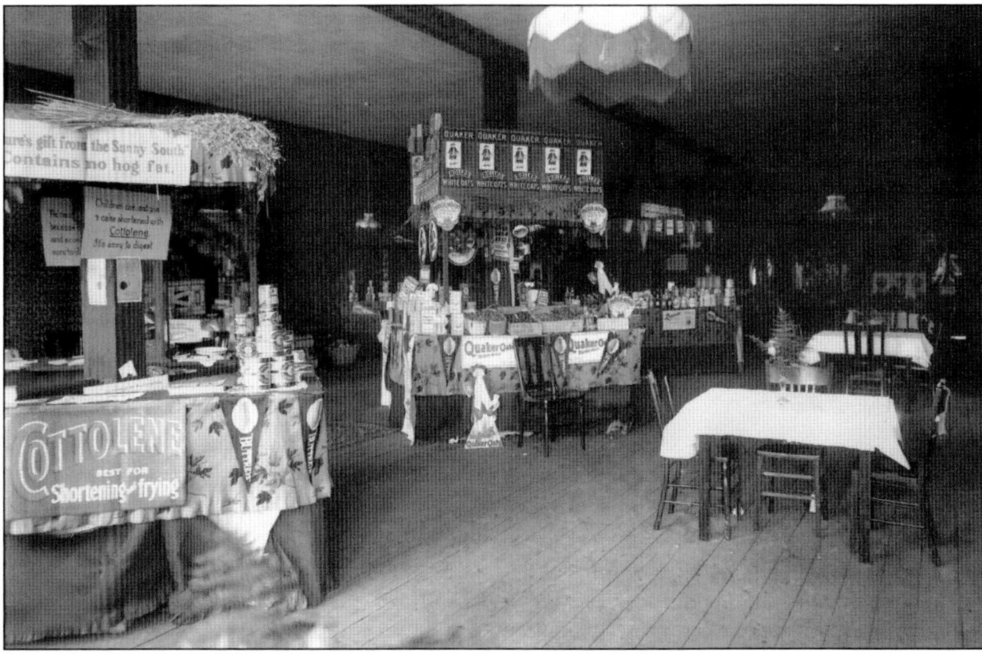

Buttrey's also participated in Merchandise Fairs, promoting the goods offered in the store. The product booth at left is promoting Cottolene, a brand of shortening. In the middle of the photograph, Quaker products including rolled white oats and puffed wheat are being promoted. Richelieu brand canned goods are to the right. (Courtesy of MSU-Northern, Al Lucke Collection.)

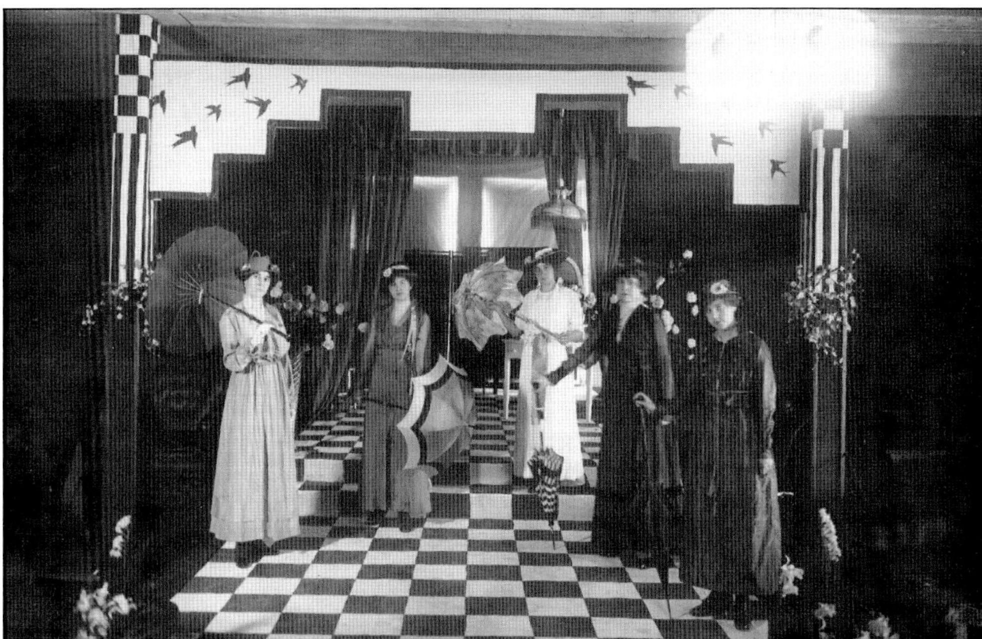

Buttrey's Department Store hosted a fashion show, promoting the clothing items offered in the store. A group of local ladies models clothing around 1913. Dresses were still long, and hats and gloves were customary during the time. A parasol offered shade from the scorching sun—or simply a fashion statement. (Courtesy of MSU-Northern, Al Lucke Collection.)

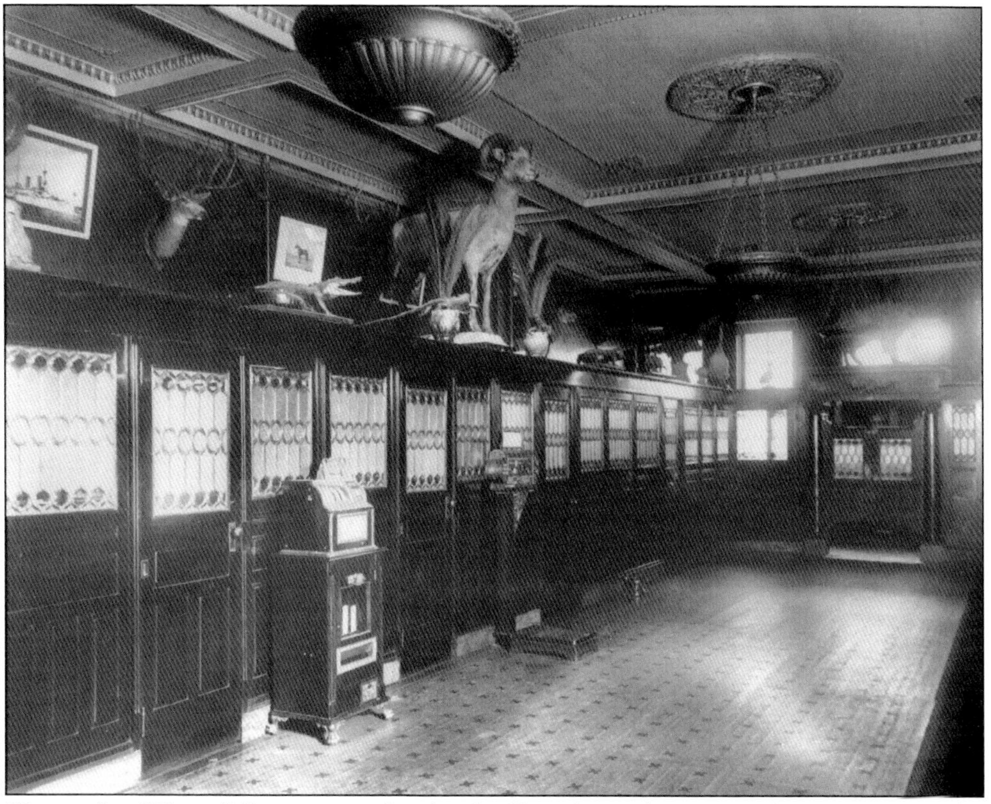

Christopher "Shorty" Young, considered to be Havre's vice king, spared no expense on the inside of the Mint Saloon. Inch-thick linoleum, leaded-glass textured windows for the booths, and stuffed animals were included. Some of the booths and two of the gold-painted plaster light fixtures are in "Shorty's" office at Havre Beneath the Streets. (Courtesy of MSU-Northern, Al Lucke Collection.)

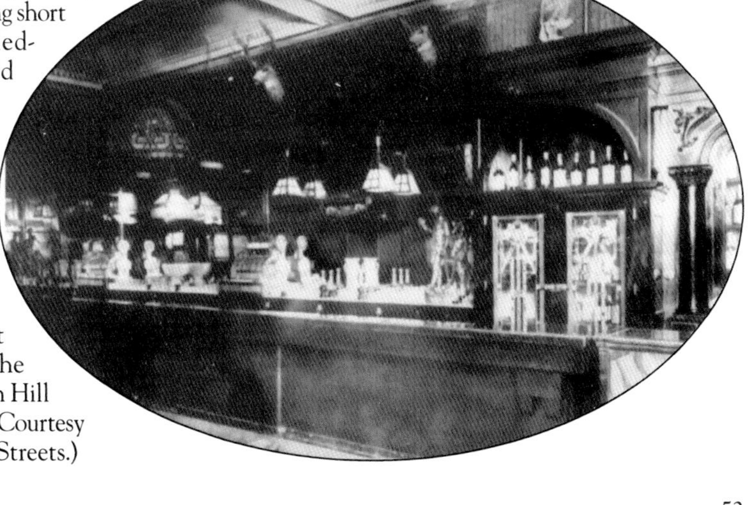

The back bar at Shorty Young's Mint Saloon was nothing short of spectacular. Leaded-glass cabinetry held the bar's inventory, and several stained-glass light fixtures illuminated the area. A coffered ceiling added architectural interest. Stuffed animals were a special feature in the Mint Saloon, showcasing the abundance of wildlife in Hill County and Montana. (Courtesy of Havre Beneath the Streets.)

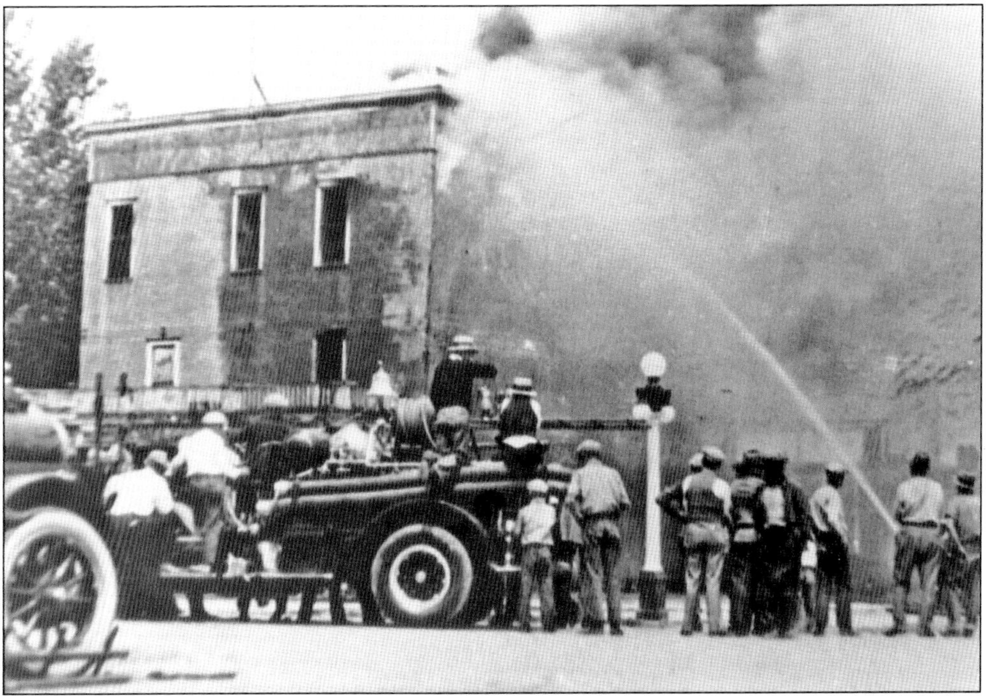

Christopher "Shorty" Young's infamous Montana Concert Hall, locally known as the "Honky Tonk," burns in 1929. It had a saloon, a stage for vaudeville acts, and a gambling hall with several different games available. However, Crib Row was located just a short distance away, and those of more polite society, as well as law enforcement, viewed it as a menace. Shorty's fortunes came and went, but a trust he established benefits the community to this day. (Courtesy of the Frank DeRosa Memorial Railroad Museum.)

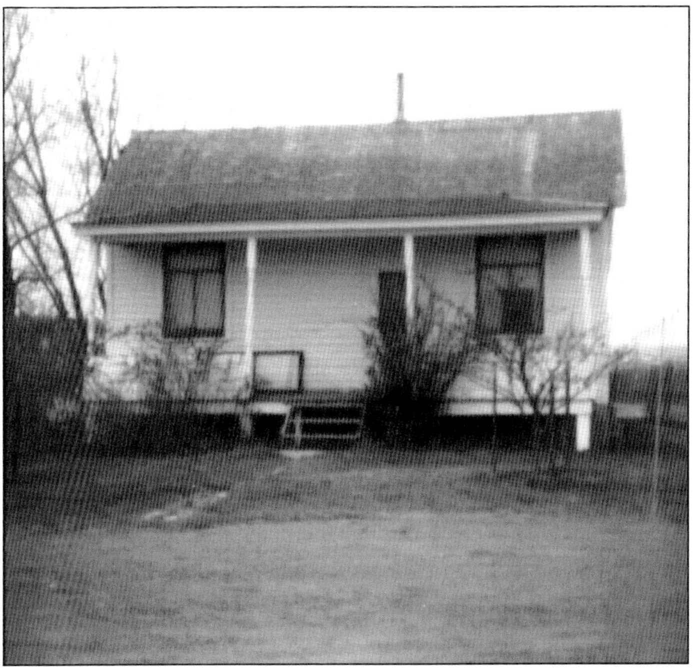

Shorty Young's interests were more than owning bars and houses of prostitution. He also had a ranch. It was located where the fairgrounds are now. His ranch house, shown in this photograph, was much more modest than his other homes. It was a simple, wood-framed structure and remained at the fairgrounds until the late 1980s, when it was razed. (Courtesy of Gary Wilson.)

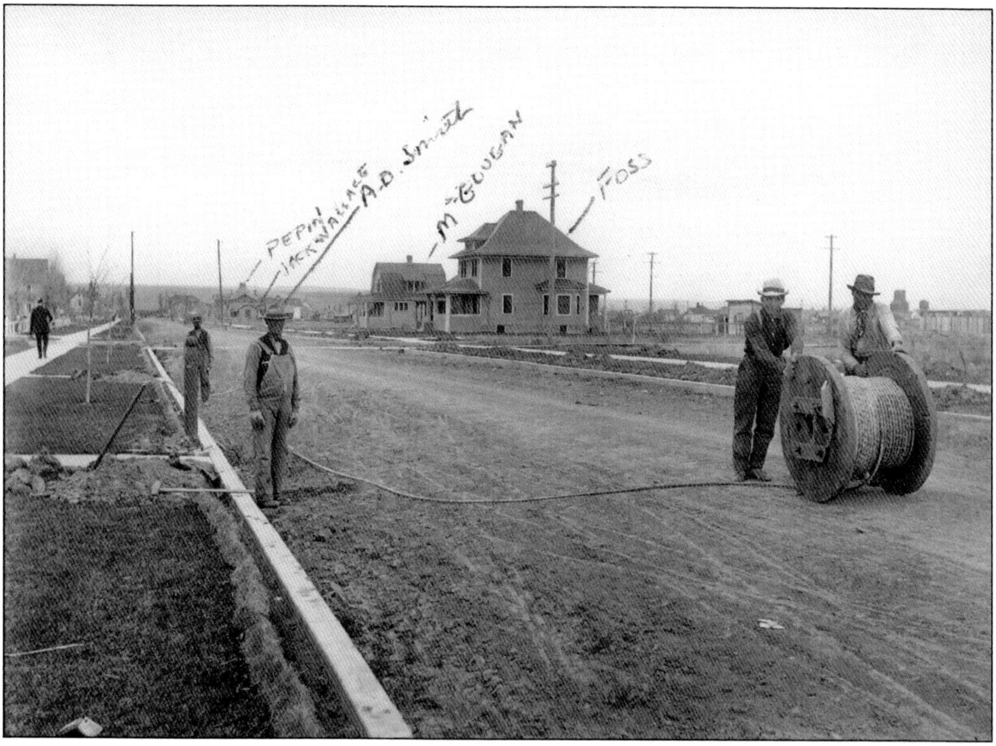

The Havre Electric Company installed the first electric streetlights in 1913. In the background is the roof of the Pepin Mansion, and in the foreground is the Foss house, located at 525 Fourth Avenue. The Havre Electric Company was incorporated in 1904. In 1914, the Havre Electric Company was acquired by Montana Power Company. (Courtesy of MSU-Northern, Al Lucke Collection.)

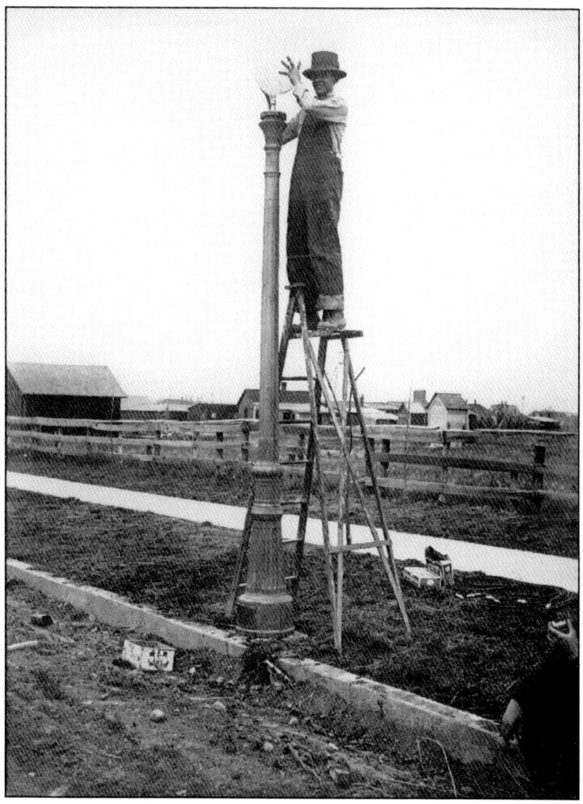

A. D. "Nosey" Smith, Havre's first parks director, puts the glass globe on Havre's first streetlights on Fourth Avenue. The lights were manufactured by the Great Falls Iron Works. The Great Falls Iron Works building is still in Great Falls, although it has found an adaptive reuse as office space and Dante's Restaurant. (Courtesy of MSU-Northern, Al Lucke Collection.)

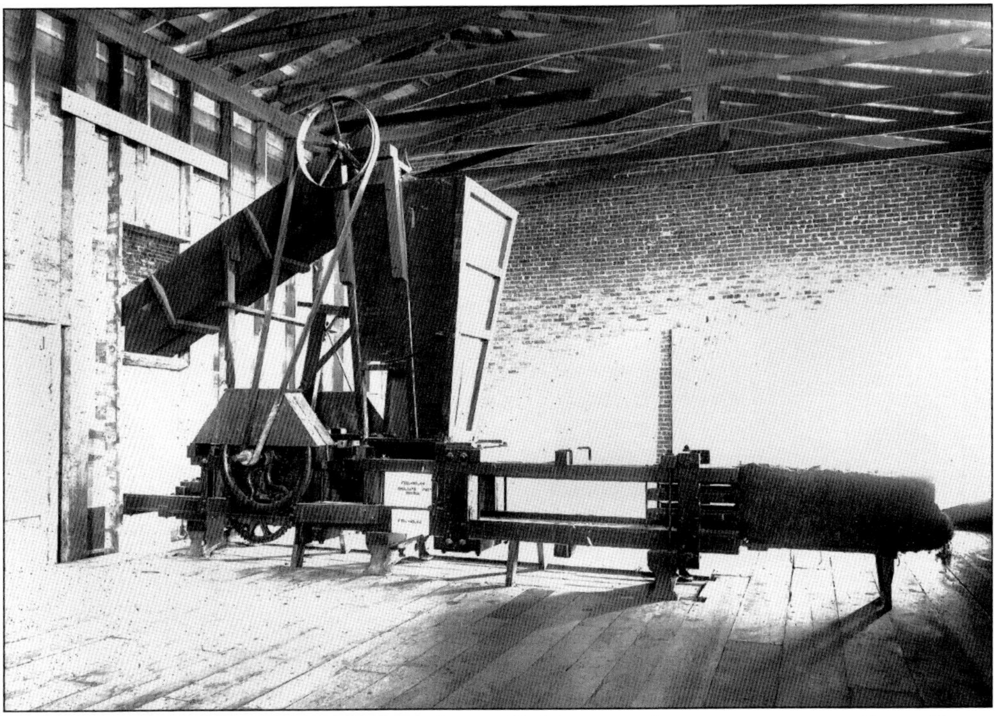

Flax was the first crop grown by homesteaders in Hill County. As a consequence, a flax mill was built. Flax was grown for its seeds, which in turn were used to cultivate crops elsewhere. A crusher with a ratchet crank was used to extract the oil from the flaxseed. Flax did not yield well, and the price could not compare with other crops, such as wheat and oats. (Courtesy of MSU-Northern, Al Lucke Collection.)

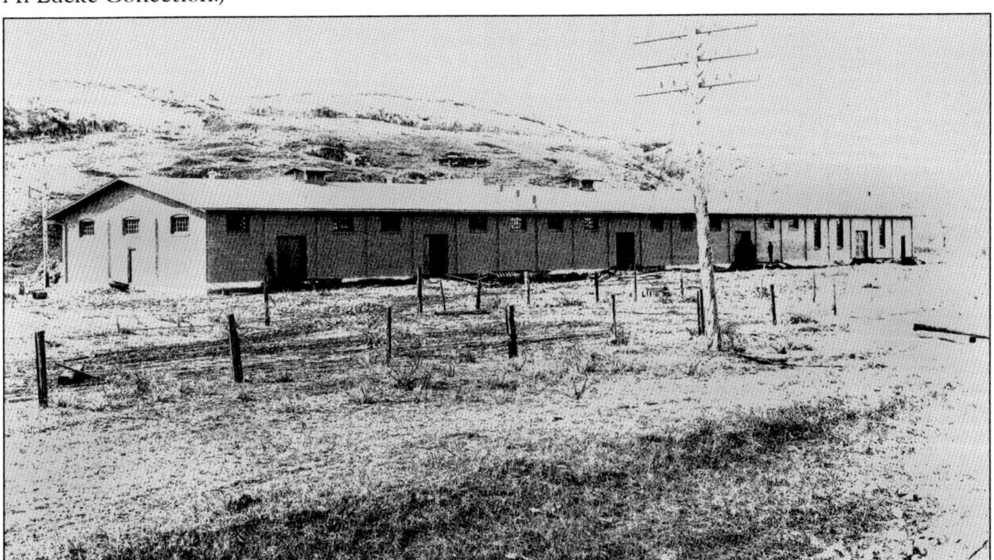

The Havre Flax Mill was located west of town near the present-day water treatment plant. It was north of the railroad tracks and south of the Milk River. It was in operation from around 1914 through 1916. After flax production ceased, the building became the border patrol for several years. (Courtesy of MSU-Northern, Al Lucke Collection.)

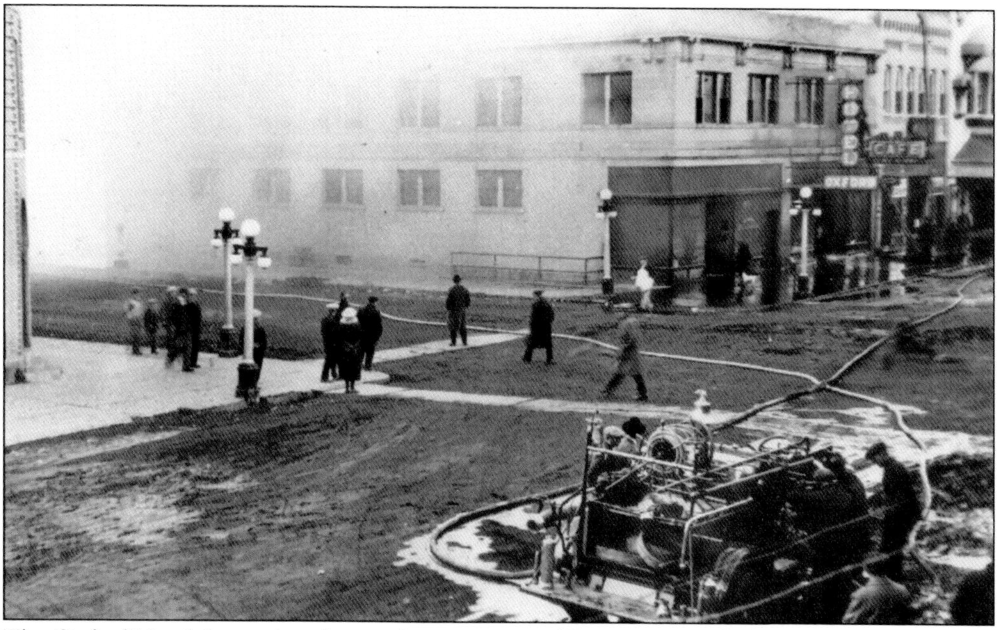

The Oxford Hotel, located at the northwest corner of First Street and Third Avenue, burned in 1924. The building also housed the Oxford Café. While the fire truck used to suppress the fire was up-to-date technologically, the streets were still dirt with concrete crosswalks to make crossing the street easier. (Courtesy of the Frank DeRosa Memorial Railroad Museum.)

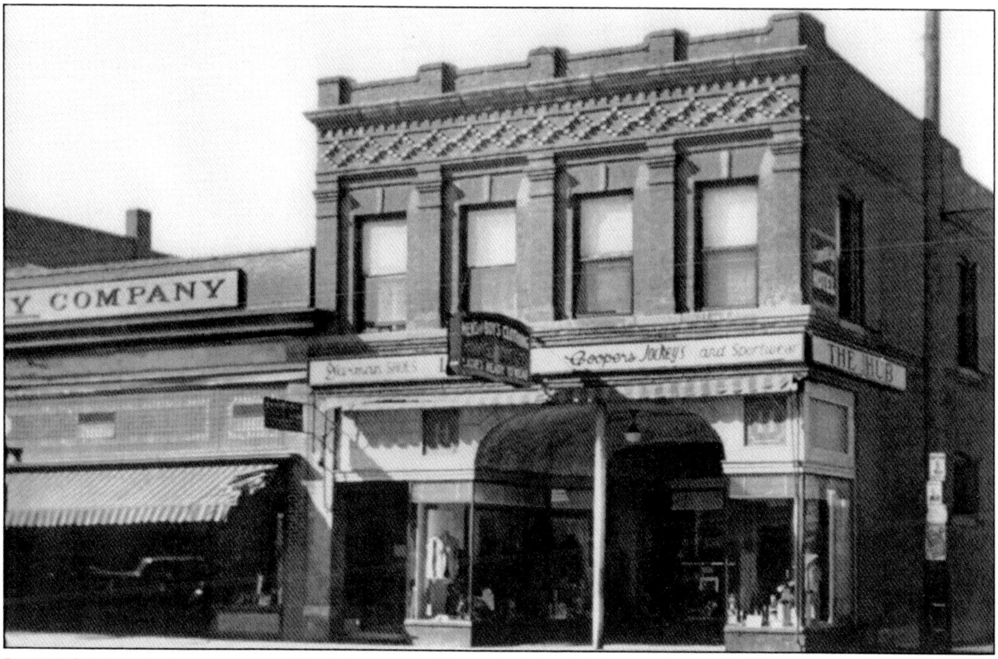

In 1925, Morris Feuer arrived in Havre and founded the Hub Clothing. The Feuers were one of the few Jewish families that lived in Havre. He was originally from Meilec, Poland, and immigrated in 1921. The Hub was a very successful business. Feuer was active in Havre and was a member of the Elks, the Masonic Lodge, the Shriners, and Montana State University–Northern. (Courtesy of the Frank DeRosa Memorial Railroad Museum.)

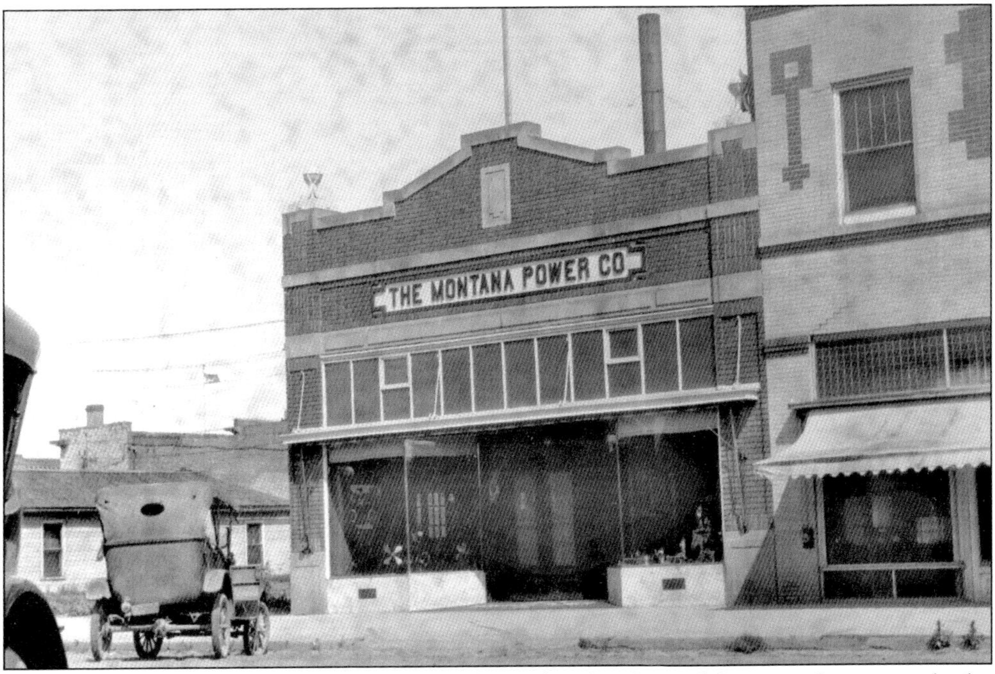

The Montana Power Company building was located at 321 Second Street and is currently the Havre Elks Lodge. The recessed doorway leads to offices. A showroom featuring products offered for sale was also in the building. In 1981, Montana Power Company sold the building to the Elks and, it was remodeled into a lodge and club. (Courtesy of the Clack Museum.)

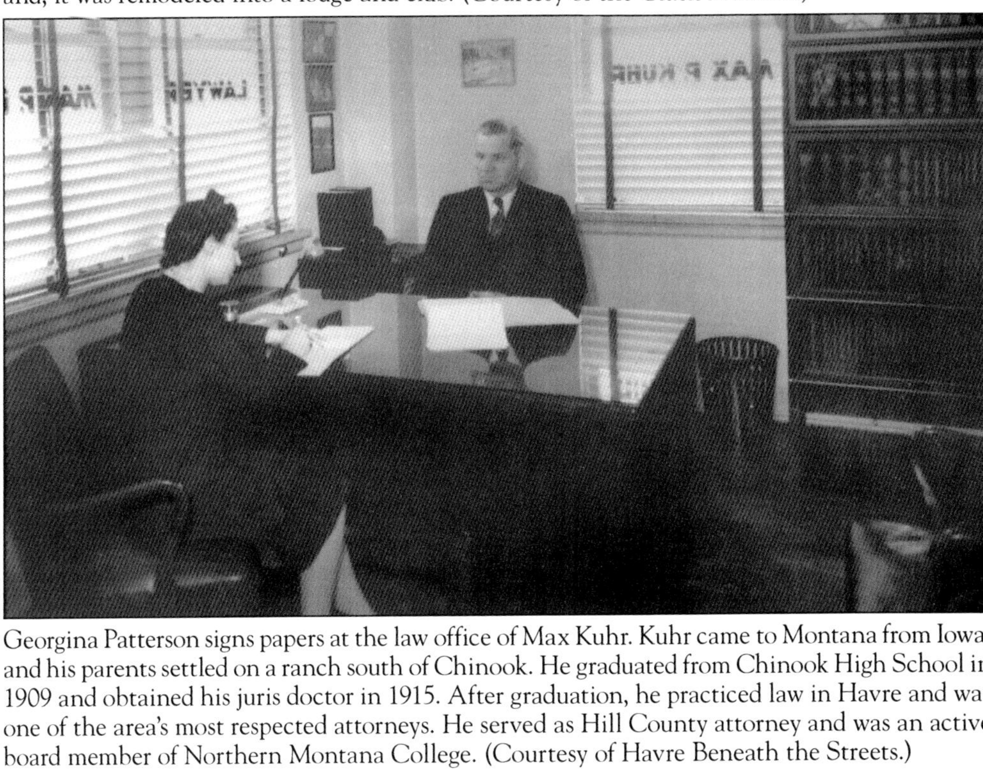

Georgina Patterson signs papers at the law office of Max Kuhr. Kuhr came to Montana from Iowa, and his parents settled on a ranch south of Chinook. He graduated from Chinook High School in 1909 and obtained his juris doctor in 1915. After graduation, he practiced law in Havre and was one of the area's most respected attorneys. He served as Hill County attorney and was an active board member of Northern Montana College. (Courtesy of Havre Beneath the Streets.)

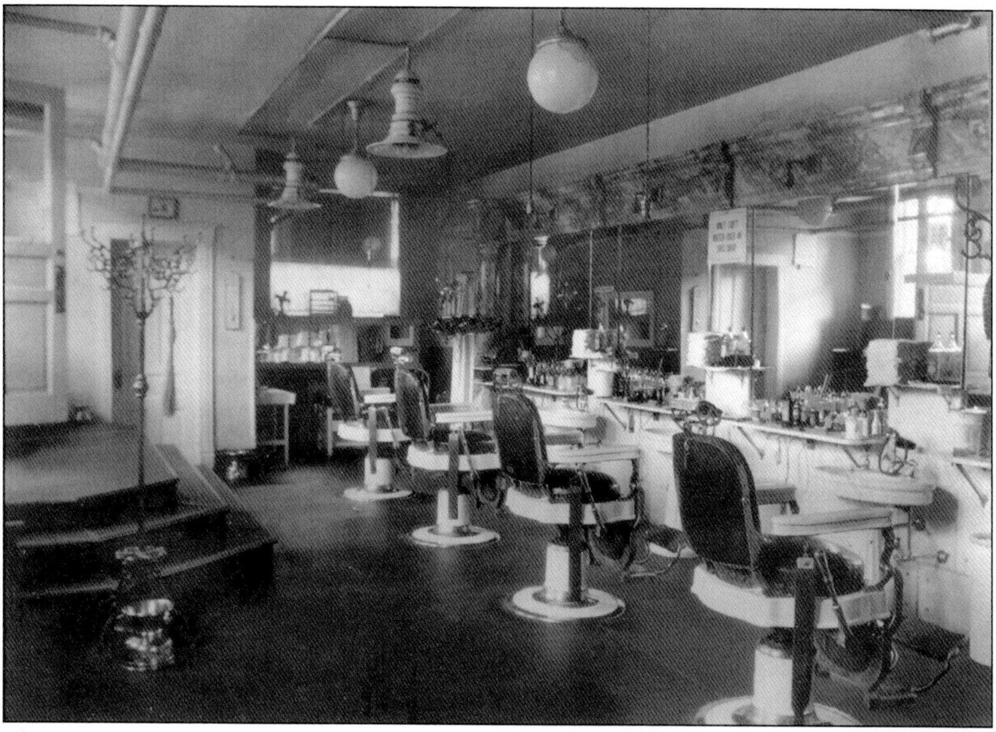

The Fountain Barber Shop was a popular place for a man to get his hair cut and a close shave. Located underground at the corner of First Street and Third Avenue, it is shown here in 1913. In later years, it moved to the 200 block of First Street and was in operation until 2000. Many of its artifacts are on exhibit at Havre Beneath the Streets. (Courtesy of Havre Beneath the Streets.)

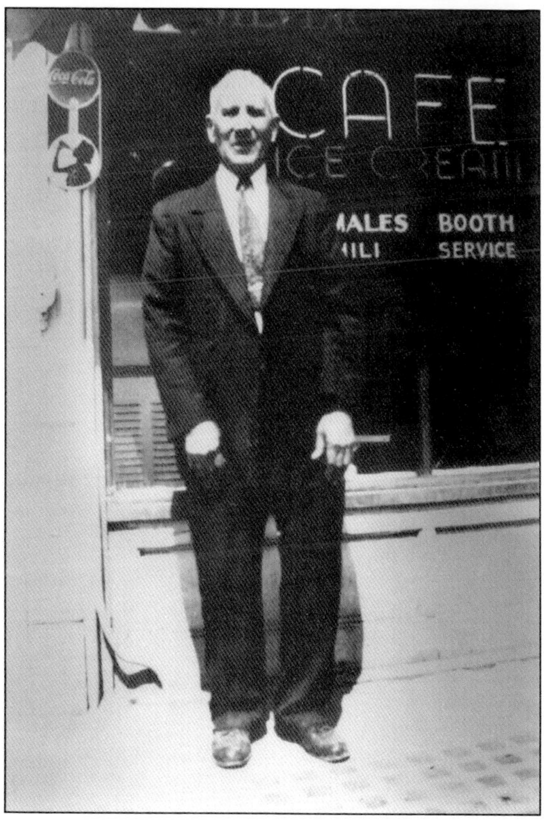

"Hot Tamale" Jim Shawlee came to Havre from Afghanistan. He started selling tamales out of a wagon and eventually in his restaurants. He is photographed in front of his Silver Grill. The squares at his feet are old glass tiles once found throughout Havre on its sidewalks. These were used to illuminate the underground passageways. There is only one place in Havre where they can still be seen, on Second Avenue next to the Eagles Club. (Courtesy of Havre Beneath the Streets.)

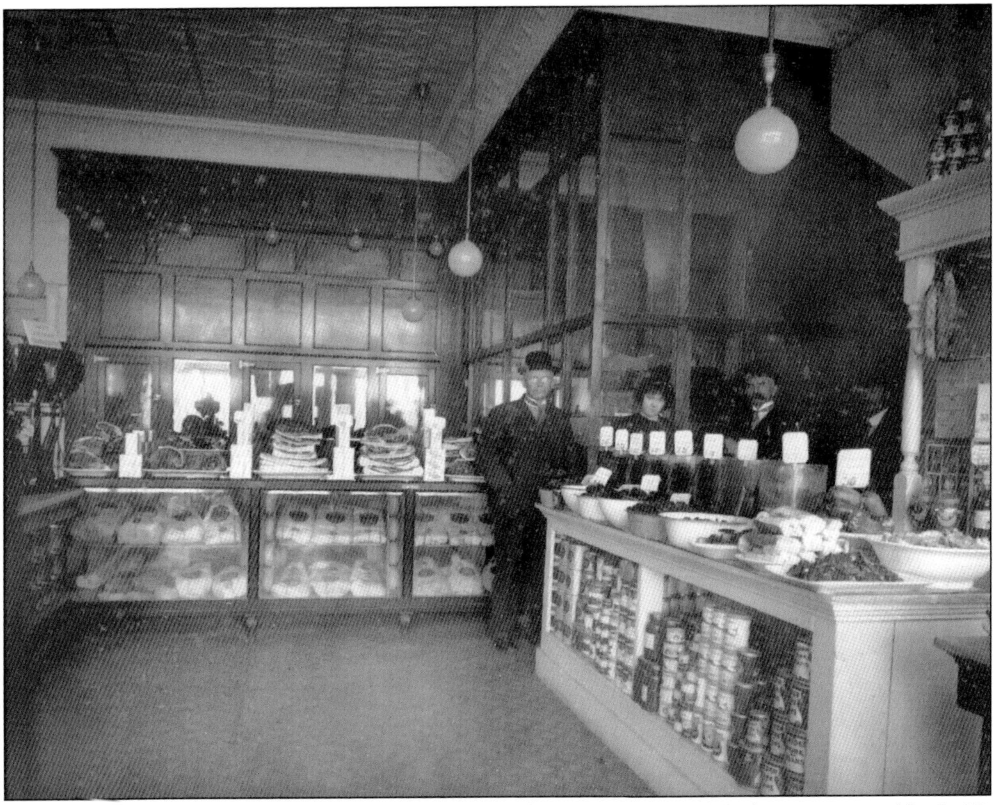

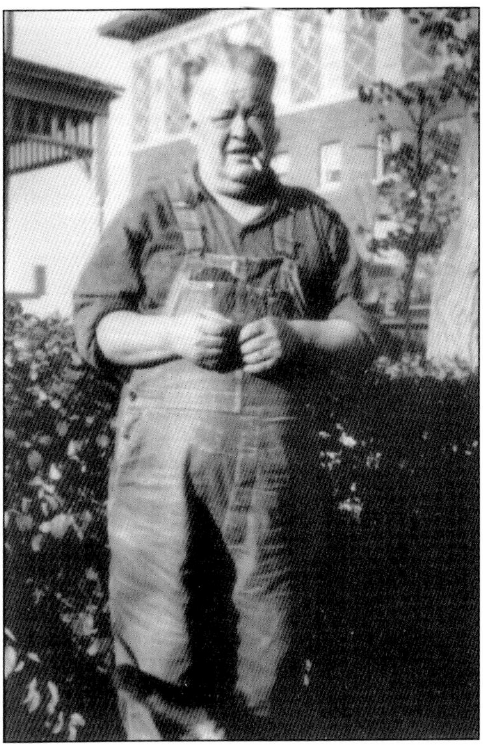

The Pioneer Meat Market was owned by L. K. Devlin and Simon Pepin. It was located at 218 First Street; the sign is still on the building facade. The store offered a variety of meats, cheeses, and canned goods to customers. Several brands of lard were also sold, a testament to the dietary customs of the time. (Courtesy of Havre Beneath the Streets.)

Cedric "Pop" Cassady owned a blacksmith shop in Havre for many years. Anyone seeking services such as sharpening shears, shoeing horses, or anything else to do with metal sought his expertise. His boys, Cedric Jr. and Elmer, helped him in the shop. Pop opened his first shop in the 1930s where Heltne's Service Center was located. Over the years, the shop moved to various locations, including just behind where Bear Paw Credit Union is today. Pop retired in the 1940s. (Courtesy of Havre Beneath the Streets.)

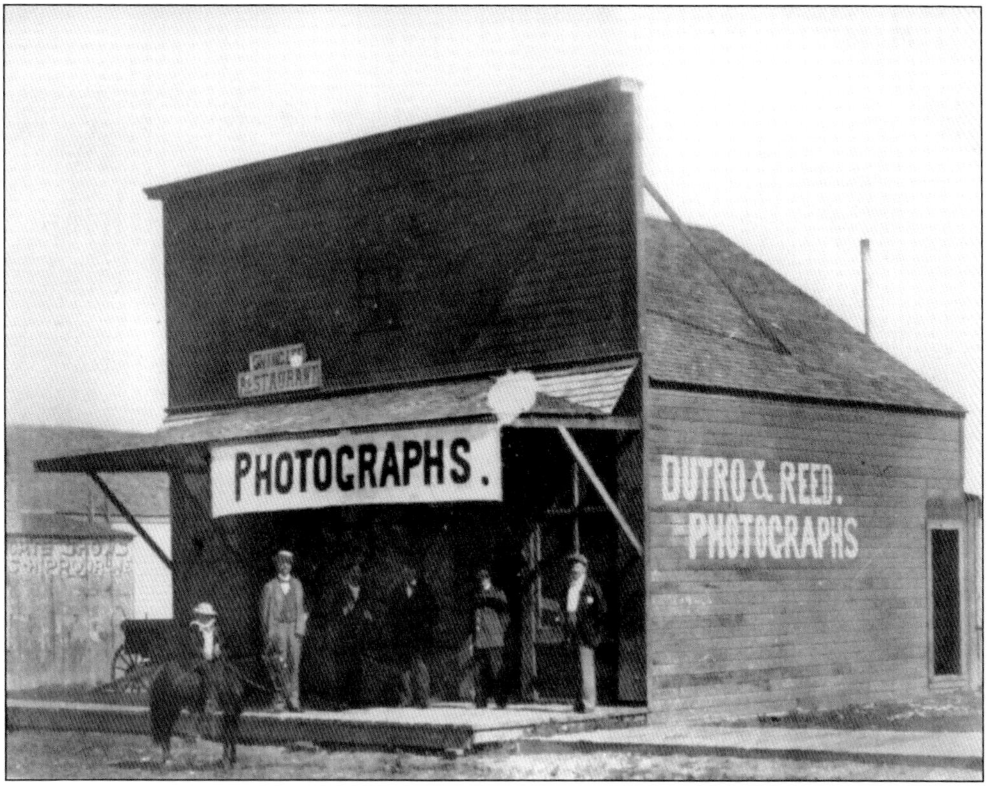

Dutro and Reed Photograph Gallery also had a restaurant as part of its building. The building was located on First Street and was a victim of the Great Fire of 1904, which destroyed most of downtown Havre. The building is typical of the era, with a false front to give the impression of a larger building when looking at it from the front and a pitched roof in the back of the false front. (Courtesy of MSU-Northern, Al Lucke Collection.)

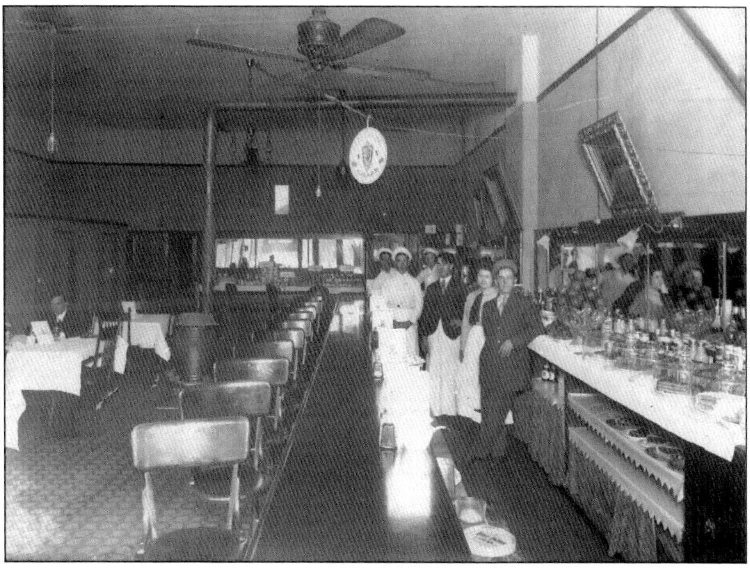

The Grill Café was located on First Street and offered food to hungry patrons. A cut-glass bowl holds citrus, and pies are offered on the shelf below. A pot-bellied stove provides an early-1900s form of central heating during the cooler months. (Courtesy of MSU-Northern, Al Lucke Collection.)

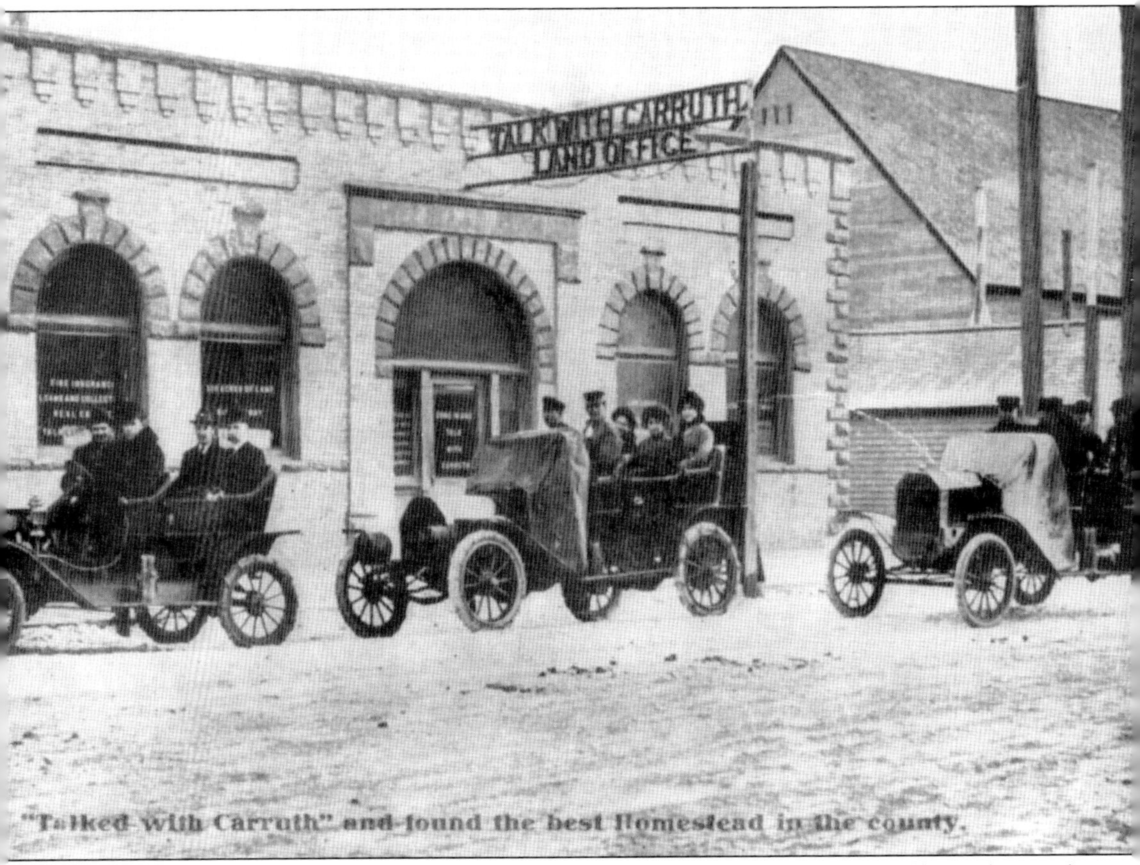

After Hill County was formed in 1912, Edwin C. Carruth opened up a real estate office and assisted homesteaders in their search for that "free farm from Uncle Sam." During the homestead era, thousands of families flocked to Hill County and made their land arrangements with Carruth. In addition, he sold insurance and was active in the development of oil and gas production and many other activities. (Courtesy of MSU-Northern, Al Lucke Collection.)

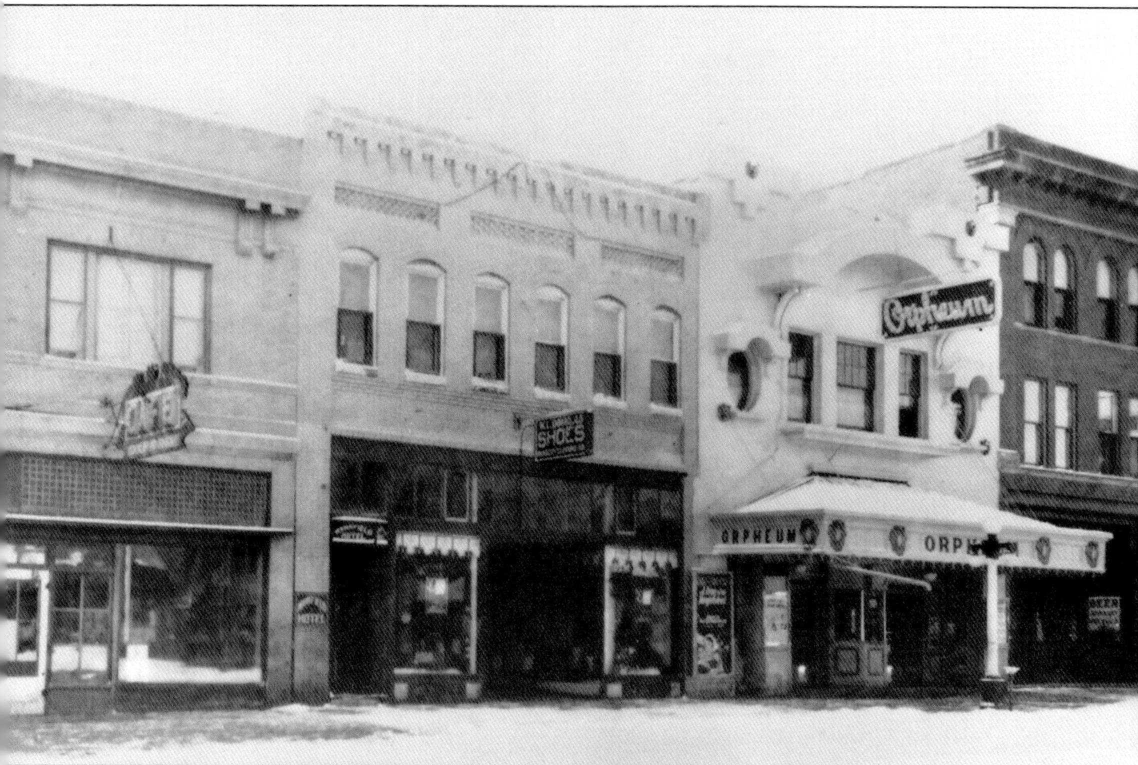

The Mansfield Hotel and Orpheum Theatre were two buildings that long stood on First Street. The Mansfield Hotel offered rooms for rent mostly on a longer-term basis. Many homesteaders rented rooms at the Mansfield Hotel while waiting for their homesteads to be filed. The Orpheum offered movie entertainment for those seeking it. (Courtesy of MSU-Northern, Al Lucke Collection.)

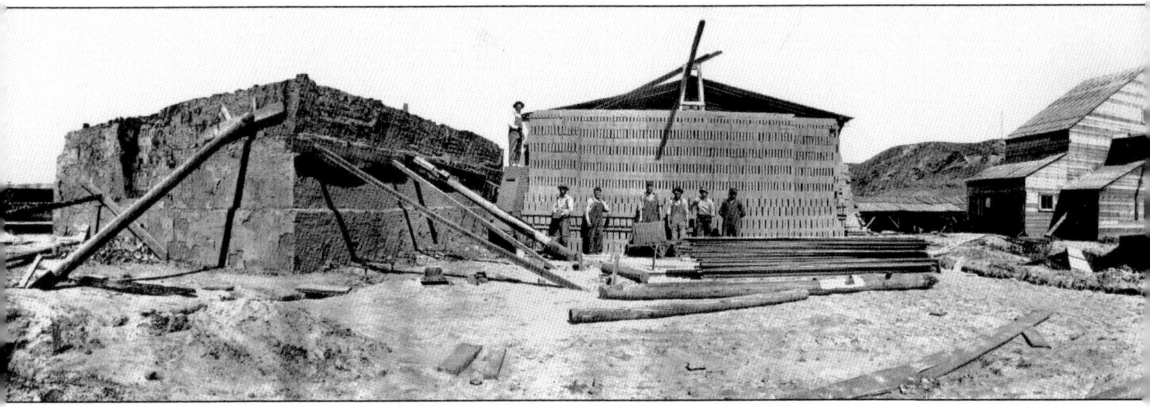

The Havre Brick Company was founded by Joseph Gussenhoven in 1902. Many homes and businesses in Havre were made from Havre brick, and today bricks that bear the town's name are highly sought after and revered. Included in that list of buildings is the Gussenhoven home, also known as "The Castle," at 26 Third Street. Gussenhoven ceased the brick business in 1910. (Courtesy of MSU-Northern, Al Lucke Collection.)

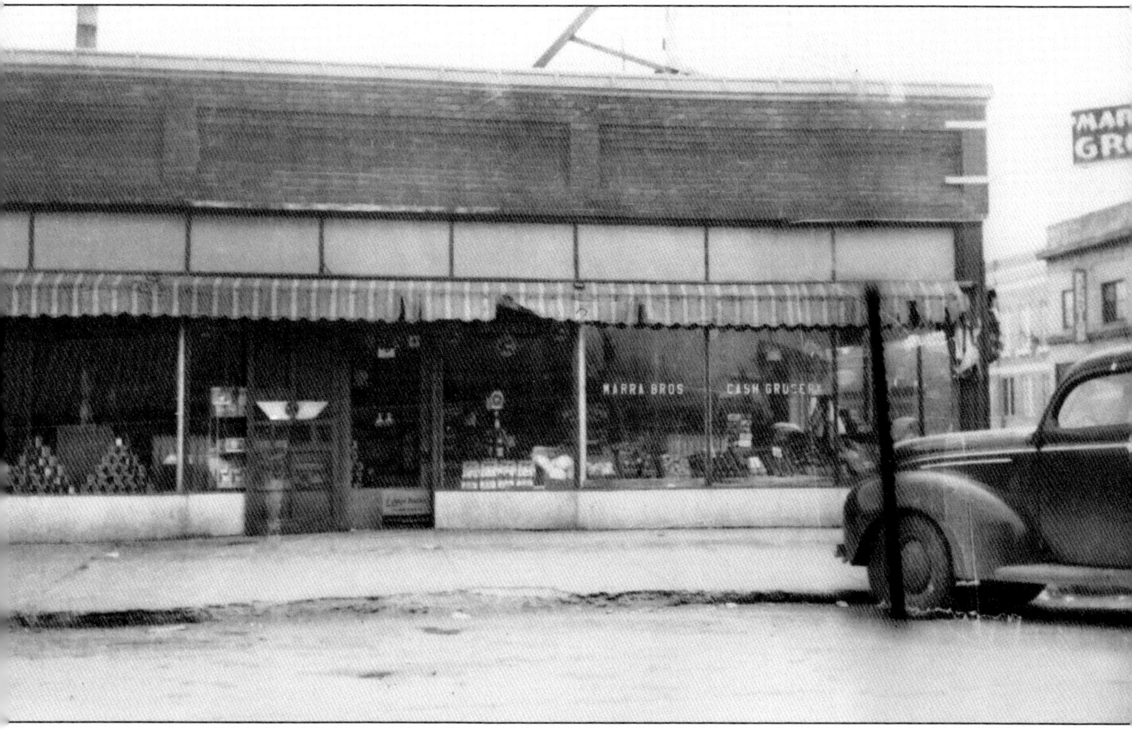

The Marra Brothers' Cash Grocery was located at the northeast corner of Third Avenue and Second Street. Frank and Joe Marra came to Havre from Italy. In 1905, they opened the grocery store. In the background to the right are the Havre Elks Lodge and Kending's, a dry goods and clothing store. William Kending served as city treasurer for Havre for several years and was an active member of the community. (Courtesy of MSU-Northern, Al Lucke Collection.)

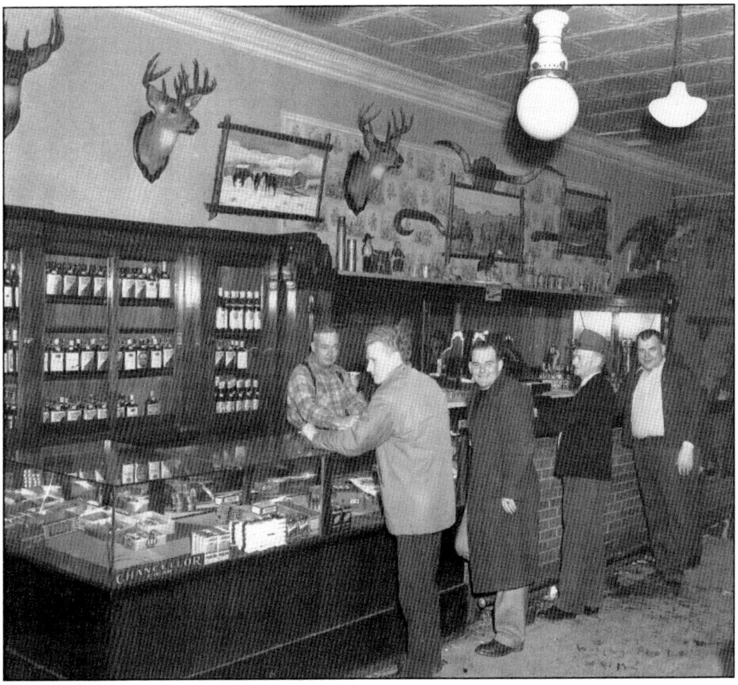

Connelly's Bar was located on Main Street and Third Avenue near the depot. PJ's is currently at its location. Connelly's Bar offered drinks, food such as sandwiches, and tobacco products to its patrons. Tom Connelly owned the bar. It was popular for railroaders and passengers because of its convenient location. (Courtesy of MSU-Northern, Al Lucke Collection.)

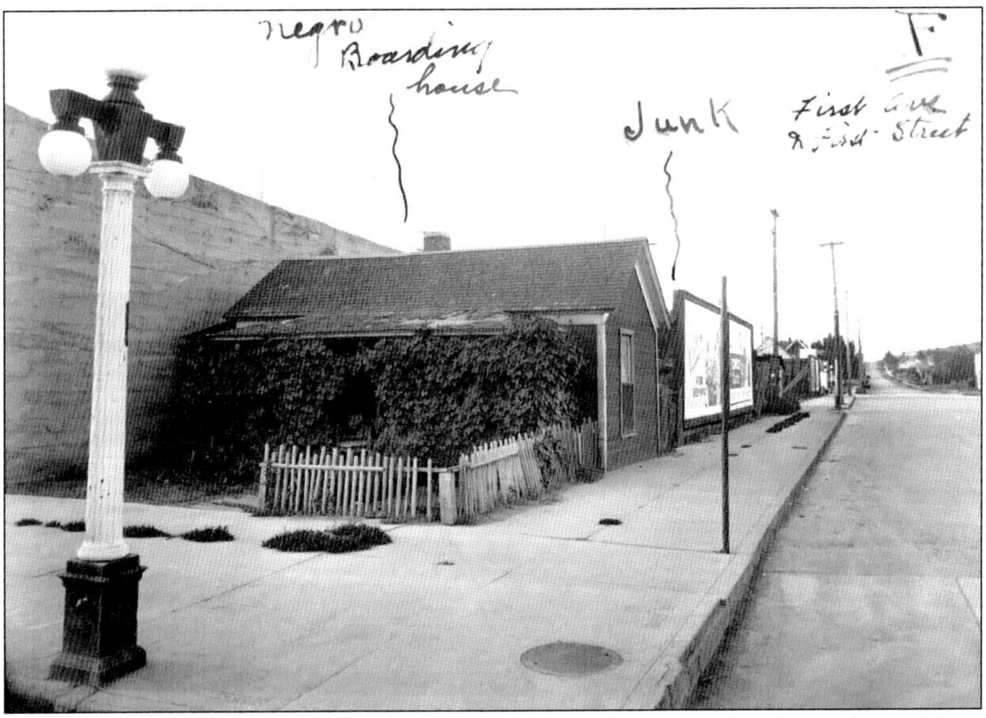

Havre's "Skid Row" was located on First Street just outside of what was then the city limits. Notes on the photograph indicate a "Negro" boardinghouse attributed to local celebrity Alice "Ma Plaz" Pleasant. A large sign disguises unsightly junk. This was a part of what some considered a rougher part of town. These were located on First Avenue and First Street. (Courtesy of MSU-Northern, Al Lucke Collection.)

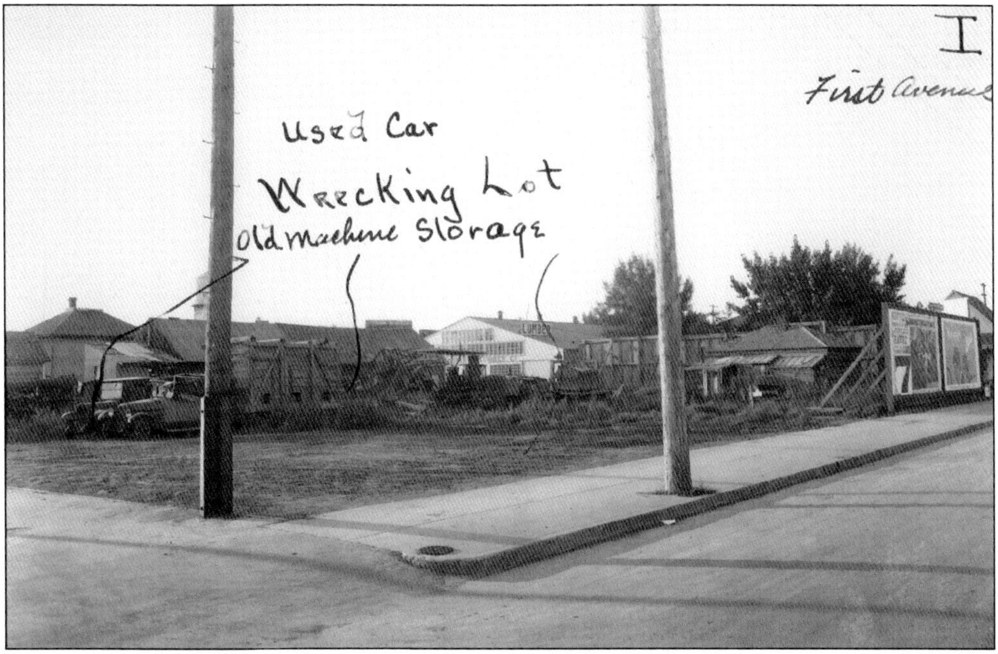

A used car wrecking lot and old machine storage were located on the northeast corner of First Avenue and Second Street. Robinson's Lumber Company can be seen in the background. The location is the part of the block where the *Havre Daily News* and Valley Motor Supply are located. (Courtesy of MSU-Northern, Al Lucke Collection.)

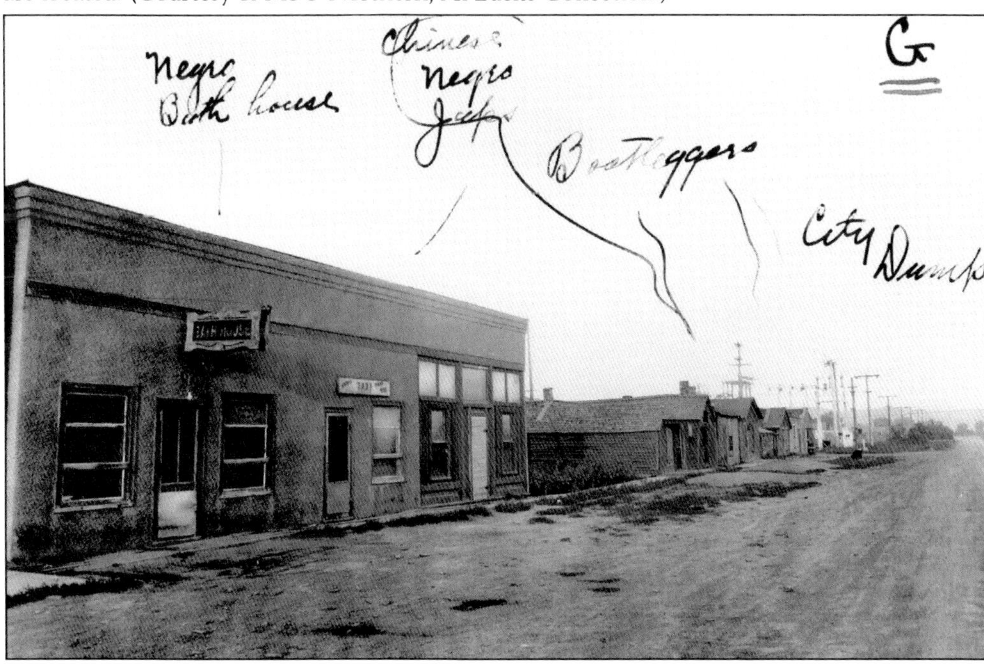

The entrance to the "Honky Tonk" and the red light district was met with a black bathhouse, a taxi service, a building apparently where bootleggers either lived or conducted business, and the city dump. These building were roughly between where Havre Rental and O'Reilly automotive store are currently. (Courtesy of MSU-Northern, Al Lucke Collection.)

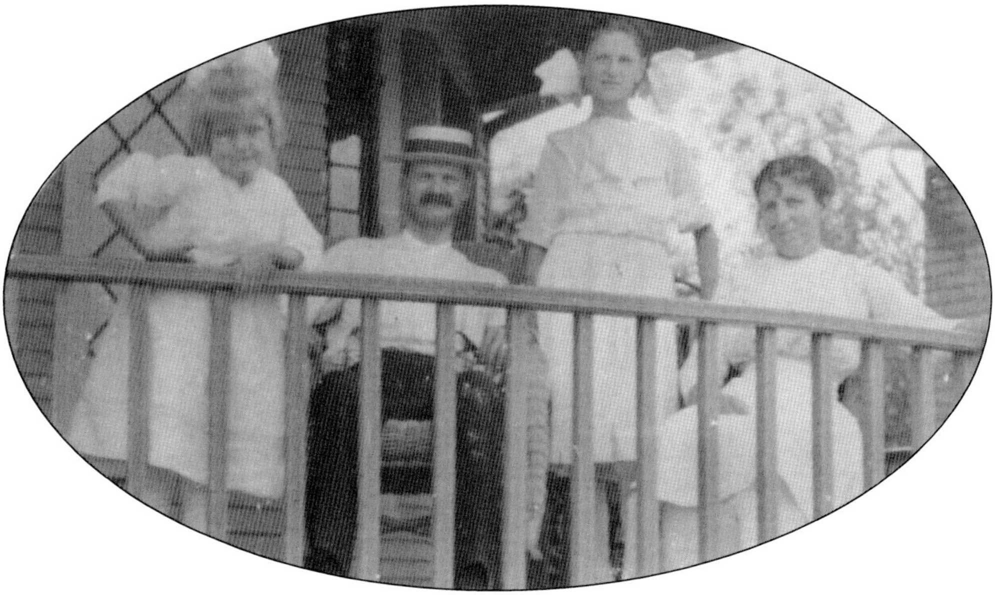

The Olaf Skylstead family is pictured on the front porch of their home located at 210 Third Street. Skylstead was an entrepreneur, engaging in such businesses as furniture, real estate, insurance, and banking, as well as serving as a Chouteau County commissioner. A native of Norway, he was in his home country when he received word that Chouteau County was splitting and was summoned home. This news brought him home early; he was scheduled to board the *Titanic*. (Courtesy of the Clack Museum.)

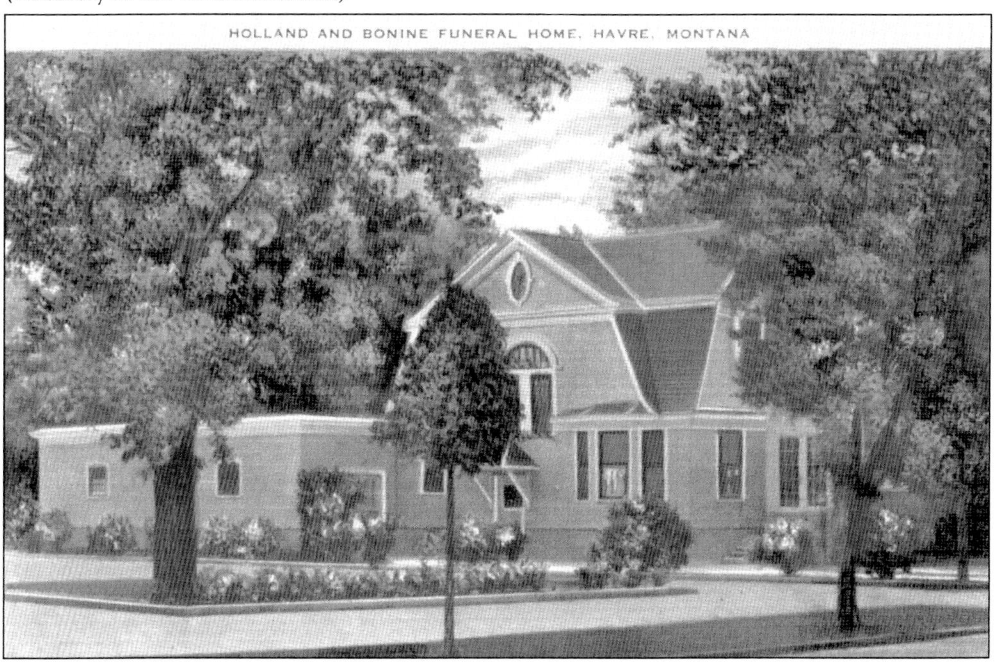

The Holland and Bonine Funeral Home, located at 210 Third Street, is the former Olaf Skylstead home. This postcard, which is color enhanced, shows the building shortly after it was converted from a private residence to a thriving business. When it opened on August 12, 1933, it proclaimed it was "modern in every respect." (Courtesy of the Clack Museum.)

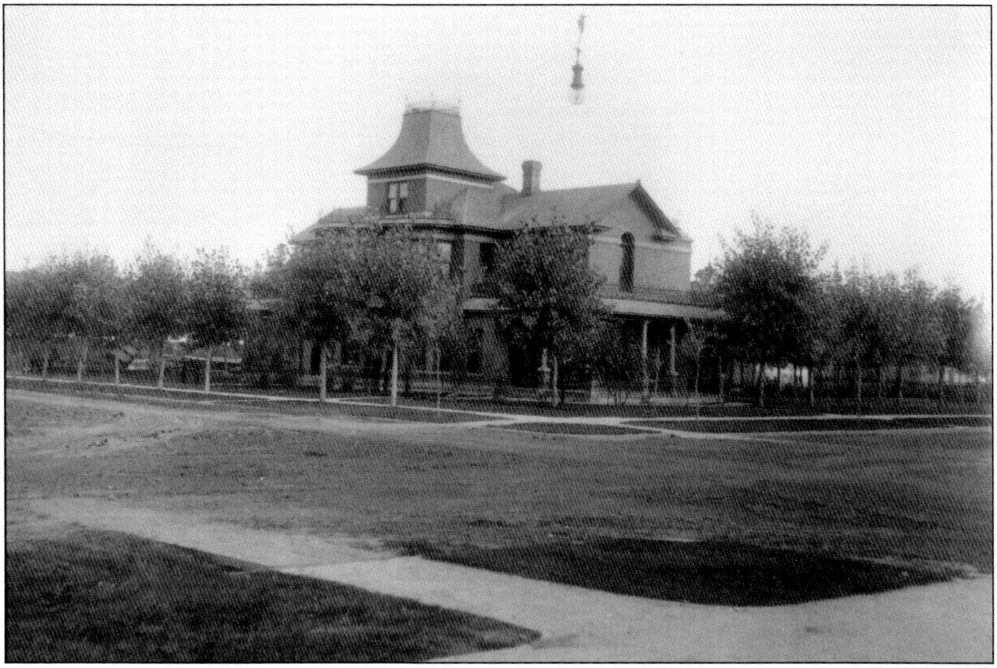

The Simon Pepin Mansion was once located where the Havre/Hill County Library is now. This 14-room mansion was constructed of brick and had a wraparound porch. Simon Pepin owned the P-Cross ranch in the Bear Paws and made his fortune in cattle ranching. He also owned the Pioneer Meat Market in downtown Havre. The mansion was razed in the 1950s to construct a clinic, which was later remodeled as the library. (Courtesy of Emily Mayer.)

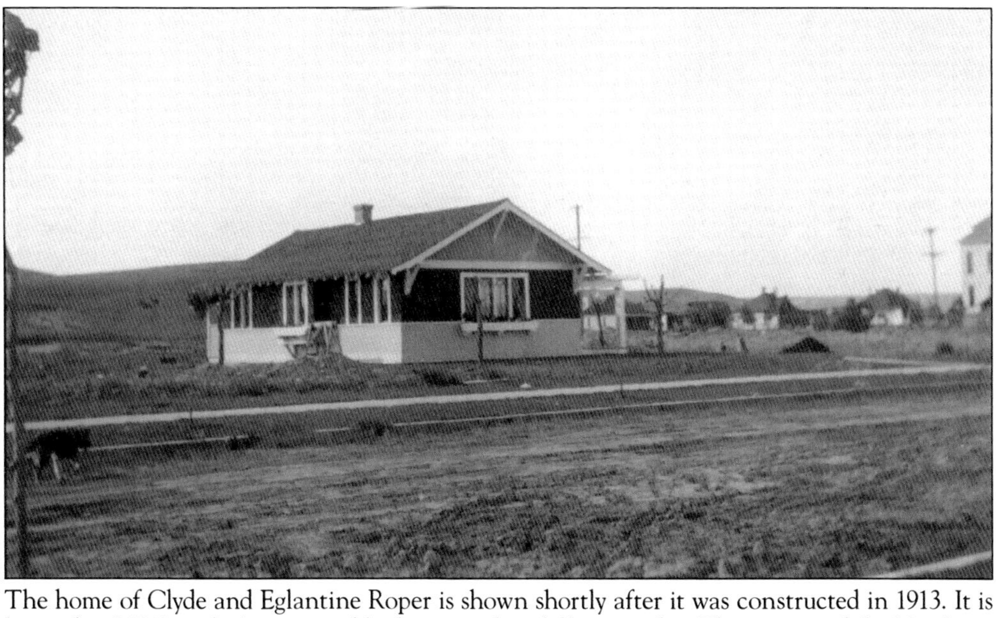

The home of Clyde and Eglantine Roper is shown shortly after it was constructed in 1913. It is located at 832 Fourth Avenue and looks somewhat different today. They operated the Northern Auto Company from 1910 to 1925. Afterward, they owned a general insurance, real estate, and loan office and also dealt in the oil business. Eglantine Roper was also an agent for U.S. Building and Loan of Butte for many years. (Courtesy of the Clack Museum.)

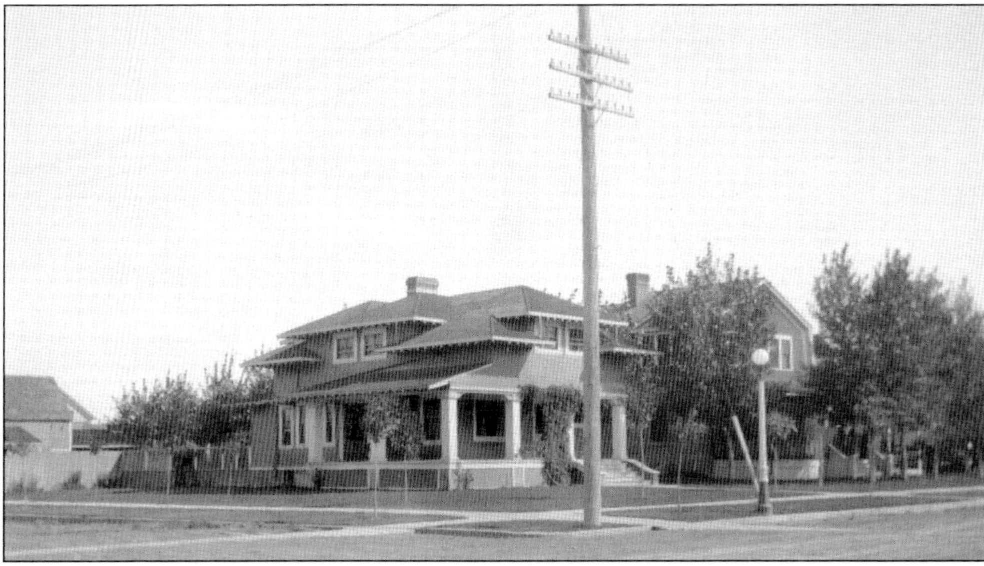

The home of Walter and Lula MacKenzie was located at 405 Third Avenue, where the Johnsrud Building now stands. Walter MacKenzie was the president of the Havre Steam Laundry. The home was moved in the later part of the 20th century to just outside of Chinook, Montana, north of the railroad tracks. The home next door belonged to L. K. Devlin. (Courtesy of the Clack Museum.)

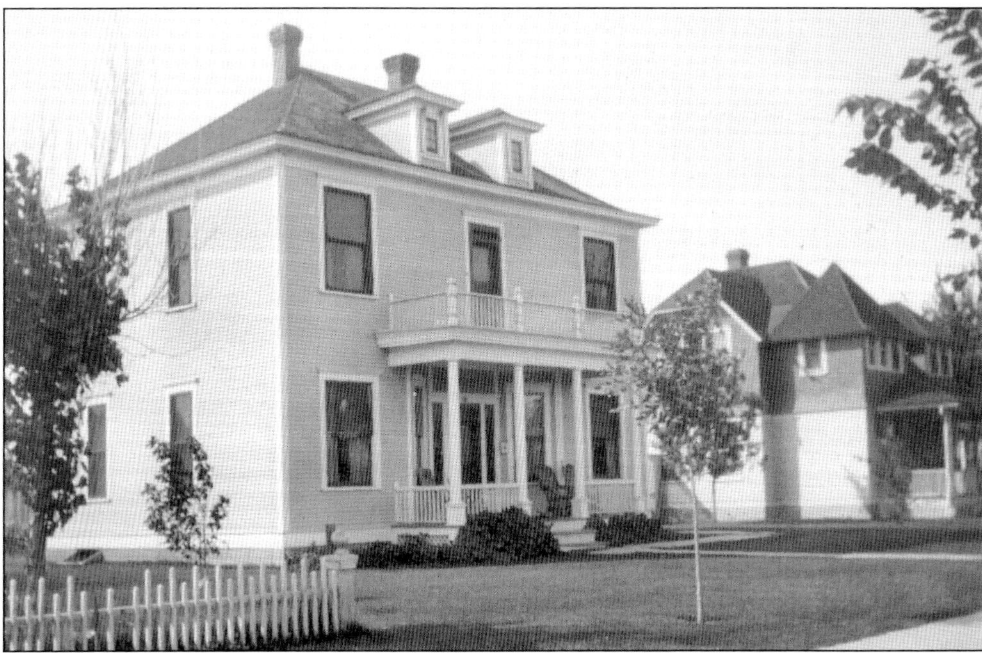

The home of Henry Spooner is located at 432 Third Avenue and looks vastly different today. He arrived in Havre in 1910. Henry Spooner worked for the Great Northern Railroad, first as a brakeman and eventually as a passenger conductor. He served as an alderman in the 1920s and in 1933 was appointed mayor. Afterward he served for several years as a justice of the peace. The house next door was razed, and Havre Optometric Clinic now occupies the site. (Courtesy of the Clack Museum.)

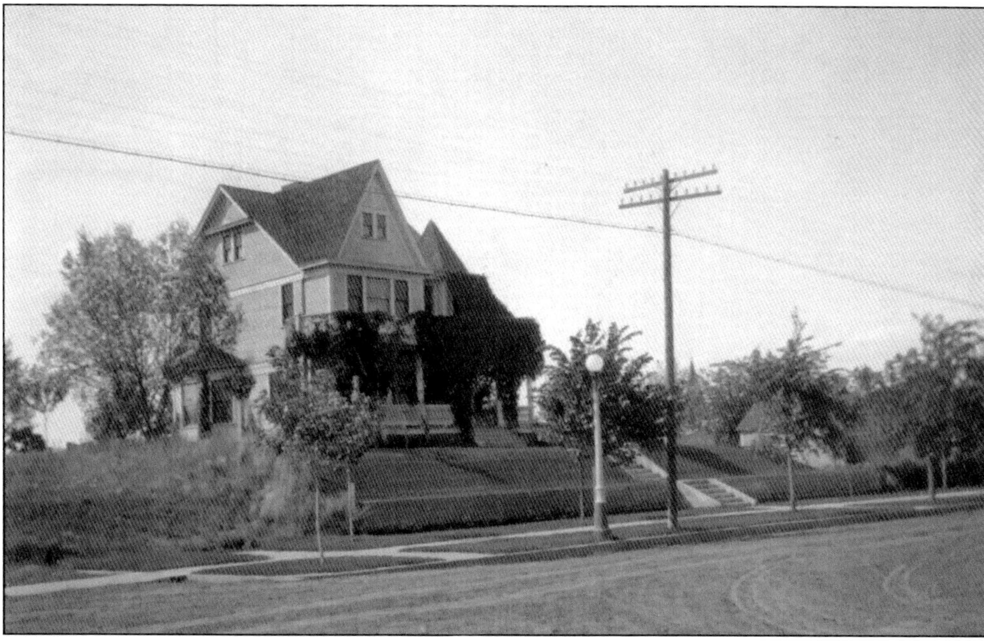

The Stringfellow House, located at 324 Second Avenue, was complete with a small tower to the right of the home that has since been removed. Henry Stringfellow arrived in Havre in 1892 and opened the first drugstore. He owned the Havre Commerical Company, which heavily competed with the Buttrey Department Store. Stringfellow also served on the Havre City Council. (Courtesy of the Clack Museum.)

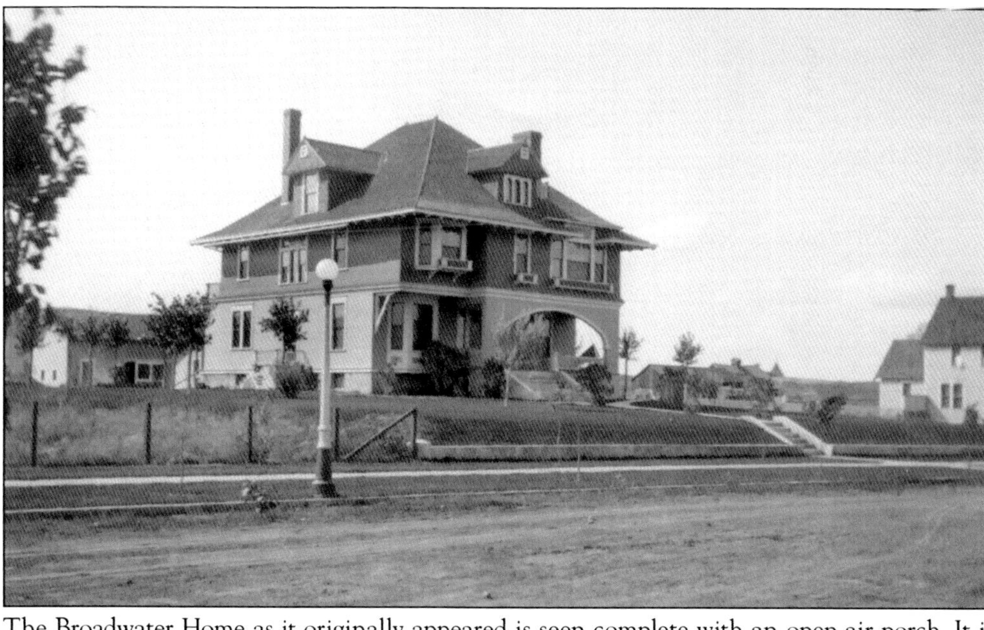

The Broadwater Home as it originally appeared is seen complete with an open-air porch. It is located at 500 Second Street and was the pride and joy of Edward Broadwater, its owner. Broadwater came to Fort Assinniboine and operated the post trader's building. When his home was under construction, a fire was intentionally lit under the staircase. It was ruled to be arson, and no one was ever charged. The house was completed in 1911. (Courtesy of the Clack Museum.)

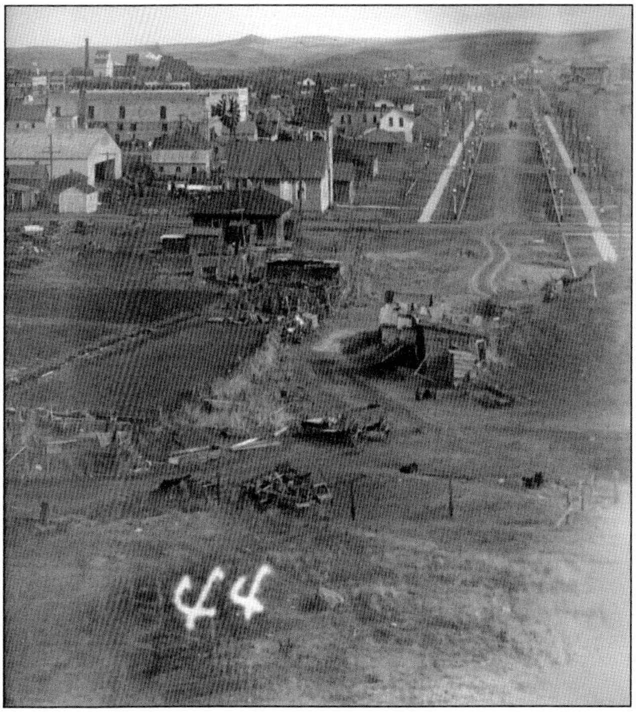

A view of Third Street shows the First Methodist Church at the corner of First Avenue. It was built in 1893, and services were conducted here until 1917, when the second Methodist church, Van Orsdel Methodist, was constructed on Fifth Avenue. Buttrey's can be seen to the left, as well as several residential homes that no longer exist. (Courtesy of Havre Beneath the Streets.)

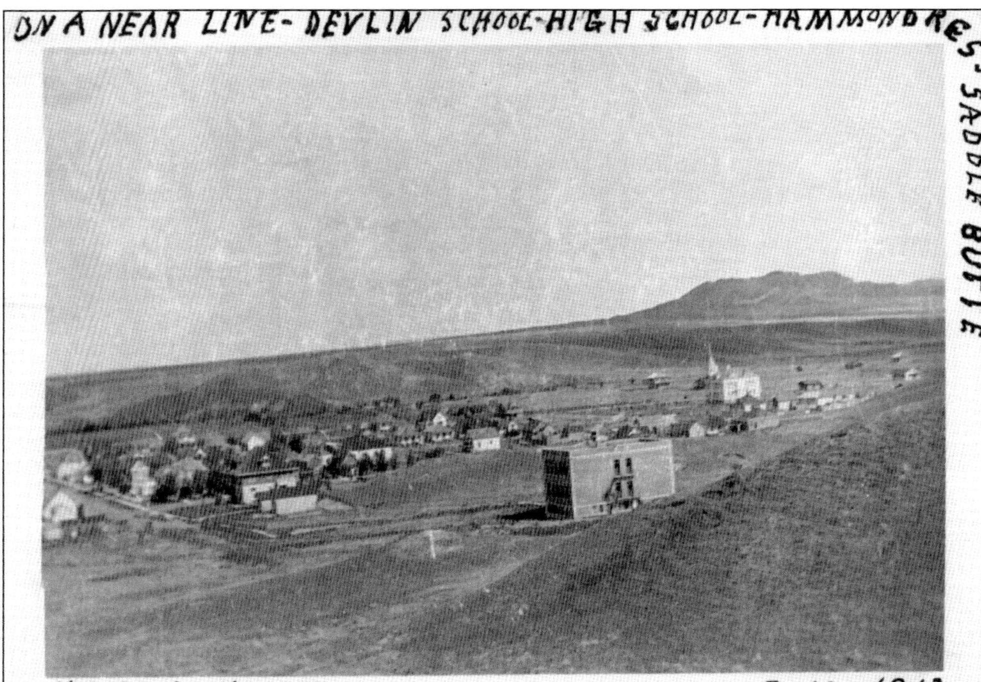

A photograph taken from the hills near Devlin School shows the progression of Havre toward the south. In the foreground is the original Devlin School, with the first high school in the middle of the photograph. Saddle Butte is featured in the background, many decades before it was developed. (Courtesy of MSU-Northern, Al Lucke Collection.)

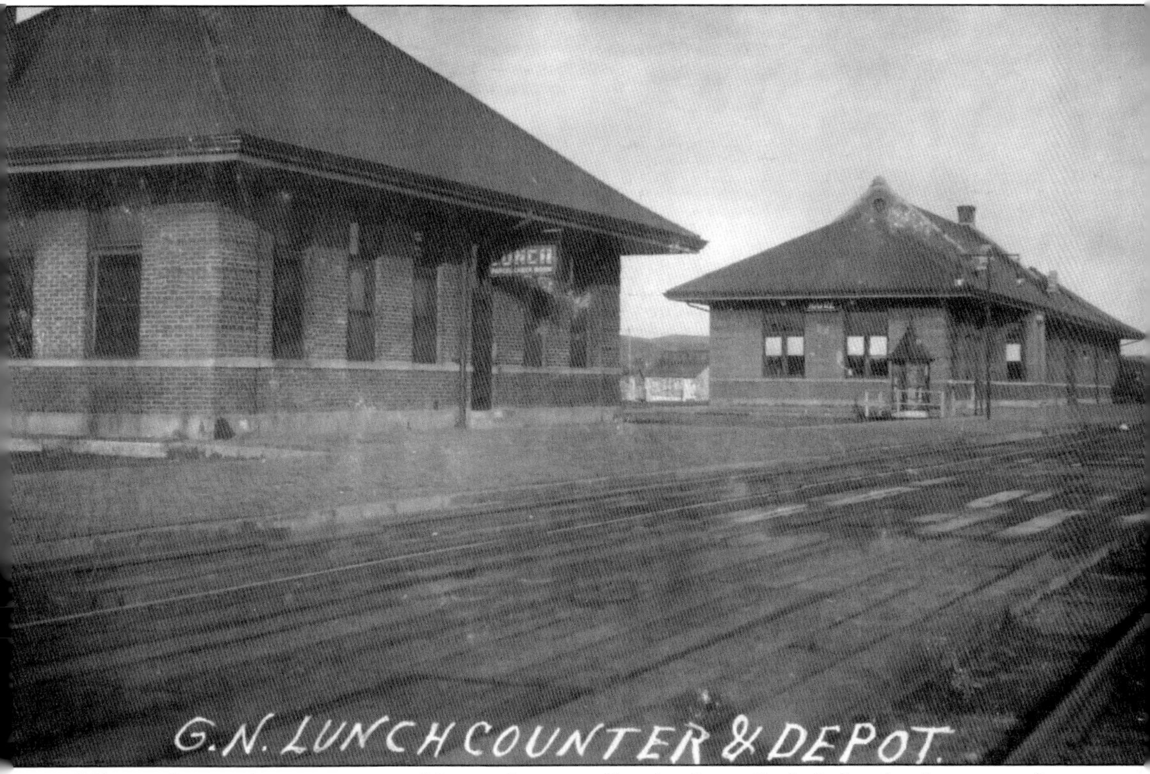

When riders on the train came to Havre, they got off at the depot. Included at the depot complex was a lunch counter named the Beanery. Chicken and beef pot pies were its specialty for the Empire Builder train line. Chili beans and baked beans were also on the menu, thus the name. A small soda fountain was also in the Beanery. It was razed in February 1968. (Courtesy of the Clack Museum.)

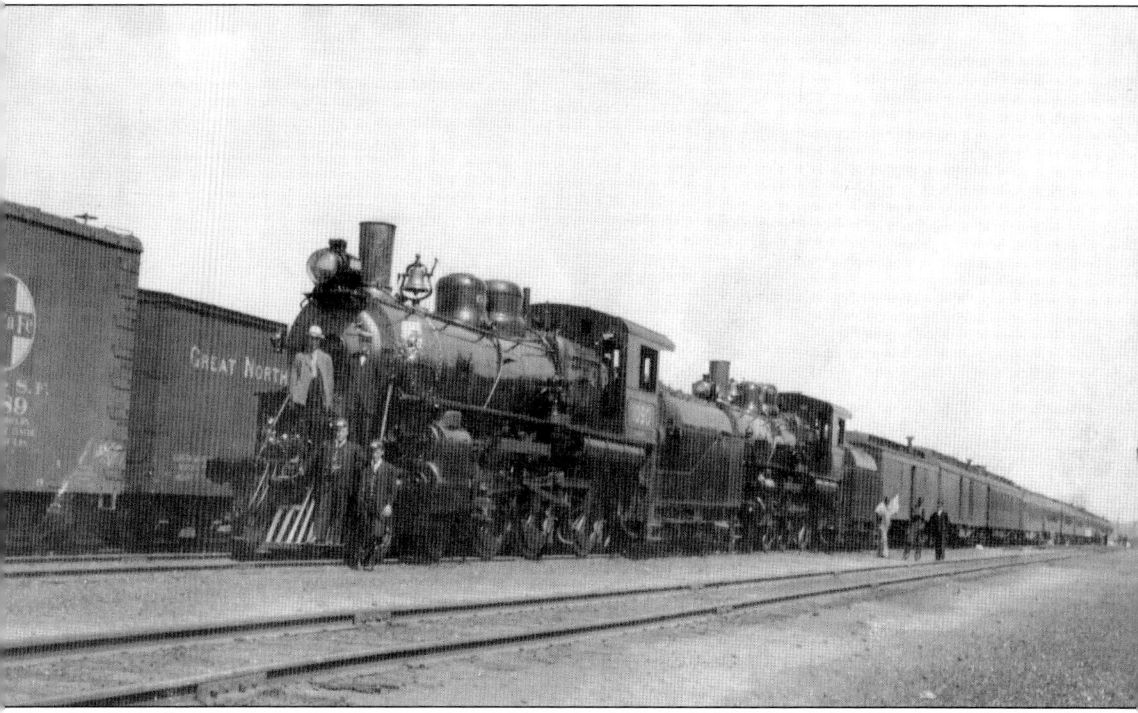

The railroad has played an important and long-standing role in the development of Hill County. The Minneapolis-Manitoba Railroad arrived in what is now Havre in September 1887 and brought with it jobs and settlers seeking a better life for themselves and their families. Early railroaders pose in front of a steam engine in the Havre yard. (Courtesy of the Clack Museum.)

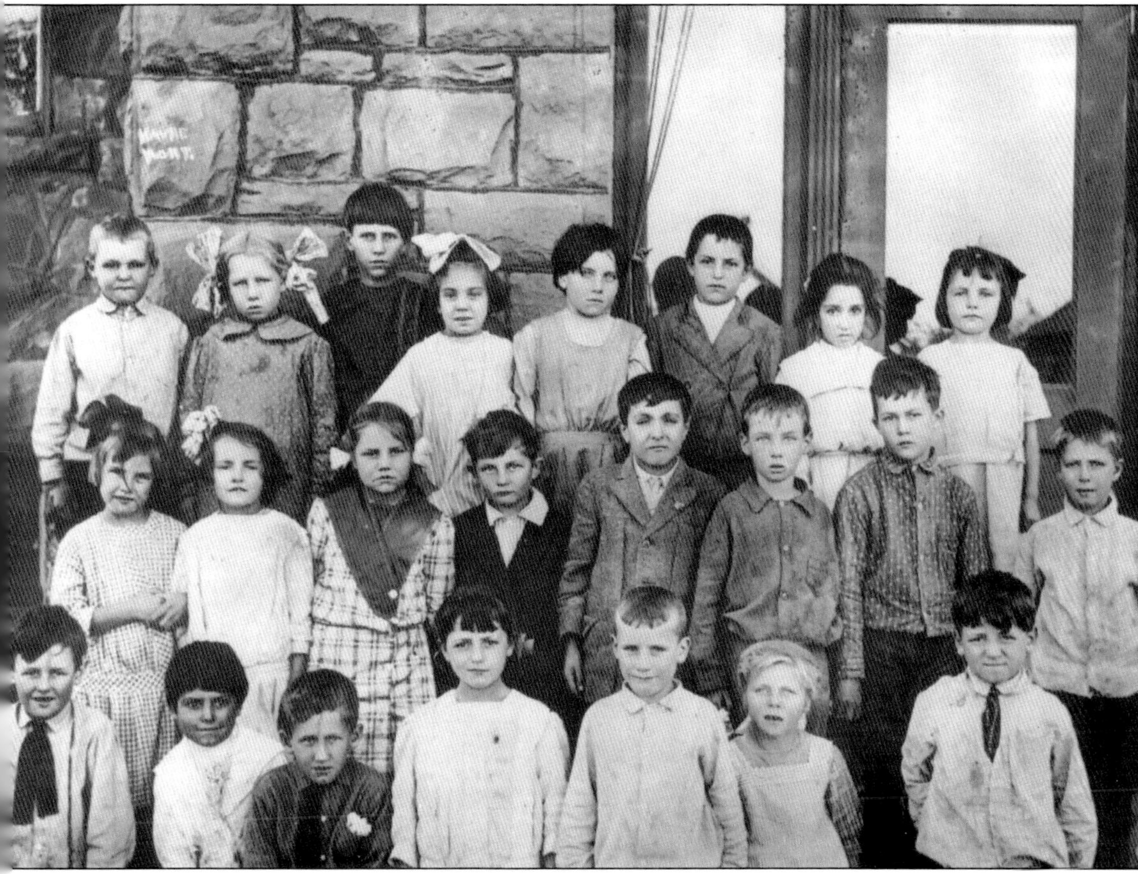

The second-grade class of the East Side School is pictured on October 1, 1913. The teacher was Selma Bonderson. Some of the identified students are William Wiltner, far left in the first row; Freda Bunton, sixth from left in the first row; Peter Hamilton, fifth from left in the second row; and Katherine Fields, second from left in the third row. (Courtesy of the Clack Museum.)

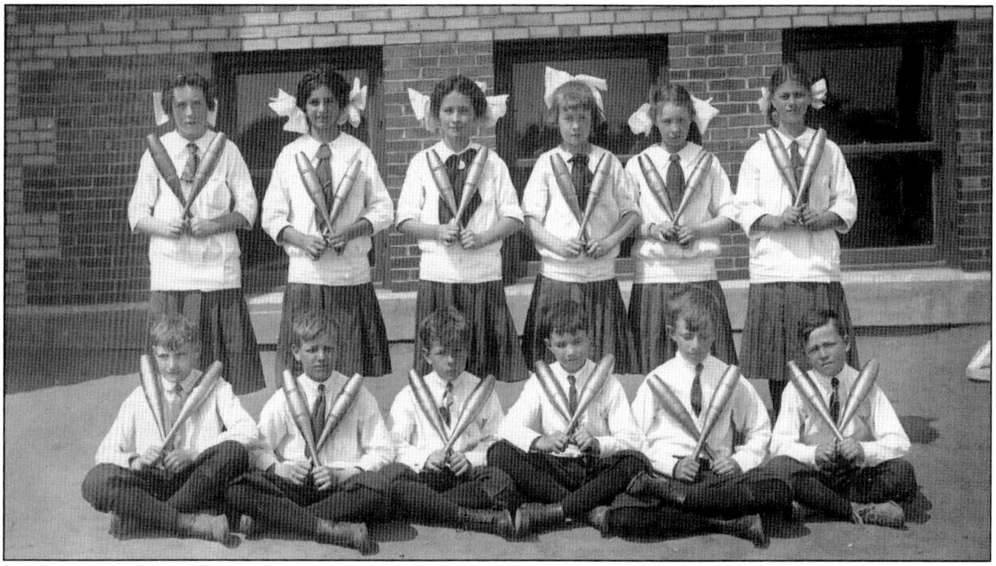

Students at Devlin School stand in a group photograph for the May Day celebration. Anonymously placing posies of flowers on doors and dancing around a pole with colored ribbons were customary observations honoring May Day. Each dance created a different woven pattern on the top of the pole. (Courtesy of MSU-Northern, Al Lucke Collection.)

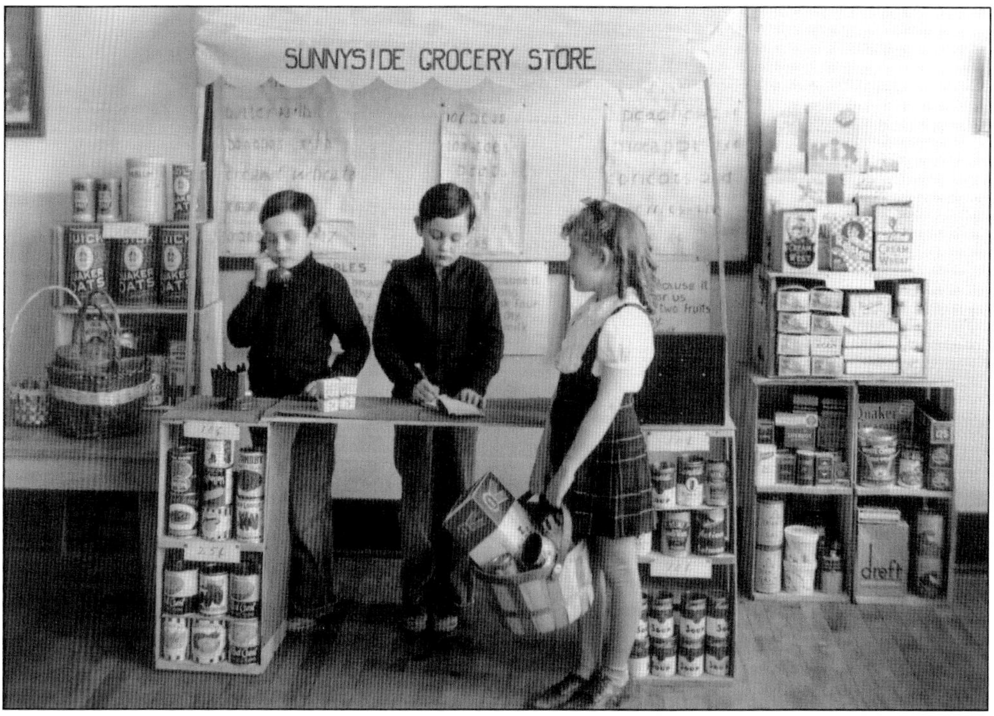

Lessons in economics were taught to children as a part of their studies. A group of children at Sunnyside School participate in a mock grocery store experience. Students were given a certain amount of money to spend on items for the home, the object being to be the most economical. The Sunnyside School where this photograph was taken was at its first location at 1115 Eighth Avenue, now a privately owned building. (Courtesy of the Clack Museum.)

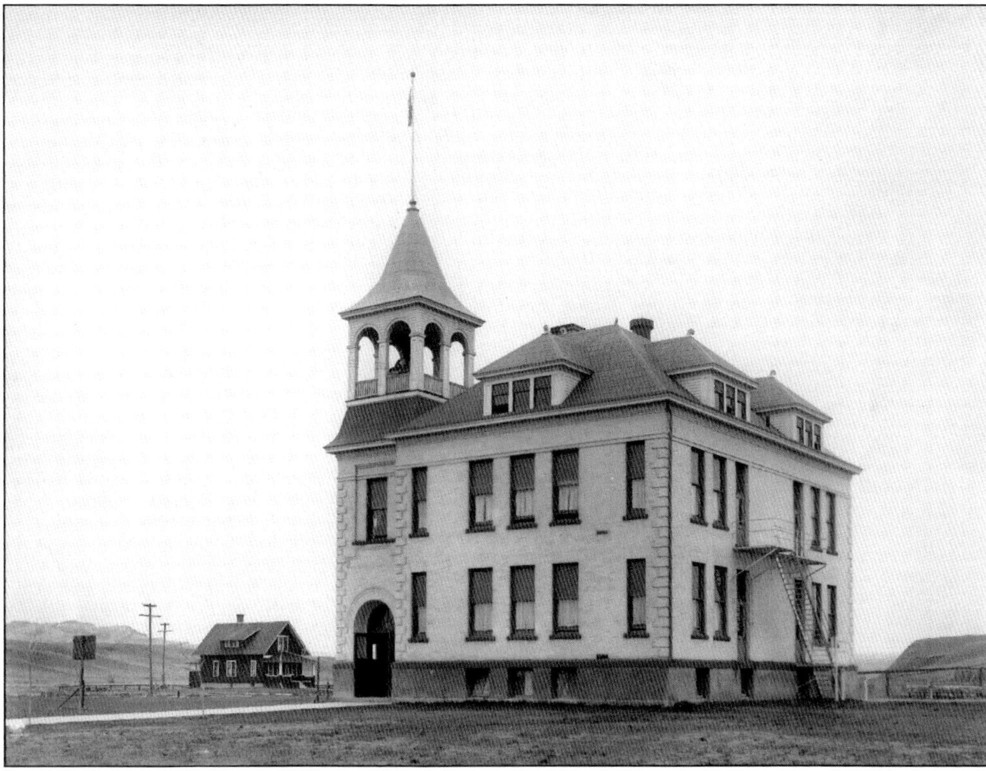

The first Havre High School building was located on the block between Third and Fourth Avenues and Seventh and Eighth Streets. It was constructed in 1909. An addition in 1914 was built for junior high students. On December 15, 1917, the high school burned. All but the auditorium was a total loss. The house in the back is at 803 Fourth Avenue. (Courtesy of MSU-Northern, Al Lucke Collection.)

F. F. Bossuot's rendition of the second Havre High School shows a building much different from the finished product. The quoins, or alternating-sized blocks on the corners of the building, are reminiscent of the first Havre High School, and the overall design hints of another of Bossuot's buildings, the Hill County Courthouse. (Courtesy of the Clack Museum.)

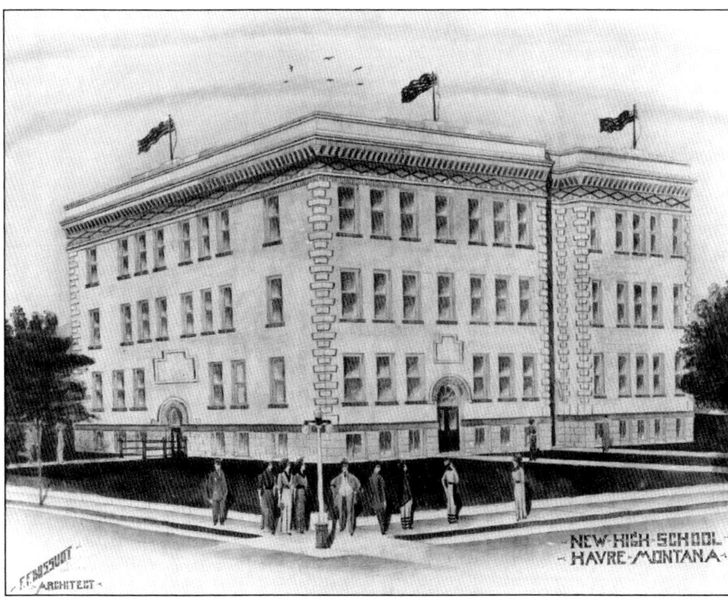

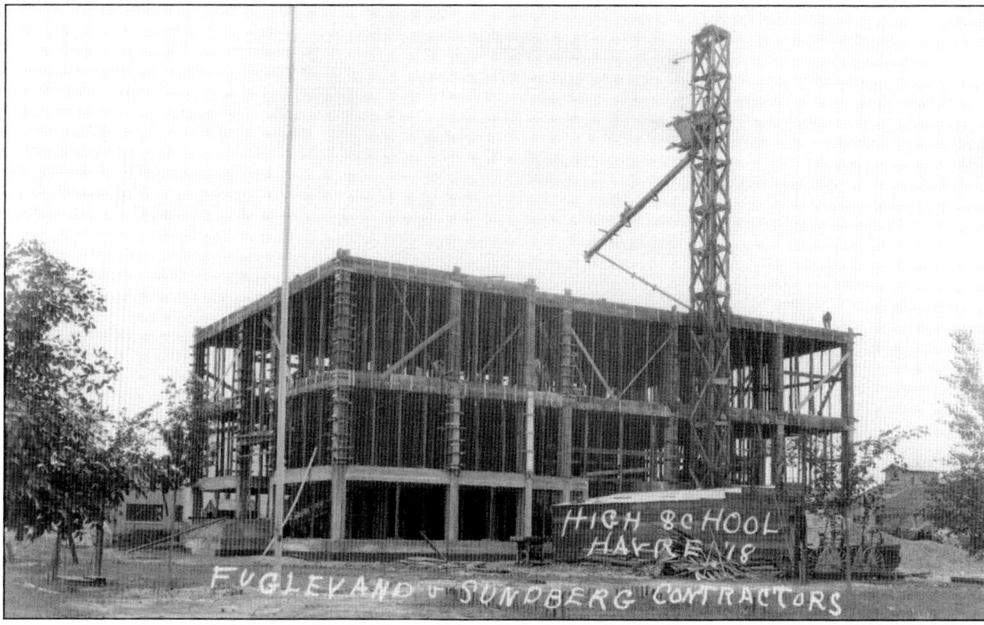

Fuglevand and Sundberg Contractors constructed the second Havre High School in 1918. Between 1913 and 1926, the team of Fuglevand and Sundberg was the most active building contractors in Havre. They partnered with Bossuot to construct the Masonic Temple and the Buttrey, the second Clack, and the Young-Almas homes. All of these pieces of architecture still stand as testament to the excellent architectural and building capabilities of these men. (Courtesy of Emily Mayer.)

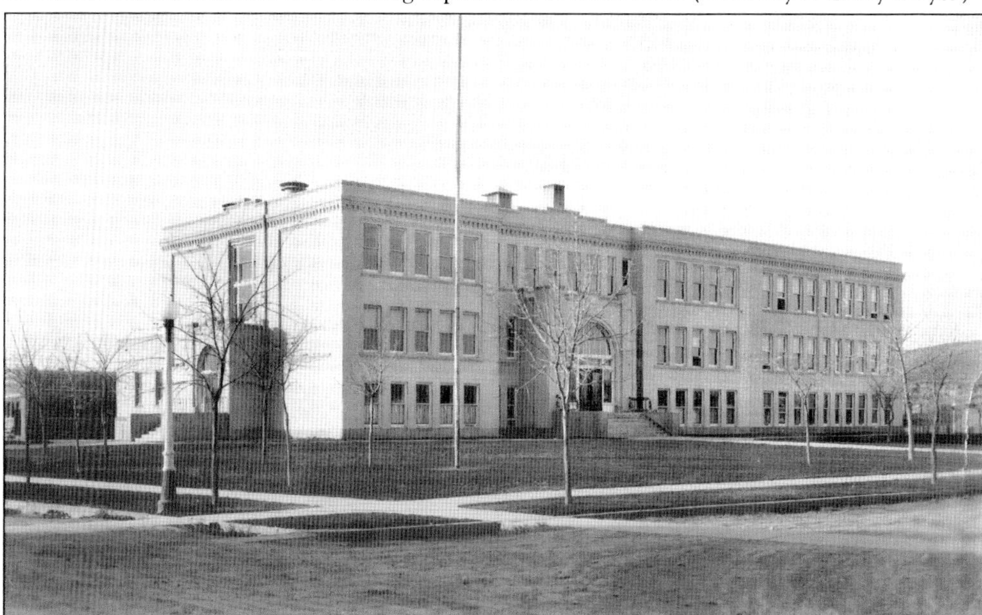

The second Havre High School building was constructed out of steel and concrete in 1918. The cost was $5,054, plus $14,160 for plumbing in the building. The curriculum included the basics, plus music, physical education, and other classes. The building was used as a high school until 1964, when the new high school was completed. The old high school then became the junior high school. (Courtesy of the Clack Museum.)

An aerial view of Havre shows the second high school in the foreground. Toward the top of the photograph at the corner of Ninth Street and Third Avenue is the Williams Gas Station. To the south of the gas station is one of Havre's many neighborhood grocery stores, Cormany's Grocery Store. It was owned by Greg and Mabel Cormany. (Courtesy of the Clack Museum.)

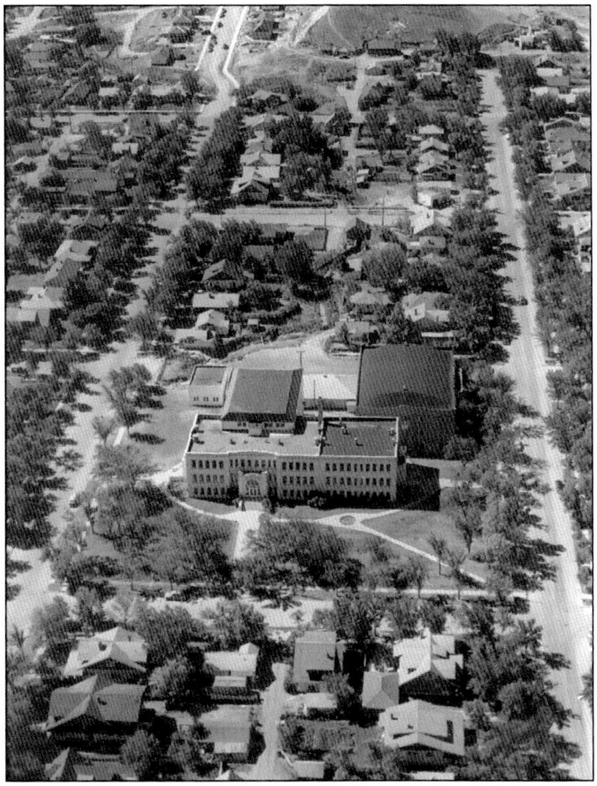

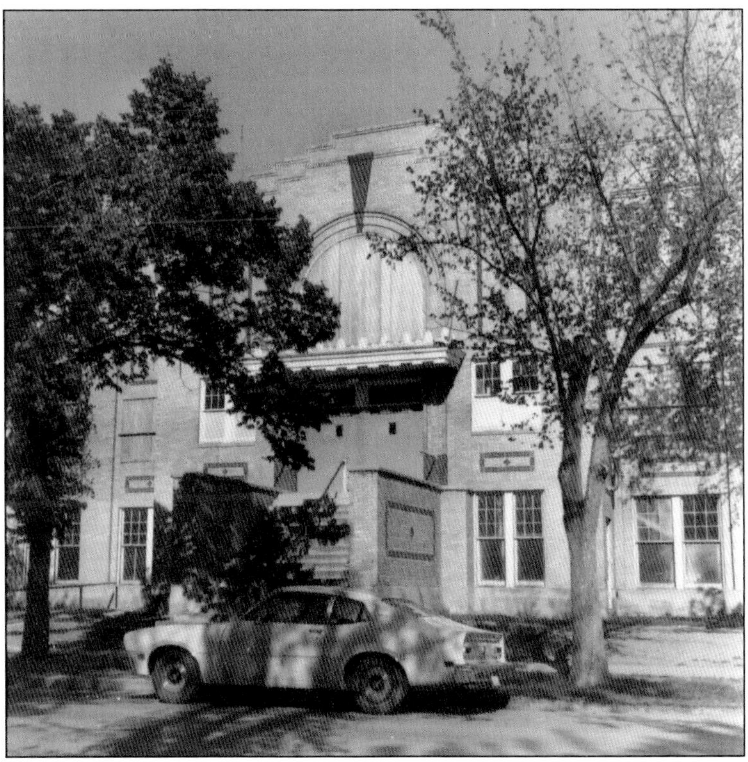

The Havre High School Gymnasium was constructed out of blond and dark-brown brick in 1928. The two-story steel-frame building hosted many basketball games, including the rivalry between Great Falls High and Havre High for the famed "Ole Goat." When the school was demolished in 1984, the gym remained in the hopes of becoming a community center. However, the dream was never realized, and the gym was demolished in the 1990s. (Courtesy of the Clack Museum.)

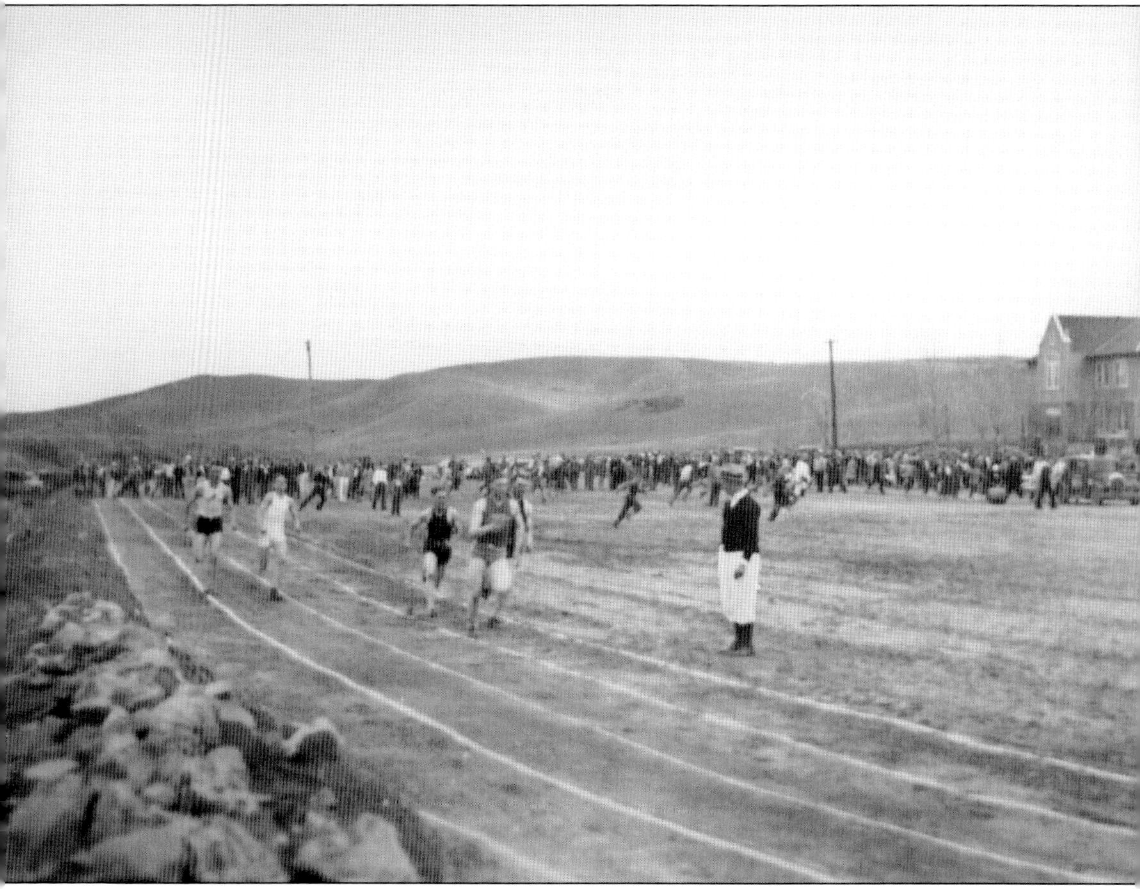

A track meet takes place on the campus of Northern Montana College. East Hall is to the right of the photograph. East Hall was the former men's dorm and was located near where the Student Union Building is today. It was abandoned in 1965 as a dorm and used for storage. Due to structural issues, East Hall was razed in 1979. (Courtesy of the Clack Museum.)

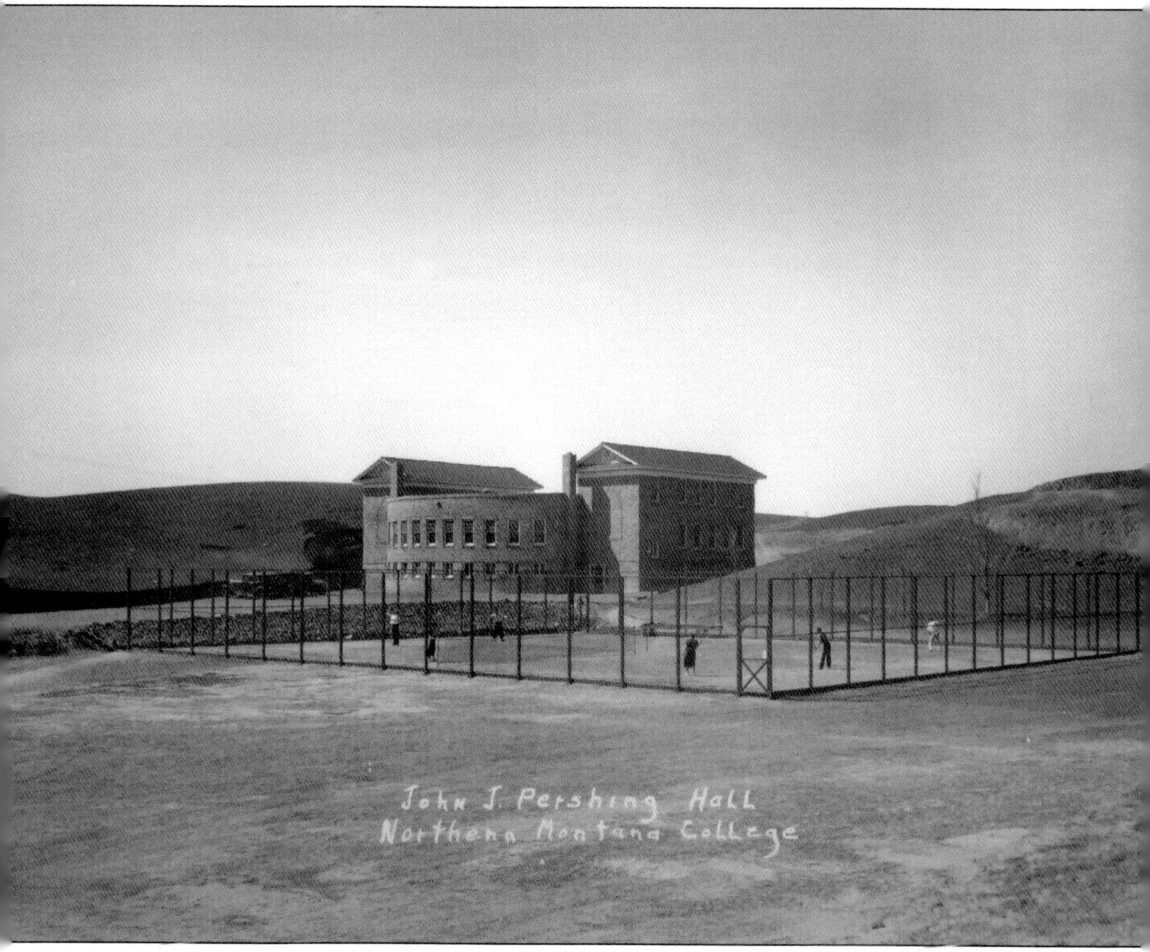

Pershing Hall and the tennis courts on the Northern Montana College campus are pictured here. Pershing Hall was named after Gen. John Pershing, who as a lieutenant served at nearby Fort Assinniboine. The building itself is believed to have been made mostly of bricks salvaged from the fort after its abandonment in 1911. The tennis courts were located where the Student Union Building is currently. (Courtesy of the Clack Museum.)

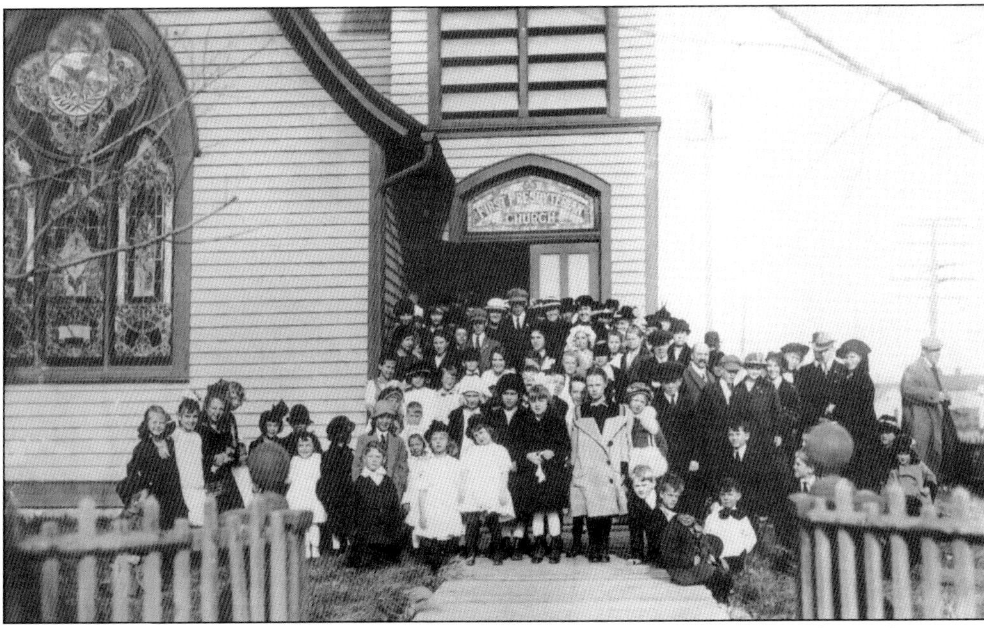

The First Presbyterian Church was once located at the northwest corner of Fourth Avenue and Third Street, where the Fuglevand building stands today. It was constructed in 1902 and later sold to the First Baptist Church, who moved the structure to its current location at 625 Fourth Avenue in 1916. The church still retains the large stained-glass window. (Courtesy of the Clack Museum.)

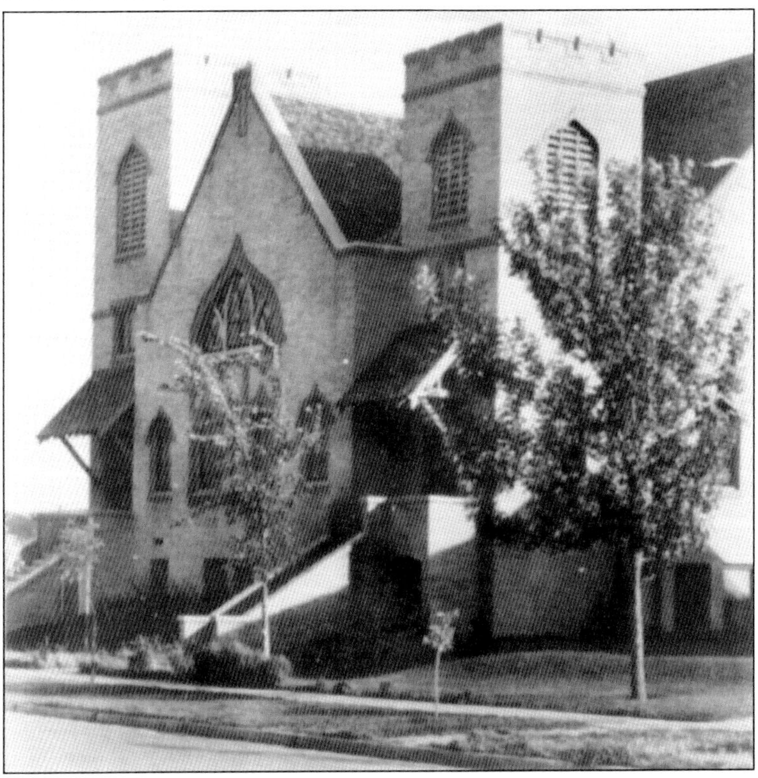

Van Orsdel Methodist Church was a stately, grand structure with Moorish-style elements. Named after Walter "Brother Van" Van Orsdel, it was constructed in 1917 and burned in 1958. The following year, the current Van Orsdel Methodist Church was dedicated. In addition to serving the needs of its parishioners, it also serves as the location for the annual Art Show. (Courtesy of Emily Mayer.)

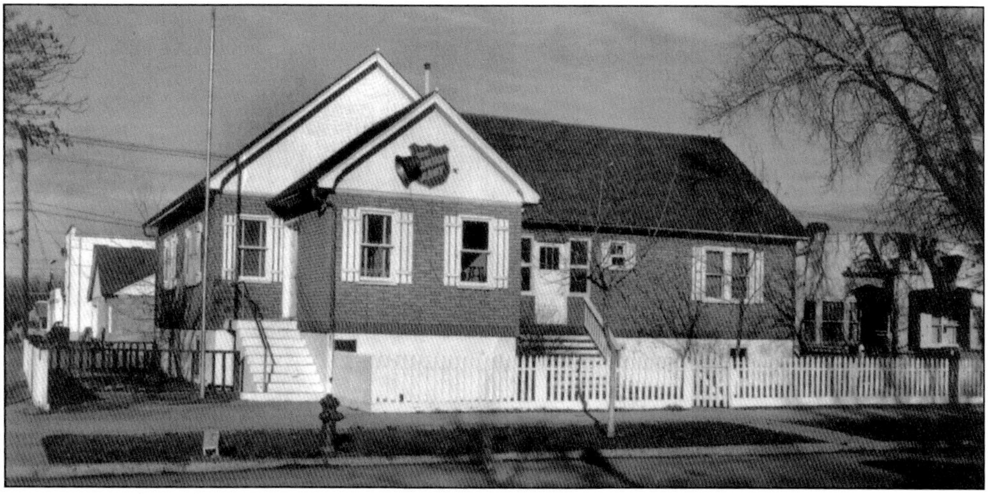

Since 1915, the Salvation Army has been a vital part of the community, assisting those in need with food, shelter, clothing, and spiritual guidance. It also offered camps at Camp Kiwanis for several years. The Salvation Army Chapel offered services until 2006. The building was eventually sold to the Havre Baptist Church. (Courtesy of Emily Mayer.)

The interior of the First Lutheran Church is shown here in 1952. In 1913, the Norwegian Evangelical Lutheran Congregation was organized, and a frame church was built on the corner of Tenth Avenue and Fourth Street. It was later named First Lutheran Church. In 1946, a fund drive was started to construct a new church. The cornerstone for the new church was laid on July 22, 1950, and on May 4, 1952, the first service was held. (Courtesy of MSU-Northern, Al Lucke Collection.)

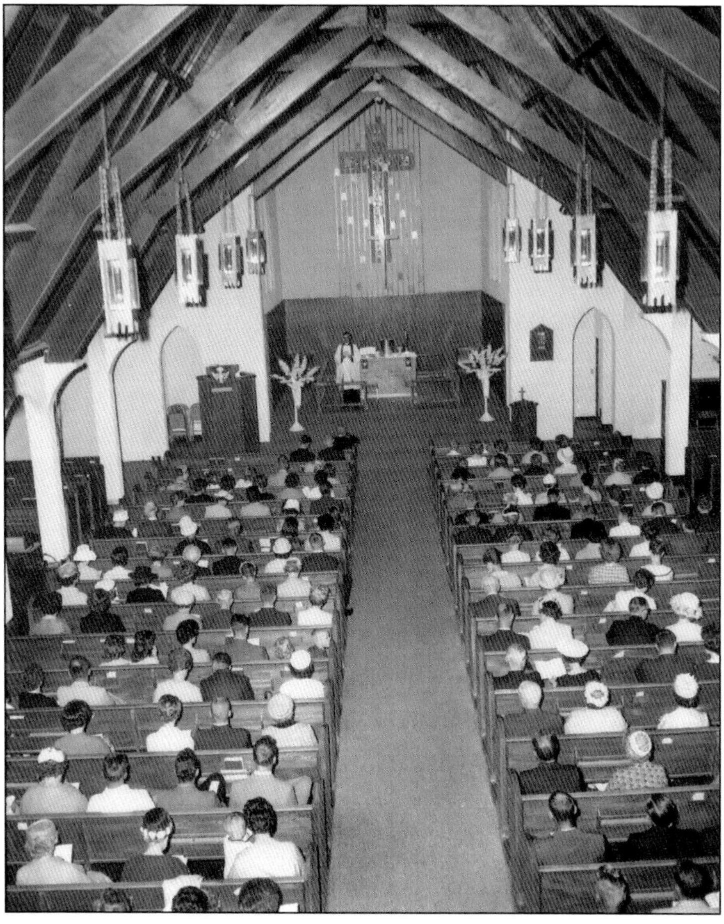

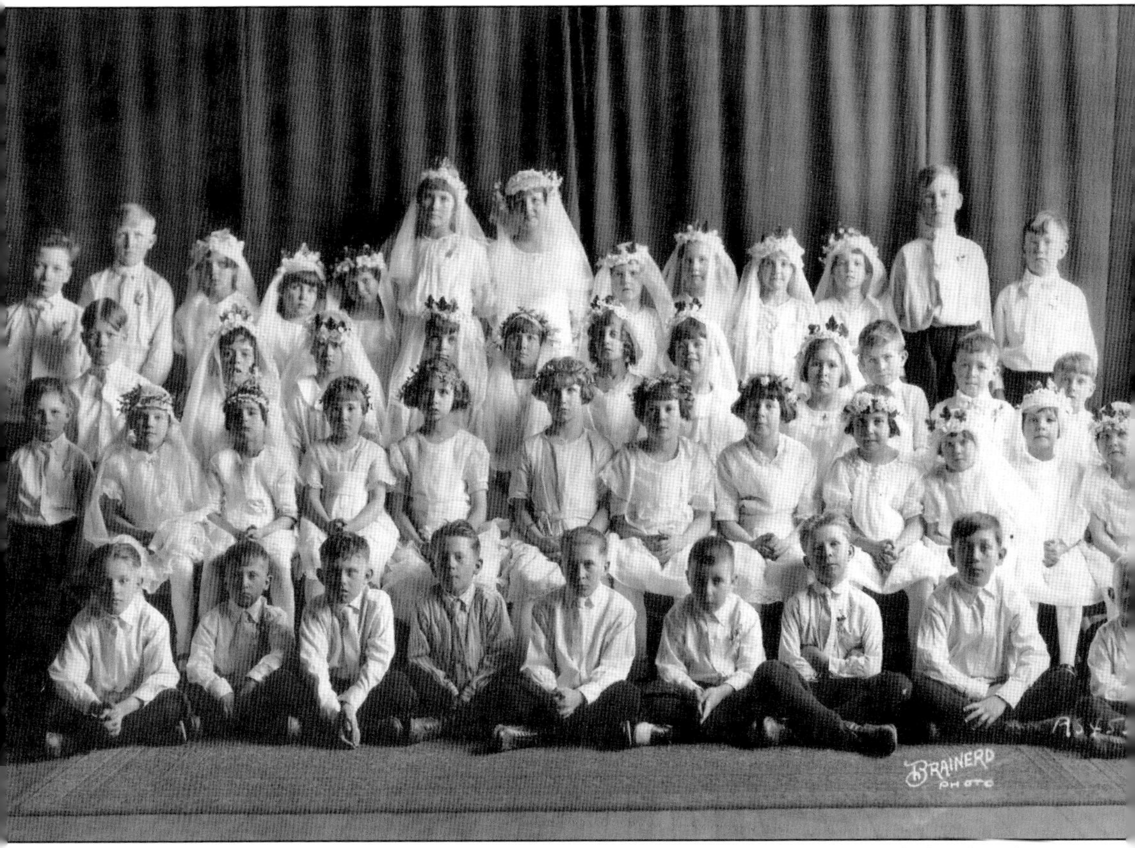

Confirmation at St. Jude Catholic Church is an annual ceremony. The first Catholic church was a wooden structure built in 1894, but it was destroyed in a storm. Mass was held in various places until 1905, when St. Jude Catholic Church was completed. It was sold in 1915 and torn down to build the courthouse. In 1925, St. Jude Catholic Church was constructed in the mission style. (Courtesy of MSU-Northern, Al Lucke Collection.)

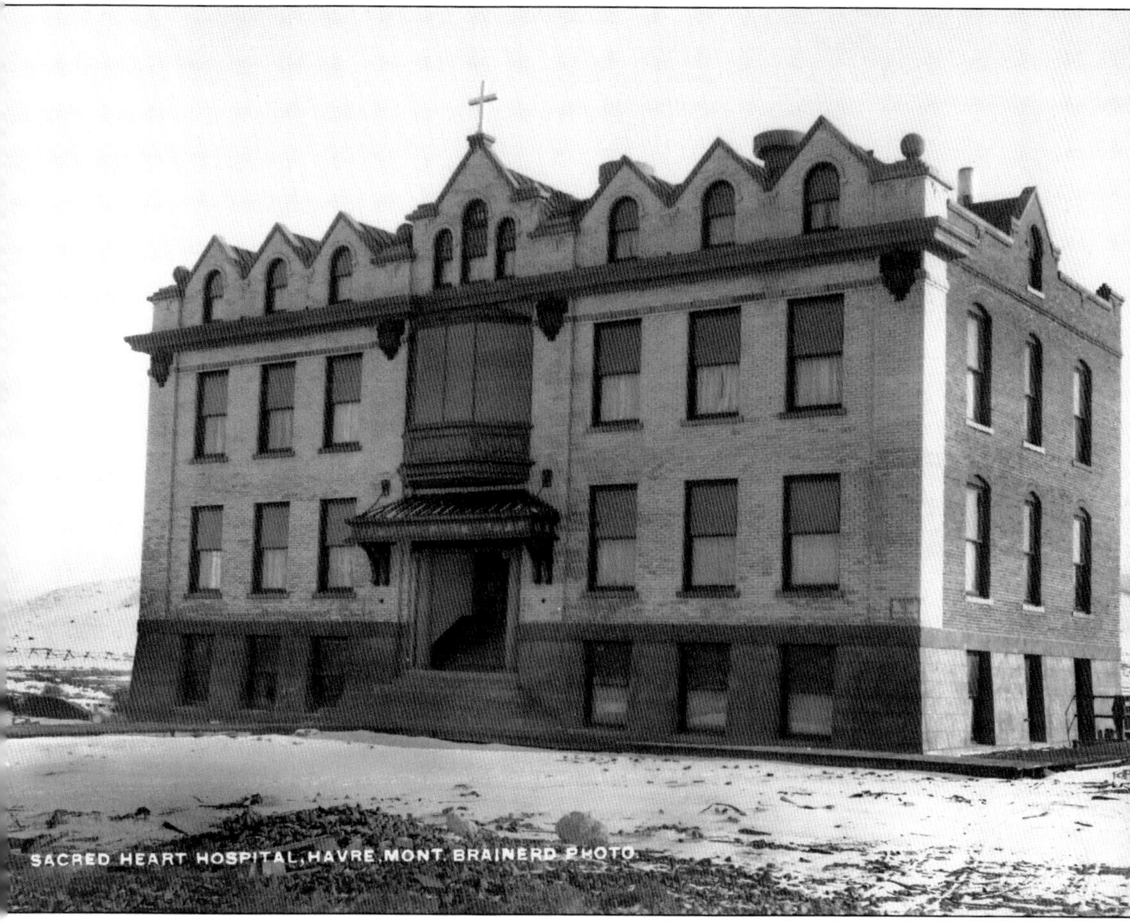

The first Sacred Heart Hospital was constructed in 1911 and completed in 1912, serving the health care needs of area residents. It burned the following year as a result of defective wiring. In 1916, plans were made to replace the hospital. It was dedicated in 1931 and was in use until the mid-1970s, when the current hospital was built. The former Sacred Heart Hospital is currently Park View Apartments. (Courtesy of MSU-Northern, Al Lucke Collection.)

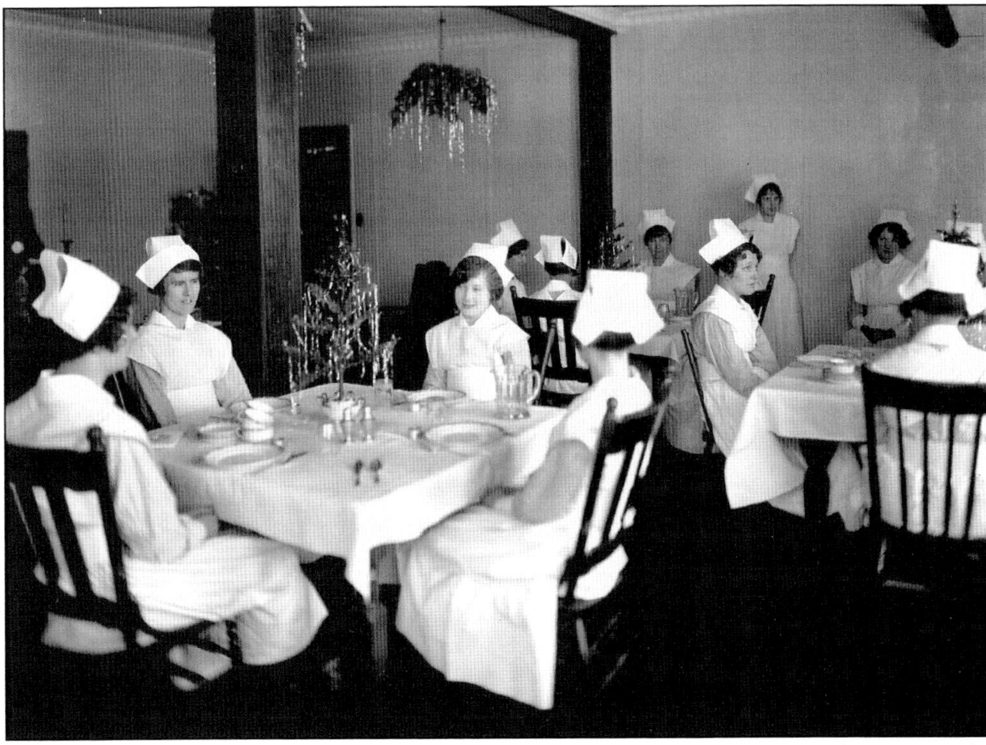

Christmas is celebrated at the Sacred Heart Hospital by its nurses around 1926. The trees on the table are feather trees, the first style of artificial tree widely used. The branches are made by dyeing goose feathers, then twisting them around a dowel. The dowels are placed in pre-drilled holes in the stem of the tree and could be re-used for many years. The tinsel would have been made of real tin, not the plastic of today. (Courtesy of MSU-Northern, Al Lucke Collection.)

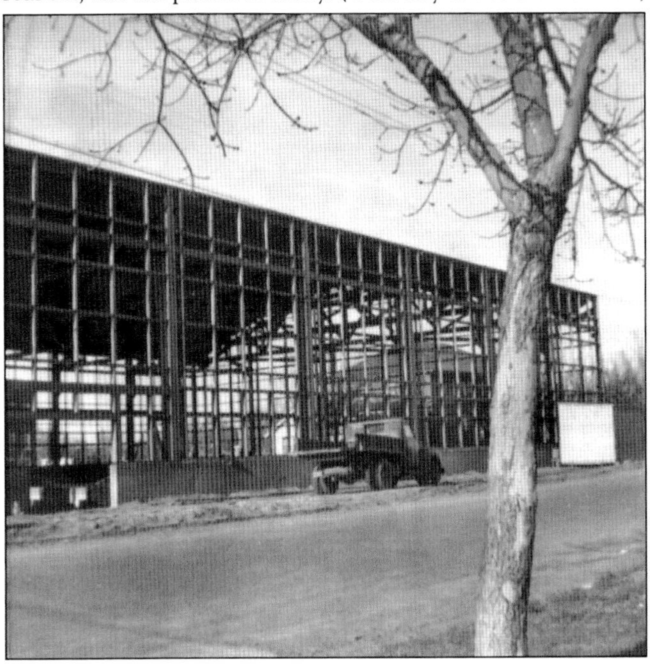

The Havre Central Gymnasium was constructed in 1951 as a part of Havre Central High School. In 1915, the combination St. Jude Catholic church and school was constructed and served that dual purpose until 1924. That same year, an attempt at a high school was made, but it ceased two years later. By 1948, a second attempt was made to establish a Catholic high school. It operated until 1968. (Courtesy of the Clack Museum.)

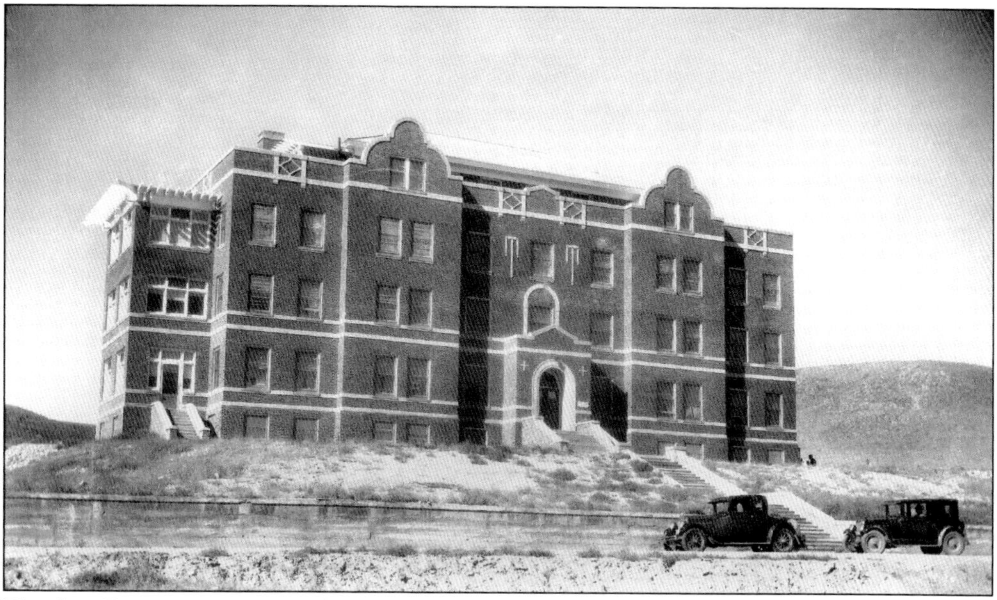

The first Deaconness Hospital was started in 1917 and finally completed in 1926 after many years of struggle and hardship. During this time, many fund-raisers were held to complete the hospital, which was badly needed. In 1958, an addition was constructed. In 1975, Deaconness and Sacred Heart Hospitals consolidated and ceased business in their separate facilities. (Courtesy of MSU-Northern, Al Lucke Collection.)

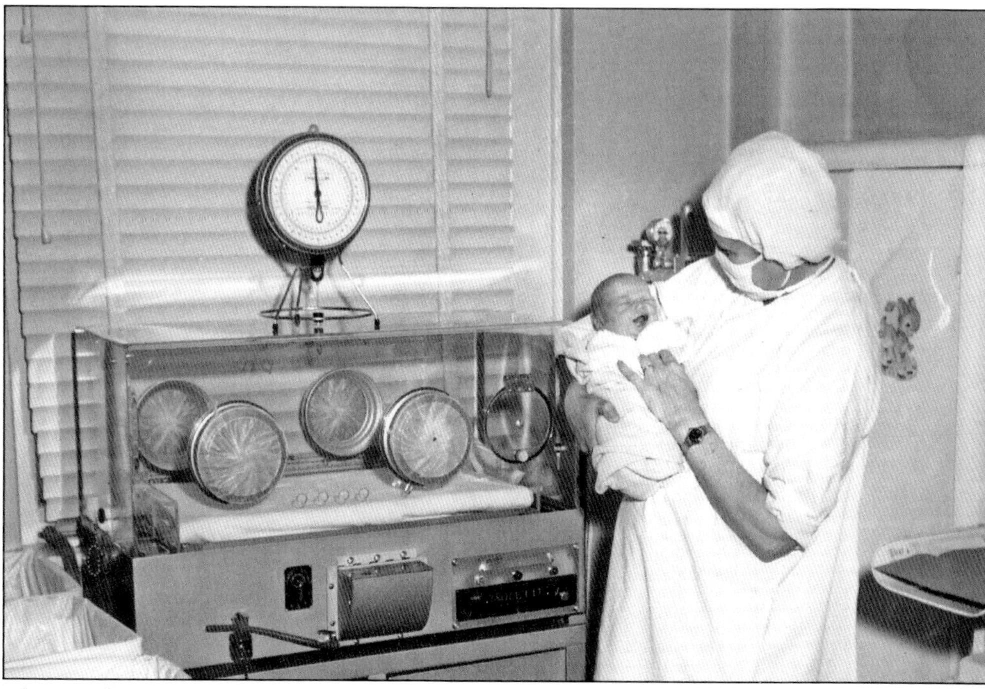

The people of Hill County have always been willing to embrace and utilize new technology. Pictured is the modern nursery of the newly constructed addition to the Deaconness Hospital. A scale to weigh the babies and a masked nurse in the customary white uniform were a part of the hospital's operation. (Courtesy of MSU-Northern, Al Lucke Collection.)

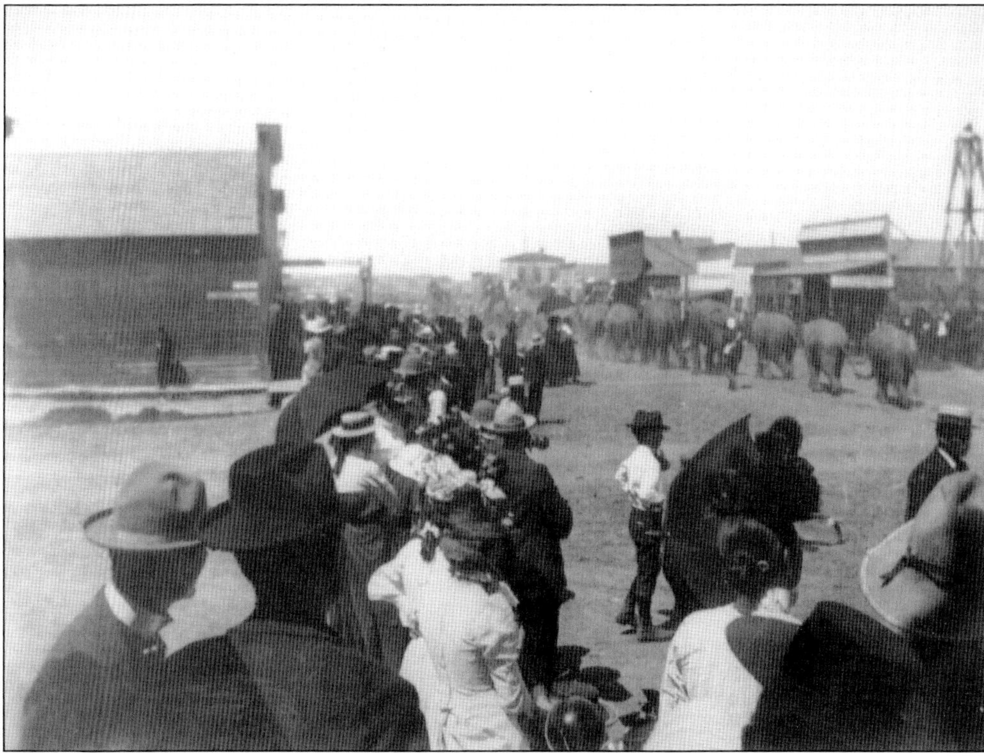

The Ringling Brothers Circus was cause for great celebration when it visited Havre in 1897. A tent was set up in the vicinity of where Devlin School would be constructed many years later. Events such as a circus were not common in rural areas, so such an occasion would attract people from many miles. (Courtesy of MSU-Northern, Al Lucke Collection.)

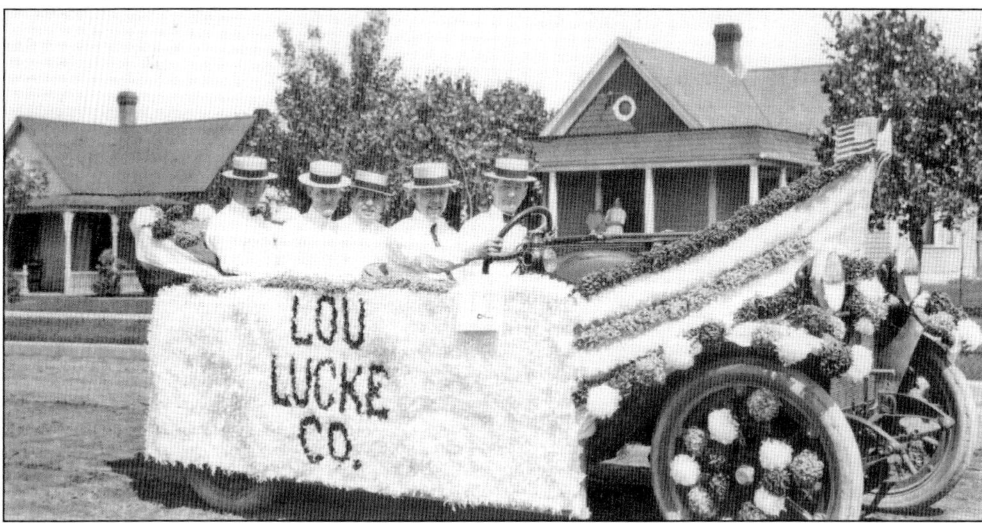

The Lou Lucke float for the 1914 Fourth of July Parade is visible here facing north. Several homes once occupied this location, along with the First Methodist Church, which was located on the corner of First Avenue and Third Street. Over the years, the buildings were razed. Safeway Grocery was located where the homes were. After Safeway moved, the building was moved to the fairgrounds and is the horse pavilion. The new post office is here currently. (Courtesy of the Clack Museum.)

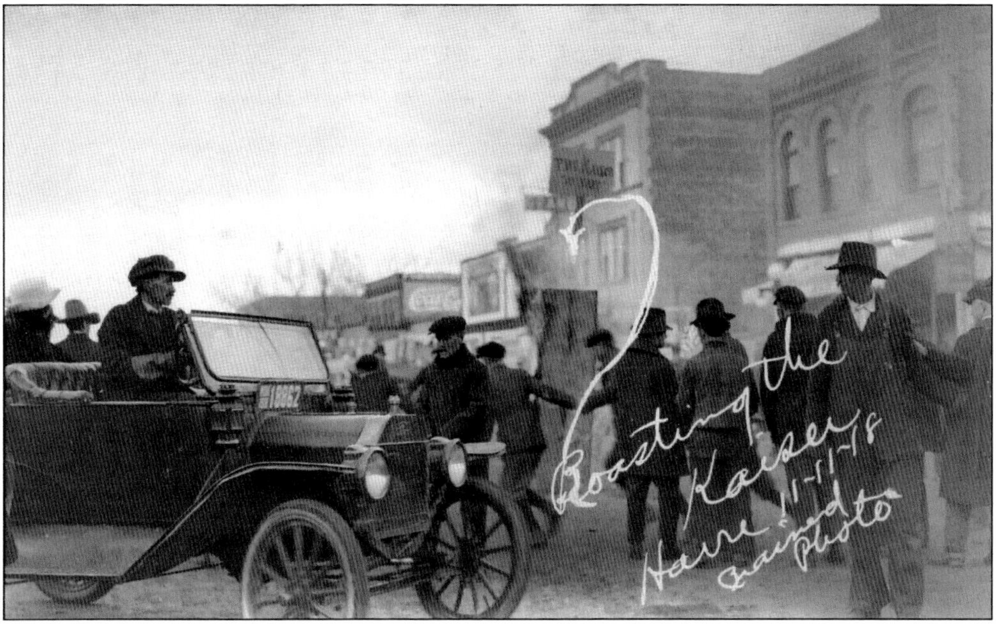

November 11, 1918, was Armistice Day, the end of World War I. Havre joined the rest of the world in celebration of the end of a long and terrible war. Havre residents enthusiastically burned an effigy of the German Kaiser in front of the Grand Hotel on First Street. (Courtesy of MSU-Northern, Al Lucke Collection.)

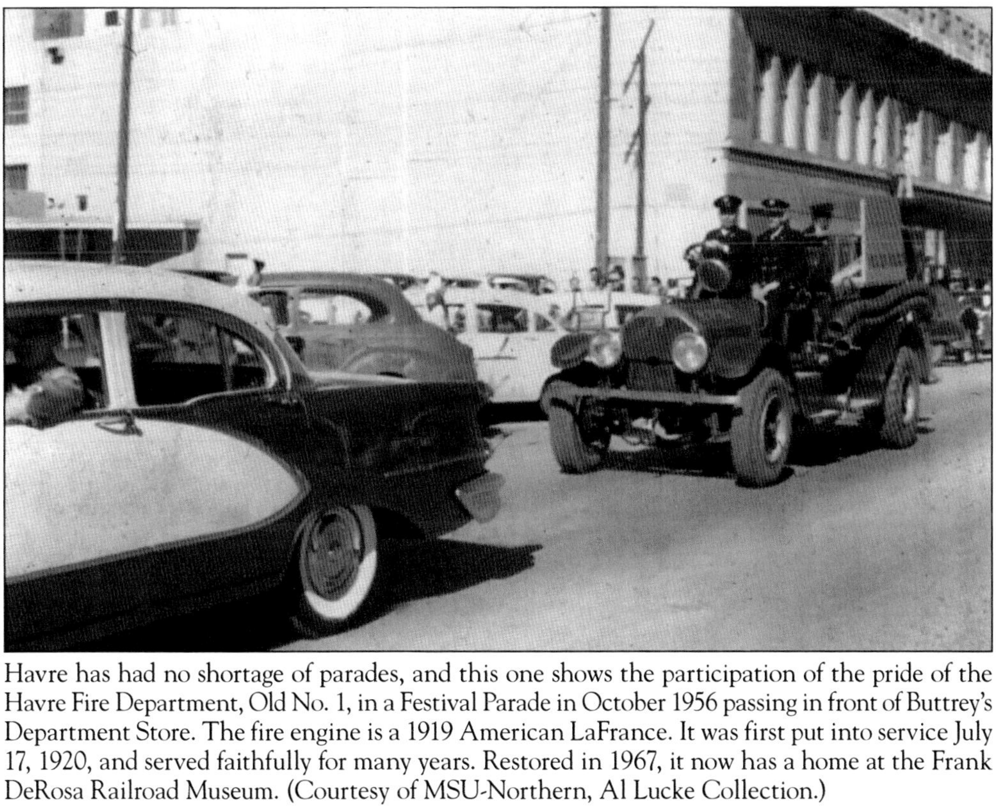

Havre has had no shortage of parades, and this one shows the participation of the pride of the Havre Fire Department, Old No. 1, in a Festival Parade in October 1956 passing in front of Buttrey's Department Store. The fire engine is a 1919 American LaFrance. It was first put into service July 17, 1920, and served faithfully for many years. Restored in 1967, it now has a home at the Frank DeRosa Railroad Museum. (Courtesy of MSU-Northern, Al Lucke Collection.)

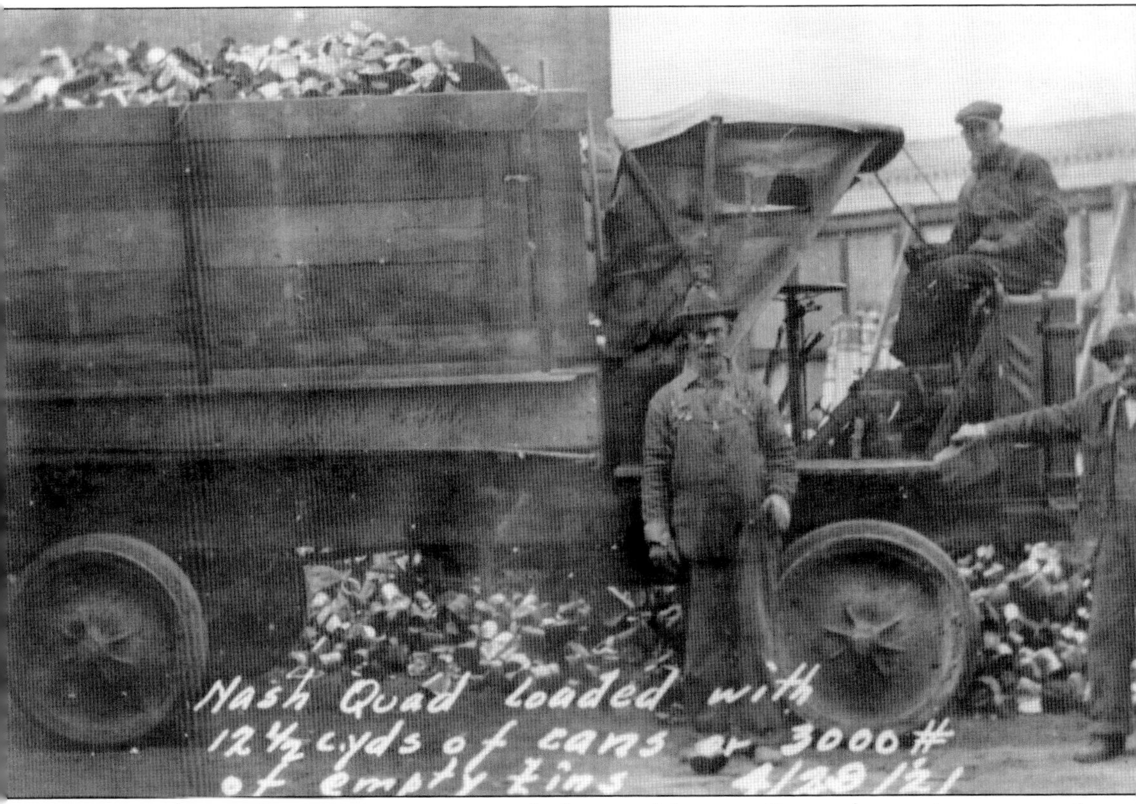

Havre clean-up days are not new events in the history of the town. Due to the massive amounts of garbage and tin cans that littered the alleys, the Havre Fire Department organized clean-ups. This particular clean-up took place in April 1921 and yielded 3,000 pounds of empty tins. (Courtesy of the Clack Museum.)

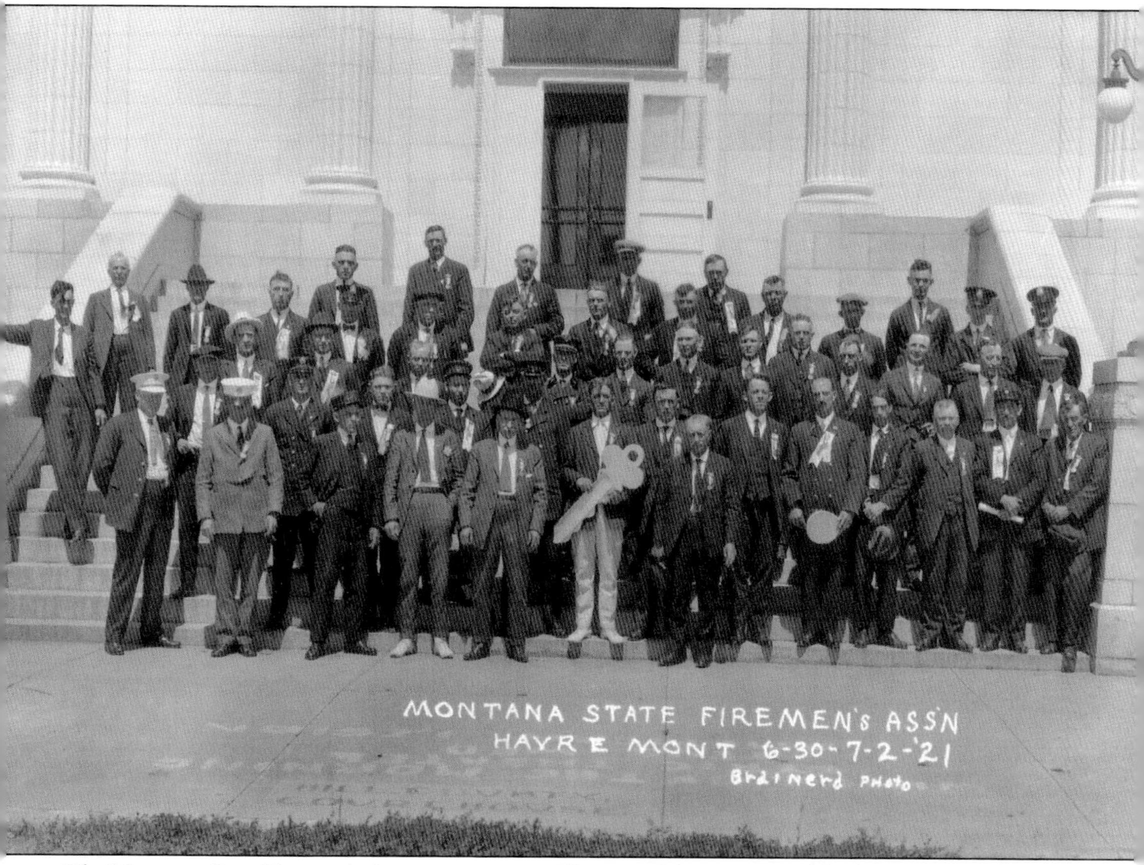

The Montana State Fireman's Association met in Havre on July 2, 1921, and had a group photograph taken at the steps of the Hill County Courthouse. The courthouse newel posts were very elaborate. Access to the courthouse was through a single doorway. (Courtesy of the Clack Museum.)

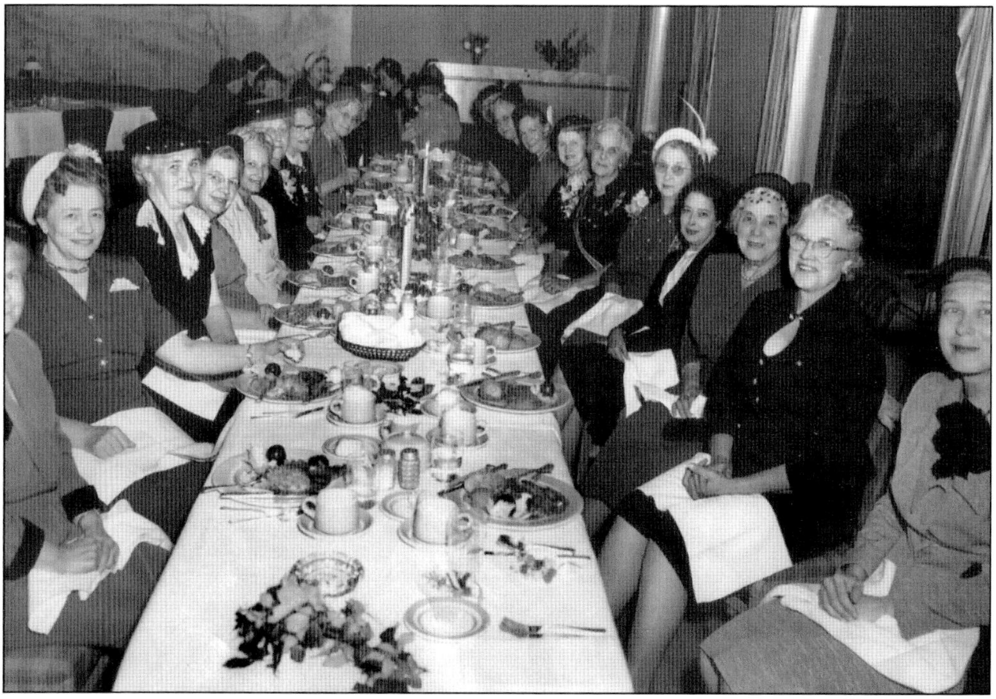

On September 28, 1950, the Assinniboine Chapter of the Daughters of the American Revolution met at the Havre Country Club. Attendees are, from front to back, (left row) Mrs. Dan Rathbone, Mrs. James Gibson, Mrs. Gus Haglund, Mrs. W. D. Williams, Mrs. F. J. Nichols, Jeannette Holesapple, Mrs. Thad Raymond, Mrs. Ray Sands, Mrs. C. J. Bonine, and Hazel Boylan; (right row) Cooley Carruth, Mrs. R. C. Monroe, Mrs. H. Earl Clack, Mrs. H. Poelher, Mrs. J. W. Pronger, Mrs. Fred May, Mrs. A. J. Midleton, Mrs. Einar Martinson, Mrs. Ira Stam, and Mrs. Bruce Travis. (Courtesy of the Clack Museum.)

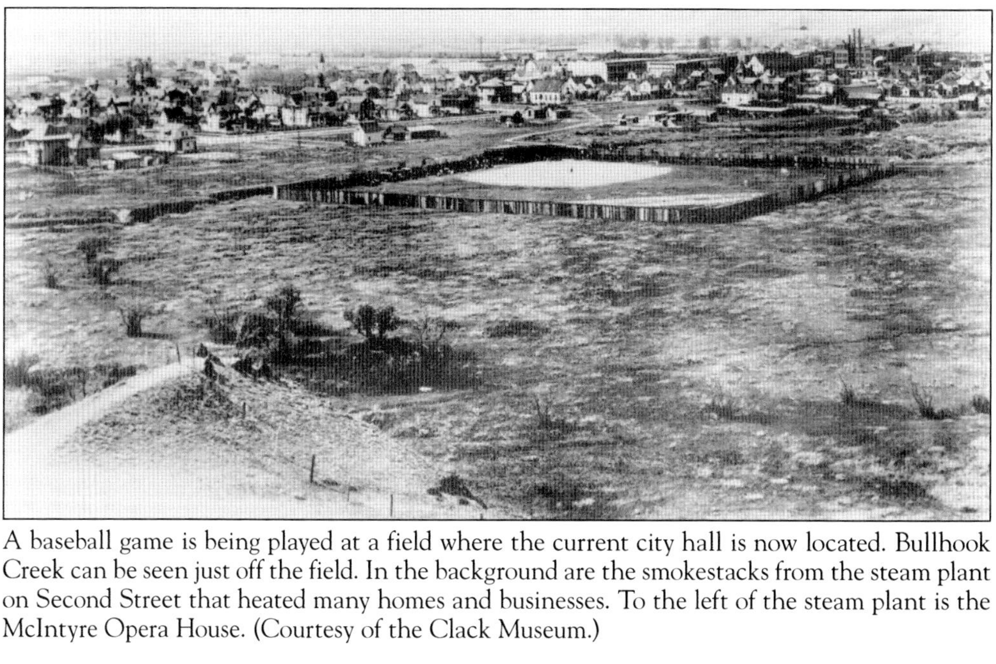

A baseball game is being played at a field where the current city hall is now located. Bullhook Creek can be seen just off the field. In the background are the smokestacks from the steam plant on Second Street that heated many homes and businesses. To the left of the steam plant is the McIntyre Opera House. (Courtesy of the Clack Museum.)

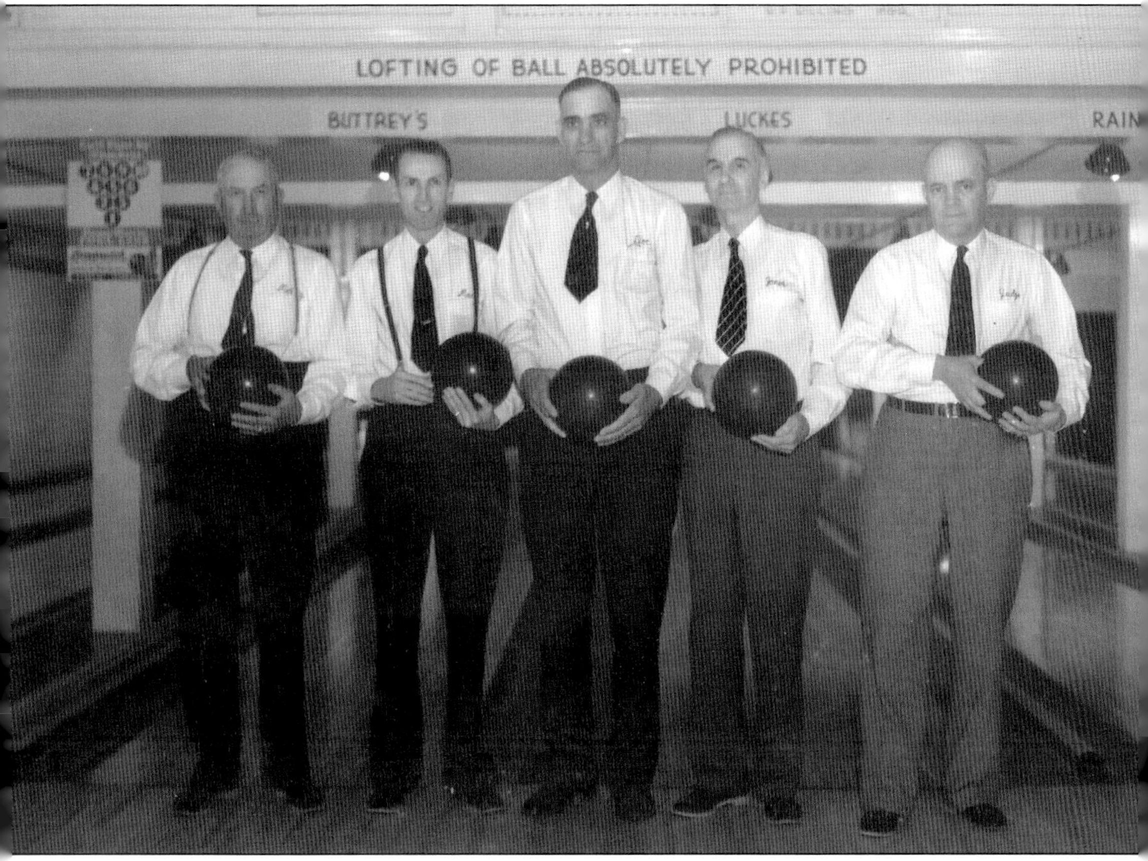

Bowling has been a pastime for Havre residents for many years. Local businesses have long sponsored bowling teams, and pictured in the background are the names of those businesses. This bowling alley was in the basement of the Oxford. Other bowling alleys in Havre have been Hi-Line Lanes on the East End and a bowling alley in the basement of the Student Union Building on Northern's campus. (Courtesy of MSU-Northern, Al Lucke Collection.)

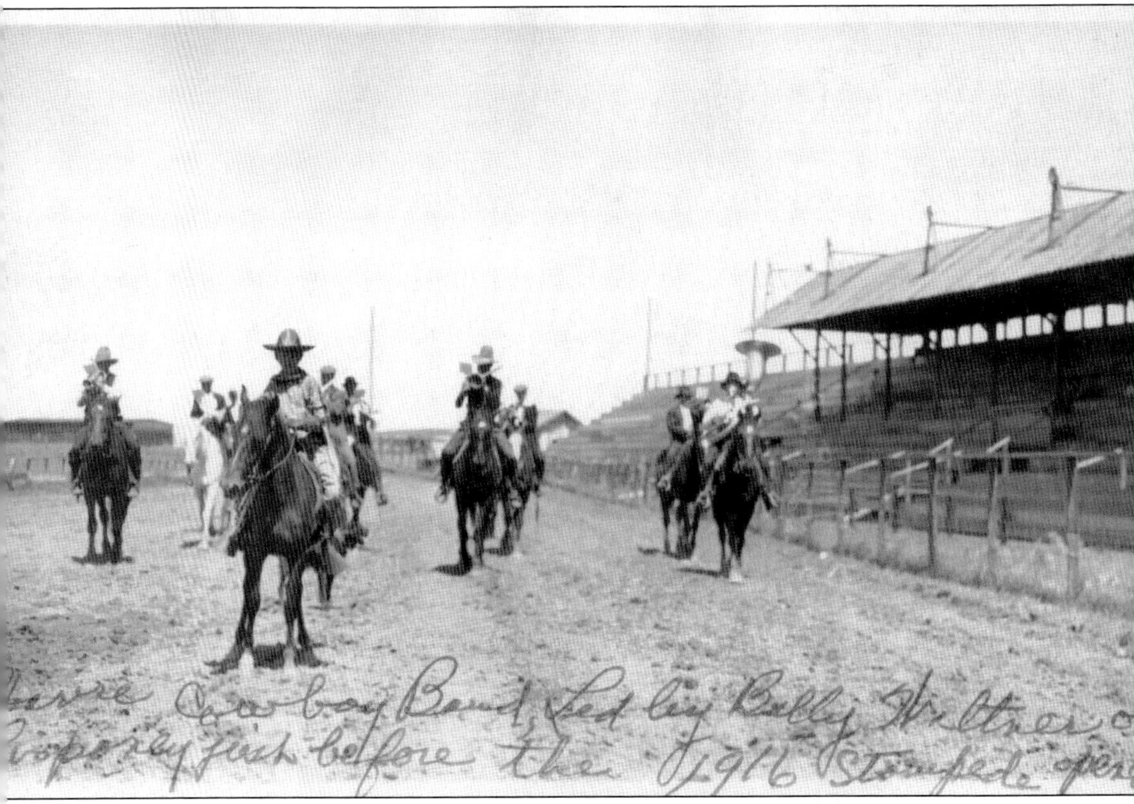

The Great Northern Stampede was once a huge event many looked forward to attending or participating in. The Stampede was held at the Hill County Fairgrounds, which was located near the current Oakwood Village east of Havre. The Havre Cowboy Band, led by Billy Wiltner, opened the 1916 Stampede. The fairgrounds were later moved to the former Christopher "Shorty" Young ranch west of Havre. (Courtesy of the Clack Museum.)

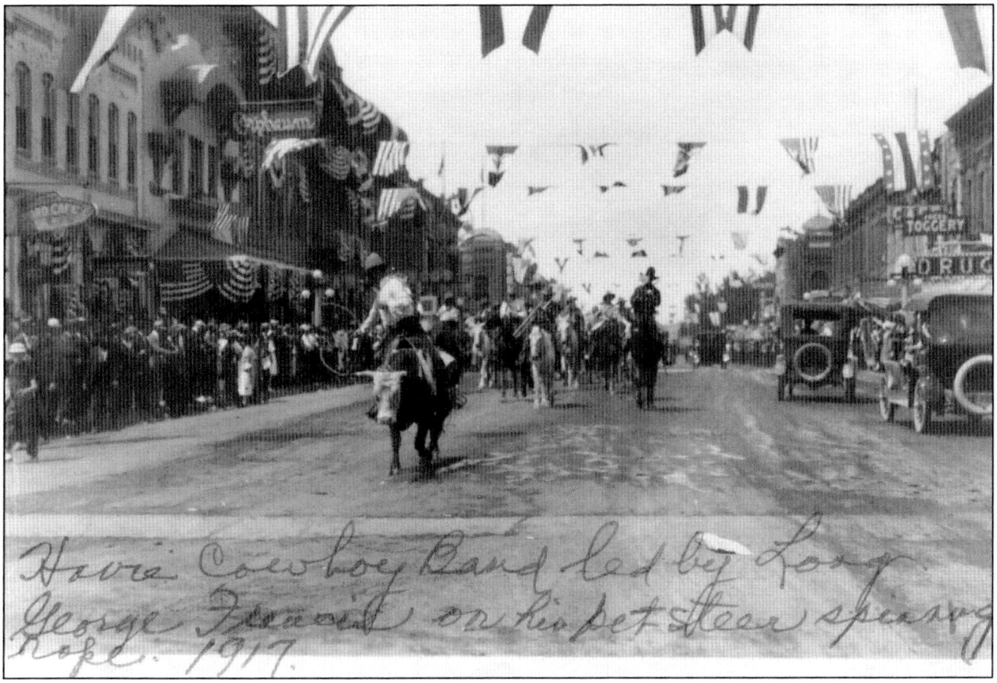

"Long" George Francis led the Havre Cowboy Band in the 1917 Great Northern Stampede Parade. A variety of buildings flank First Street, including the Ford Café, Mansfield Hotel, Havre Hotel, drugstores, and a toggery store. As a sign of progress, automobiles are to the right of the photograph, showing residents' willingness to embrace new technology. (Courtesy of the Clack Museum.)

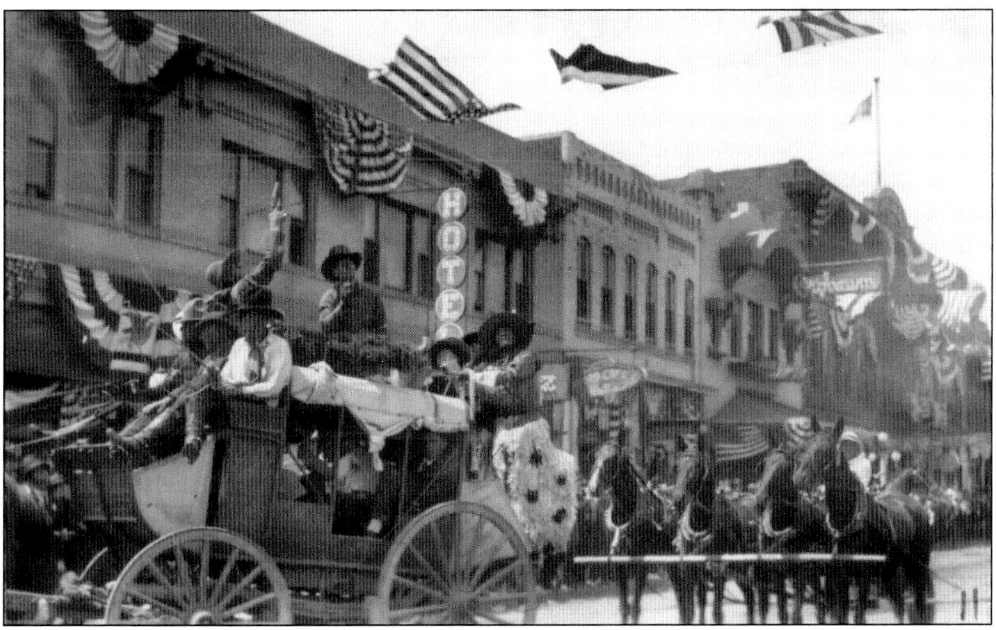

A parade down First Street shows how big the Great Northern Stampede was, along with the ever-present wind. Behind the stagecoach is the Oxford Hotel; to its right is the Ford Café and Mansfield Hotel, followed by the Orpheum Theatre and Havre Hotel. (Courtesy of the Clack Museum.)

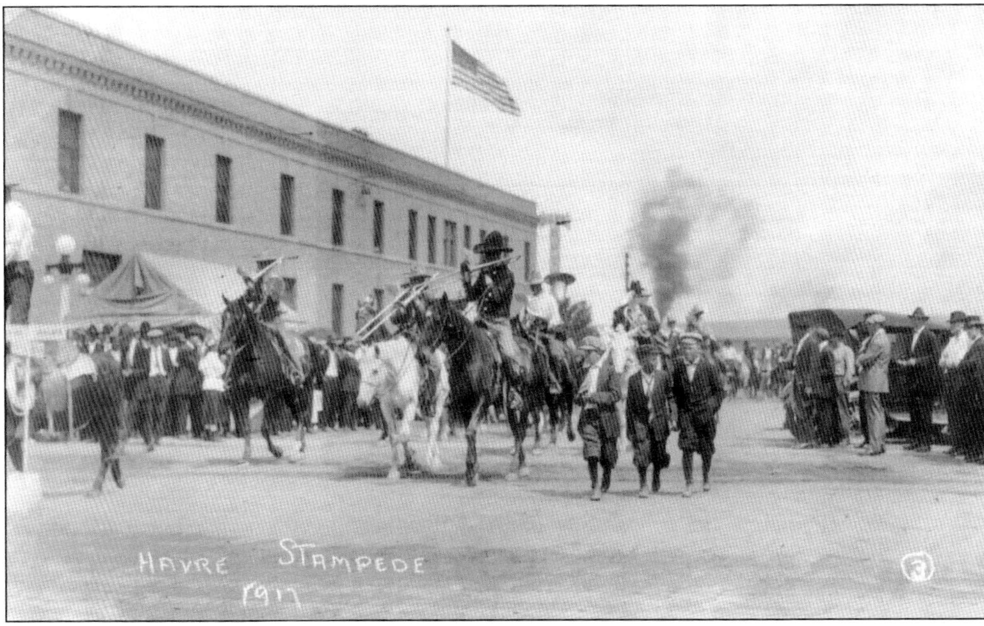

The Great Northern Stampede celebrations were not solely confined to the fairgrounds. In 1917, a parade down Fourth Avenue commemorated the event, complete with cowboys and bands on horseback. The Park Hotel is in the background. (Courtesy of the Clack Museum.)

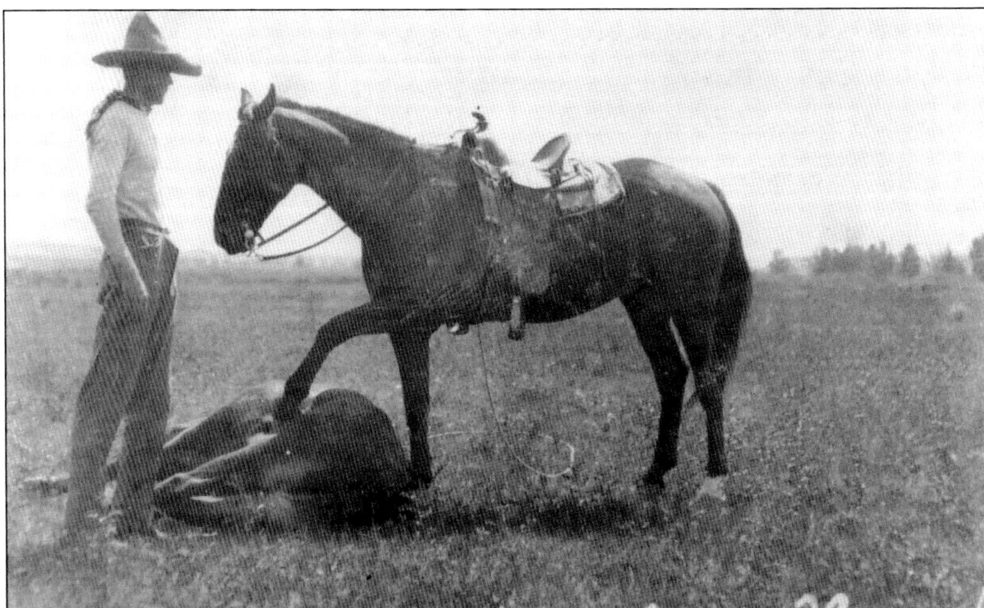

"Long" George Francis was a colorful character in Havre's past. At 6 feet 6 inches tall, "Long" George made quite an impression. His passion was the rodeo, and he enjoyed competing in and organizing them. However, in 1918, an arrest warrant was issued for "Long" George for the theft of a bay mare belonging to Phil Clack. On February 28, 1918, he was found guilty of horse theft but did not live to serve his sentence. (Courtesy of the Clack Museum.)

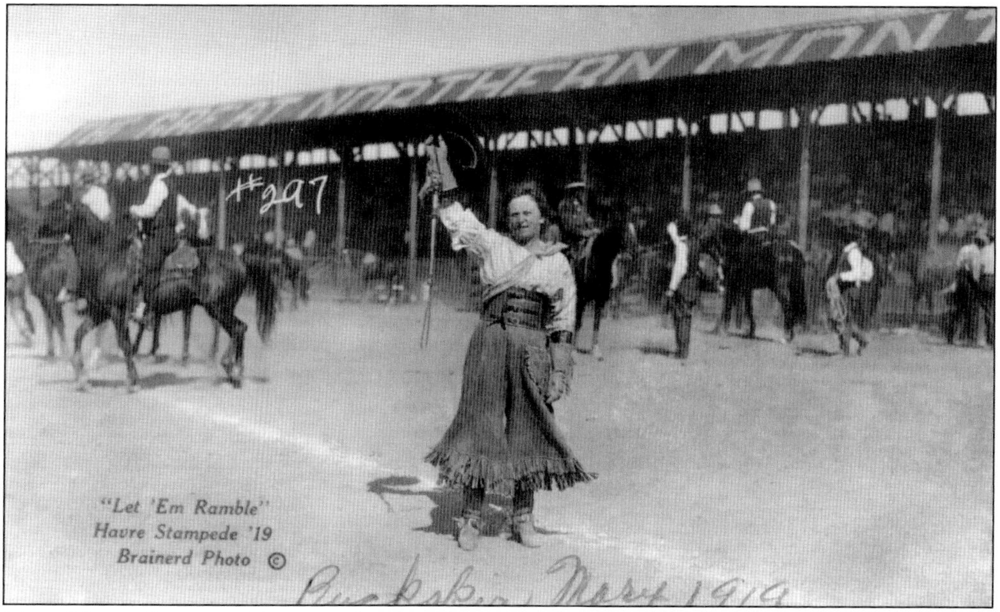

Marie Massoz Dumont Gibson was born in Belgium and came to the Havre area in 1914. She began trick riding as a girl and continued this skill, competing at fairs and rodeos. Her professional career took off in 1917, and she was very successful. Her career took her all over the world, including London, where the Prince of Wales saw her ride. He was so impressed with her skills that he presented her with a horse. (Courtesy of the Clack Museum.)

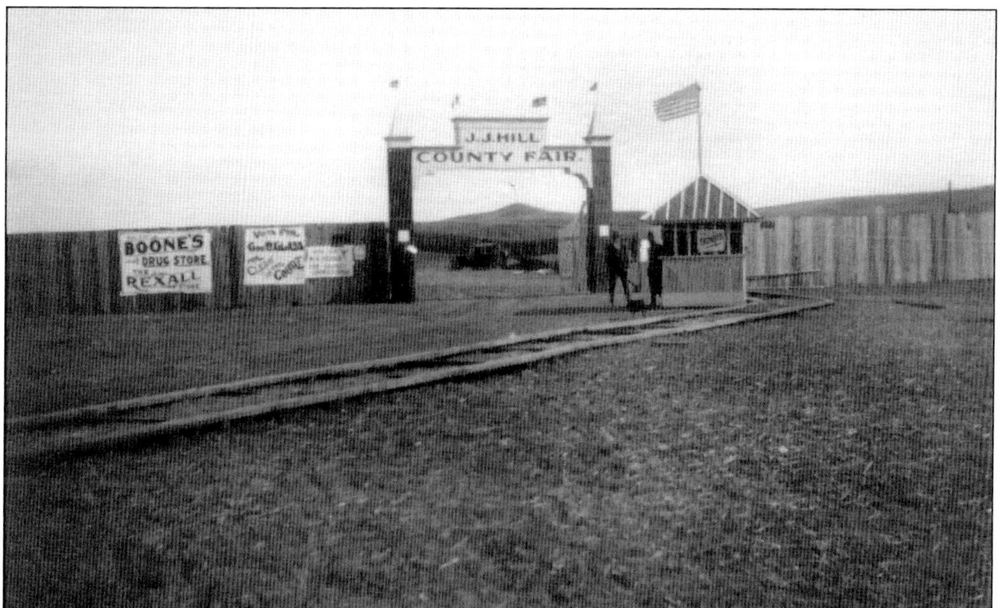

The entrance to the original J. J. Hill Fairgrounds east of Havre is pictured along with the ticket booth. Advertising at events is not a recent occurrence, as evidenced by the signage on the wall. Boone's Drug Store was owned by Daniel and Elizabeth Boone, who moved to Havre from Virginia. Hill County was named after James Jerome Hill, founder of the Great Northern Railroad. (Courtesy of the Clack Museum.)

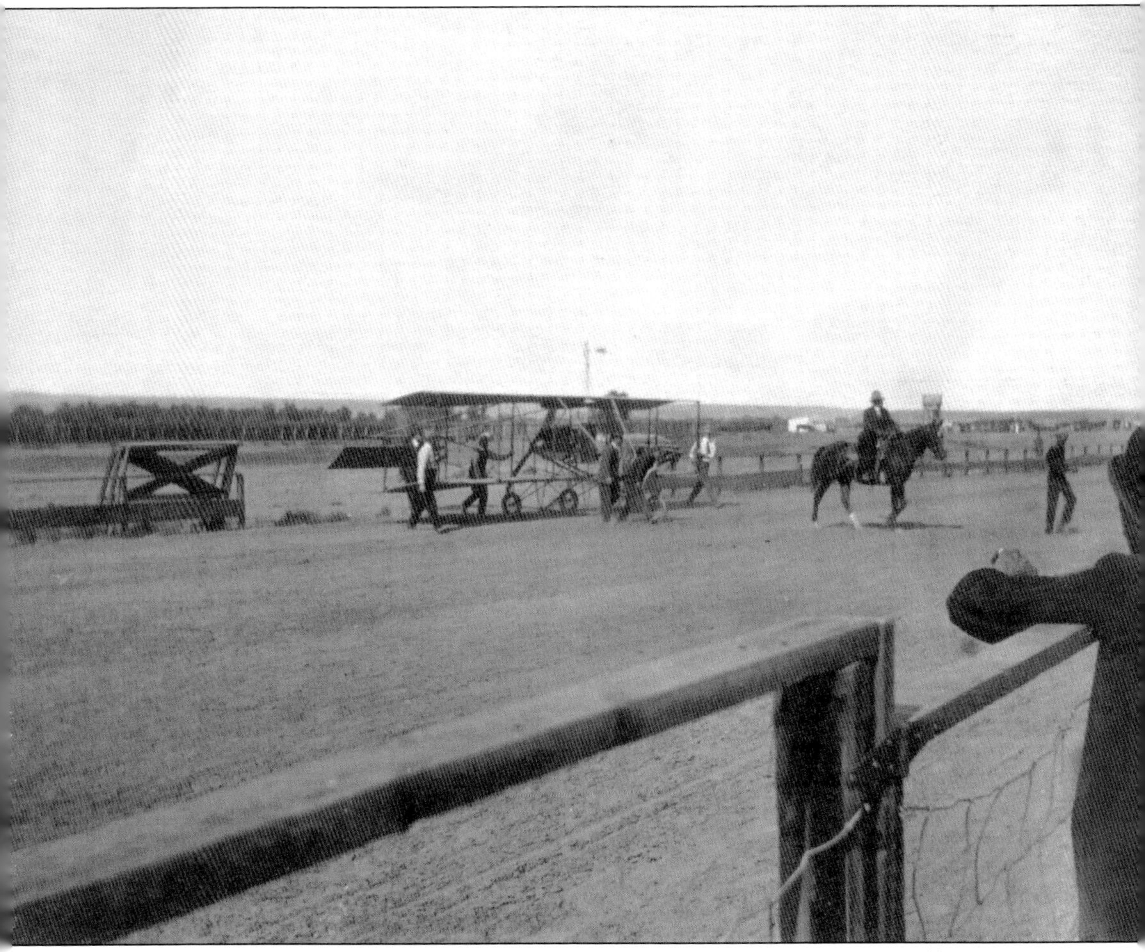

Aviator Maroney and his flying machine made an appearance at the 1913 Hill County Fair. Airplanes were a new technology then, and its arrival in Havre for an air show was cause for great excitement in the community. At the time, they were a curiosity, but aircraft became much more important in Havre in 1939 with the establishment of the Civilian Pilot Training Program, a part of Northern Montana College. (Courtesy of the Clack Museum.)

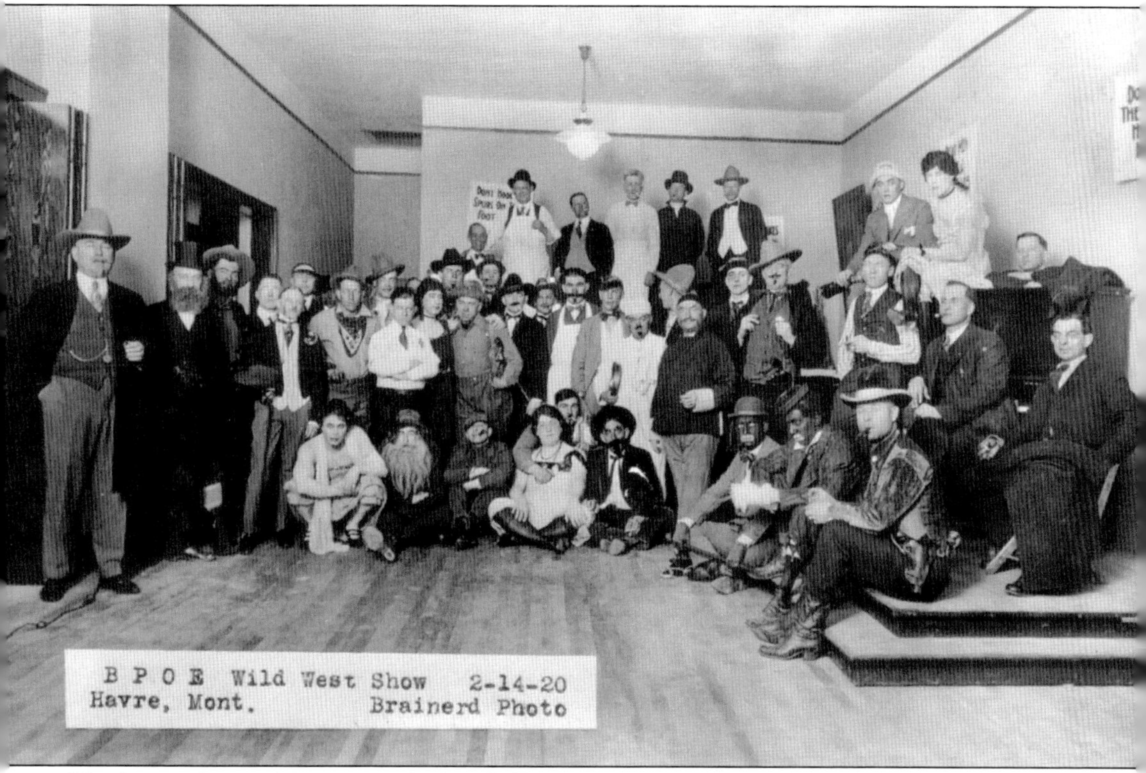

The Benevolent and Protective Order of Elks Lodge No. 1201 was established in 1910 and was located where the Cottonwood Theatres are now. The building had a lodge room and a club, accessed by separate doors. It was once a men's-only fraternal order; the photograph shows those participating in a Wild West Show. It is unclear if the women in the picture are indeed females or if they were men playing a part in the show. (Courtesy of the Clack Museum.)

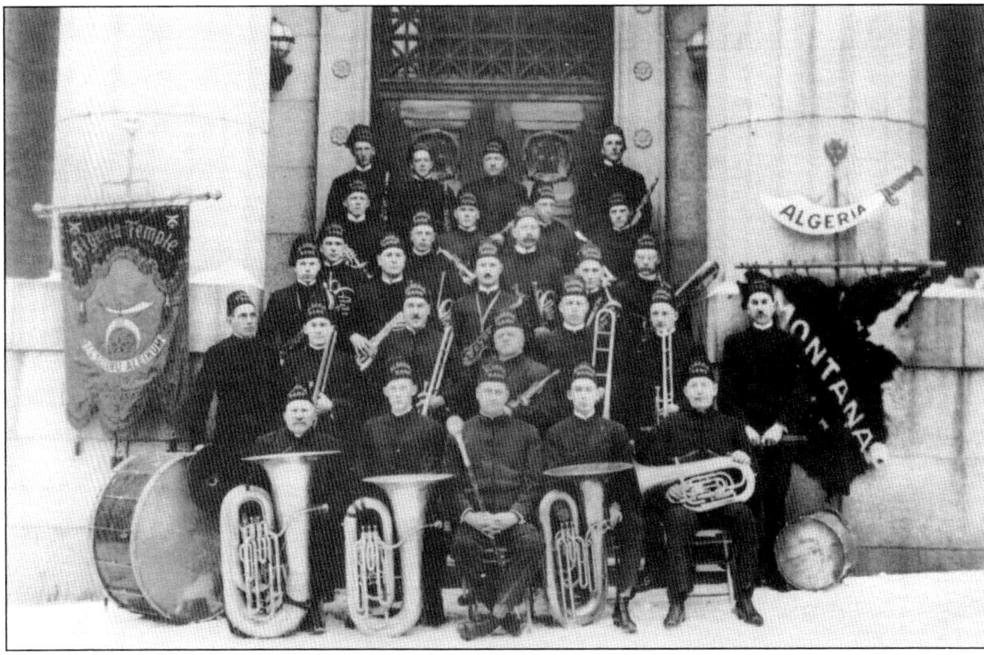

The Shrine Club of Algeria Temple is an order of the Masonic Lodge. It met in the Havre Masonic Lodge, located at 305 Third Avenue. The Egyptian Revival–style building was designed by Frank Bossuot. The cornerstone was laid on November 12, 1915, and the first lodge meeting was held the following year. The first three floors were intended for businesses, while the fourth and fifth floors were dedicated to Masonic functions. (Courtesy of the Clack Museum.)

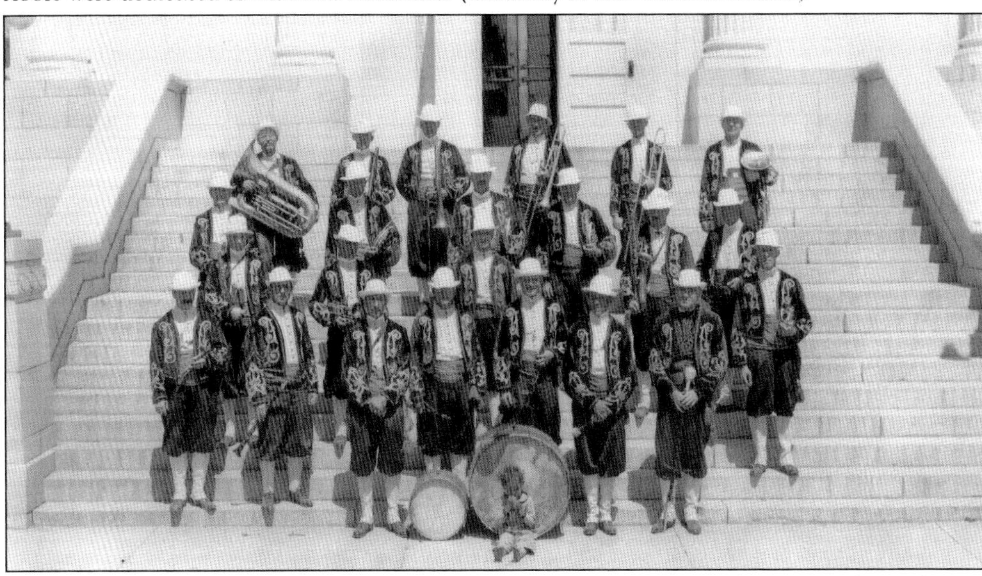
On July 13, 1921, the Grand Commandery, Knights Templar, held their annual conclave in Havre. Local members organized an event that surely impressed those who attended: a parade, a band concert, luncheons for the ladies, and a basket picnic at Fort Assinniboine followed by an evening of entertainment and dancing. In addition, the Elks Club granted privileges to the Knights Templar. People were encouraged to display the American flag for that weekend. (Courtesy of MSU-Northern, Al Lucke Collection.)

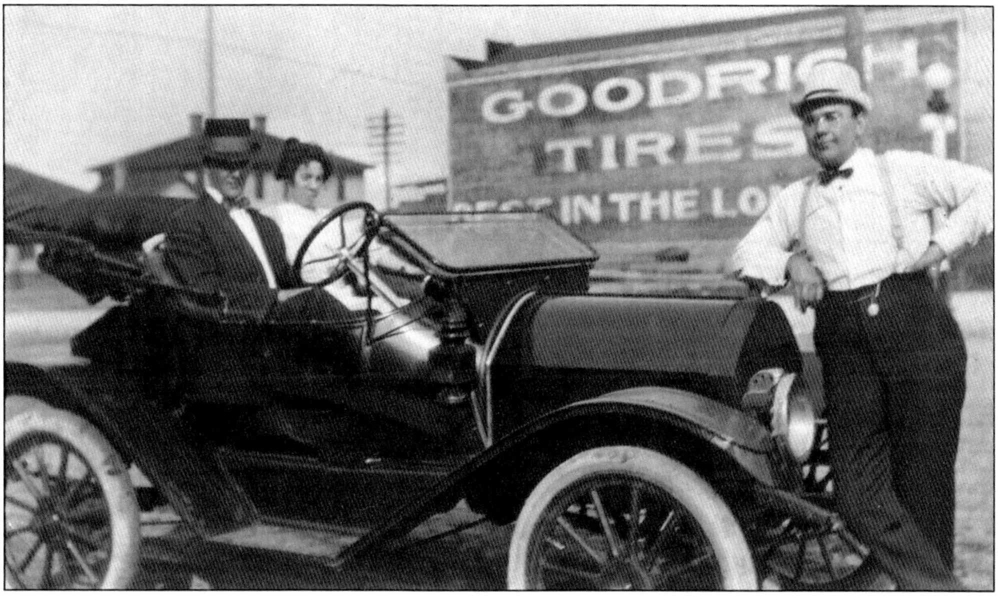

The people of Hill County have long been proud of their automobiles. Otto Ash shows off his four-cylinder Little Monroe, the beginning of what is now Chevrolet, in 1908. The first automobile in Havre arrived in 1905 for E. C. Carruth. It was built by Locomobile Company of Toledo, Ohio, and was an old crank-type model. (Courtesy of MSU-Northern, Al Lucke Collection.)

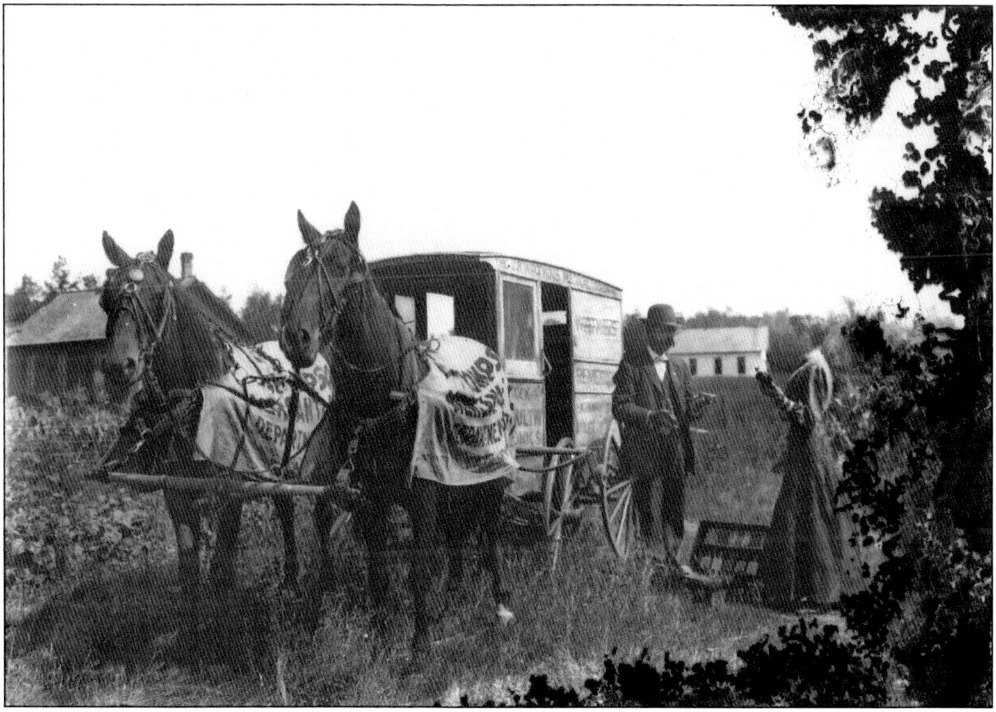

The Watkins salesman was making his rounds in Hill County when this photograph was taken in 1912. Salesmen such as this offered their goods and services by traveling door-to-door and to rural homesteads. The Watkins salesmen sold elixirs and "cures for what ailed you," along with other products for the choosy housewife. (Courtesy of MSU-Northern, Al Lucke Collection.)

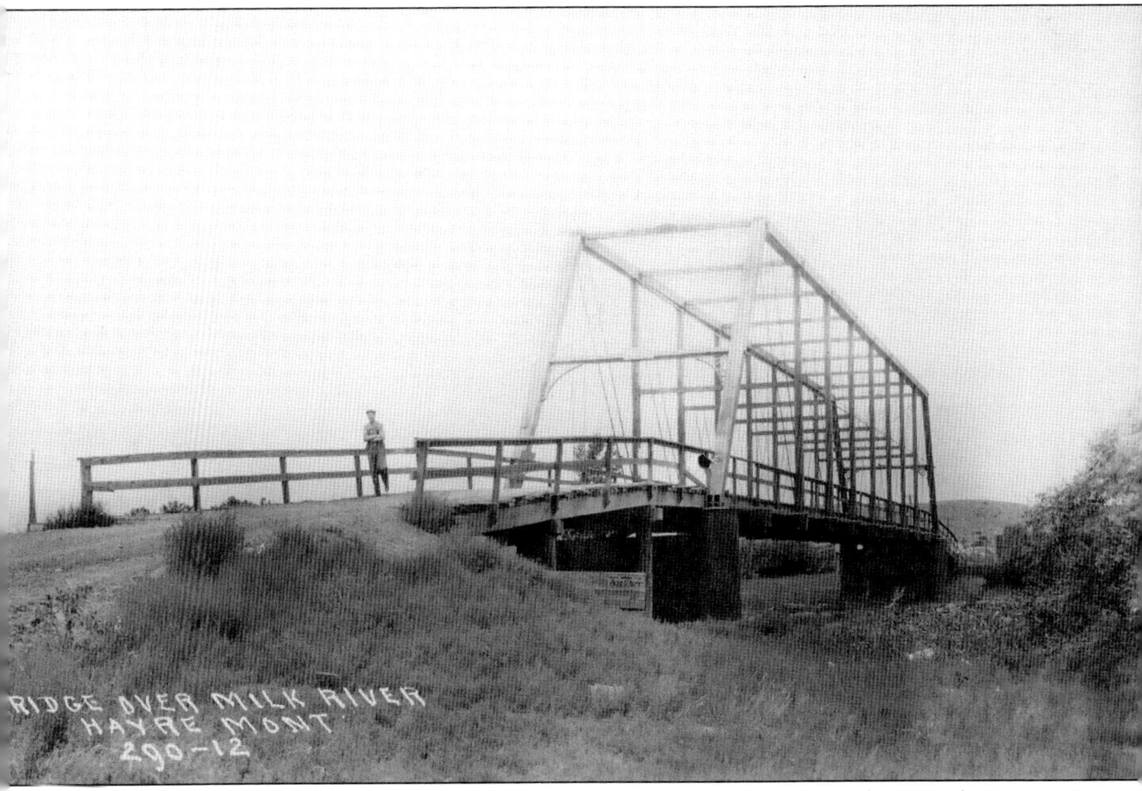

The bridge over the Milk River served as a crossing between those from the "North Country" and the city of Havre for many years. The bridge itself was constructed of wood. Sometimes the wood would give way and leave a hole open to the river below. Those who crossed on foot were very careful when crossing the bridge. The bridge was rebuilt in the 1980s into a concrete one. (Courtesy of MSU-Northern, Al Lucke Collection.)

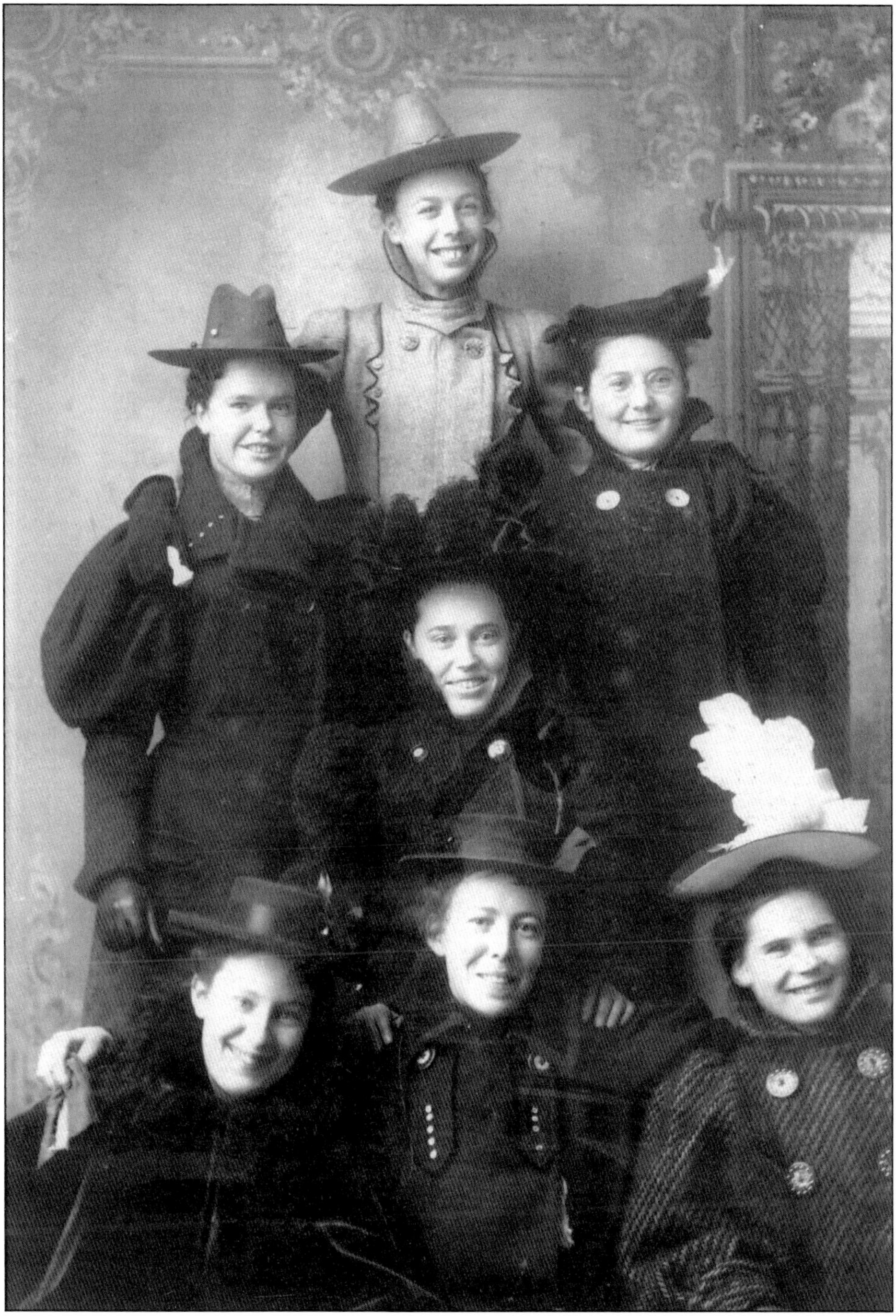

The daughters of some of Hill County's founding families gather for a *c.* 1916 photograph. Pictured from left to right from the top are Gertrude Gowerie, Nell Thackeray, Susan Gallow, Kate Thackeray, Alma Reardon, Mary Gowerie, and Margaret Auld MacKenzie. The hats and dresses worn in the picture are typical of the time. No self-respecting young lady would have been seen in public without being properly attired, including a hat and a pair of gloves. (Courtesy of MSU-Northern, Al Lucke Collection.)

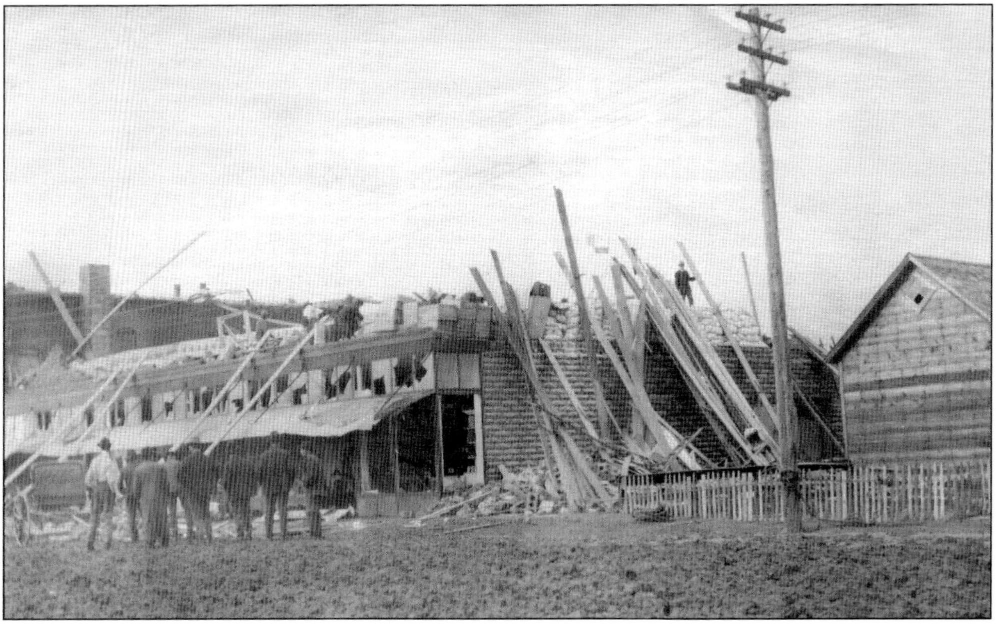

The Havre Hurricane, or cyclone, ripped through Hill County on June 22, 1906. It did considerable damage throughout Hill County. The Havre Commercial Company was severely damaged, and a portion of a wall of the post trader's building at Fort Assinniboine caved in. Along with the hurricane-force wind was hail. An at-the-time record-breaking hailstone measuring 4 inches in diameter fell, and considerable livestock losses were reported. (Courtesy of MSU-Northern, Al Lucke Collection.)

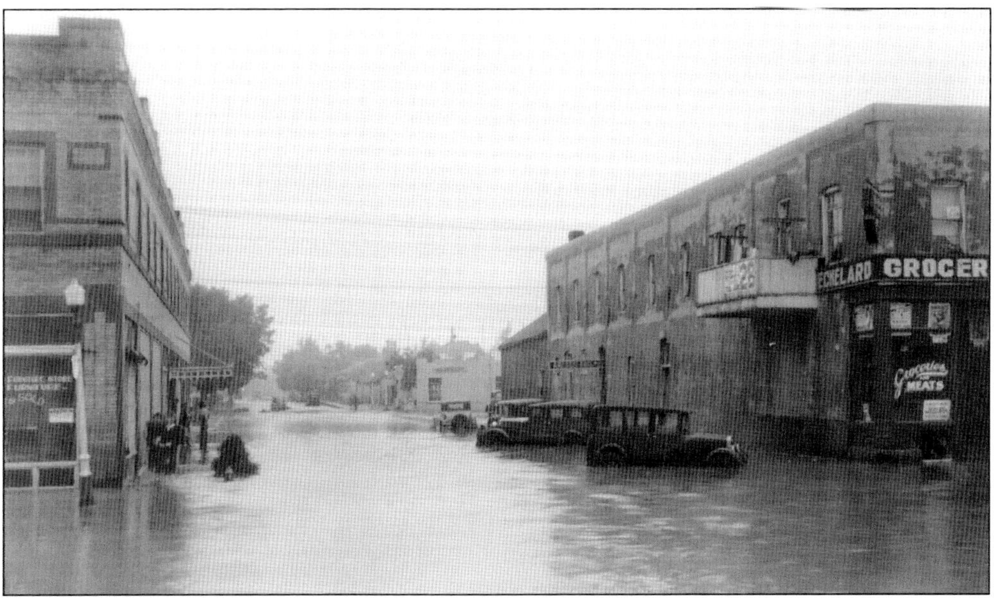

Flooding was a major problem in Havre, and the flood of June 1938 was particularly brutal. A cloudburst occurred in the Bear Paws, and the water cascaded into low-lying areas, including Havre. In the town of Laredo, south of Havre, several people were killed in the floodwaters. The photograph shows the Echelard Grocery, which later became the Corner Bar, the Shell gas station, and the Yeon Building. (Courtesy of Susie Leonard.)

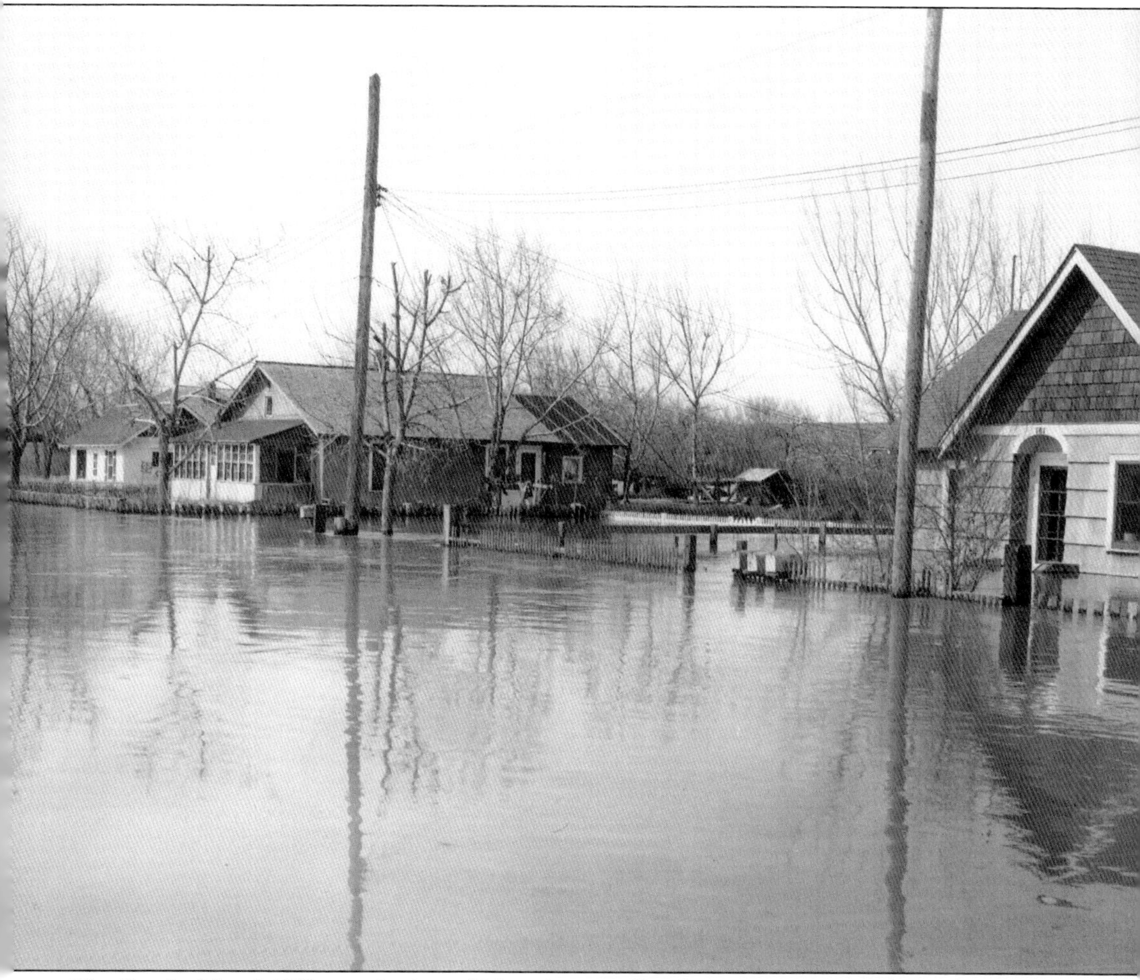

The flood of April 1952 was the last of Havre's major floods. Many Havre residents alive at the time remember this disaster vividly. Pictured are the Don and Violet O'Donnell residence at 161 Farley Avenue (now 1127 Fourth Street North) and the home of Eugene "Gino" and Emelia Priete. (Courtesy of the Clack Museum.)

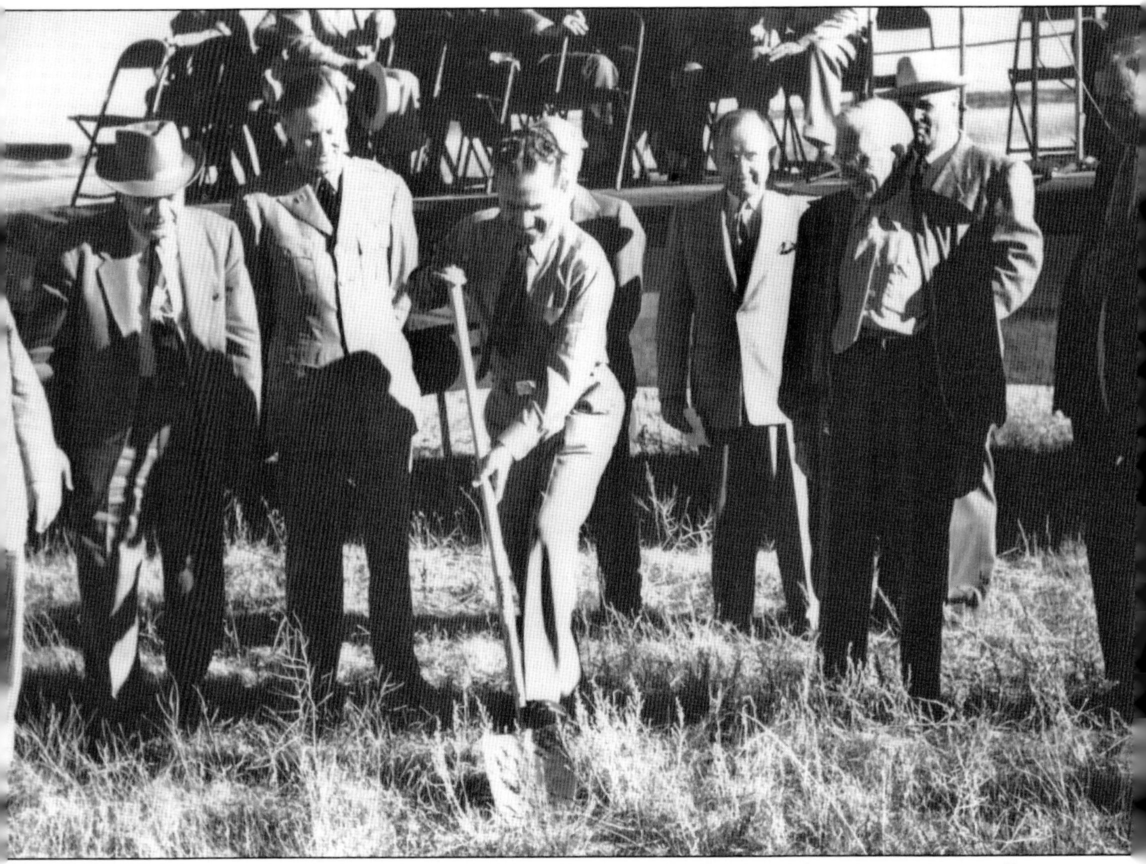

On September 17, 1953, the Bullhook Diversion Project broke ground in an attempt to alleviate the flooding that occurred all too often. From left to right are R. M. Lockwood, Judge C. B. Elwell, Lt. Col. Erland Tillman, Brigadier General Potter, Earl Bronson, Dr. G. A. Jestrab, Fred Buck, Jack Travis, and Mayor Oval Hatler. (Courtesy of the Clack Museum.)

Three

Modern Times, Bits and Pieces, and Lost History

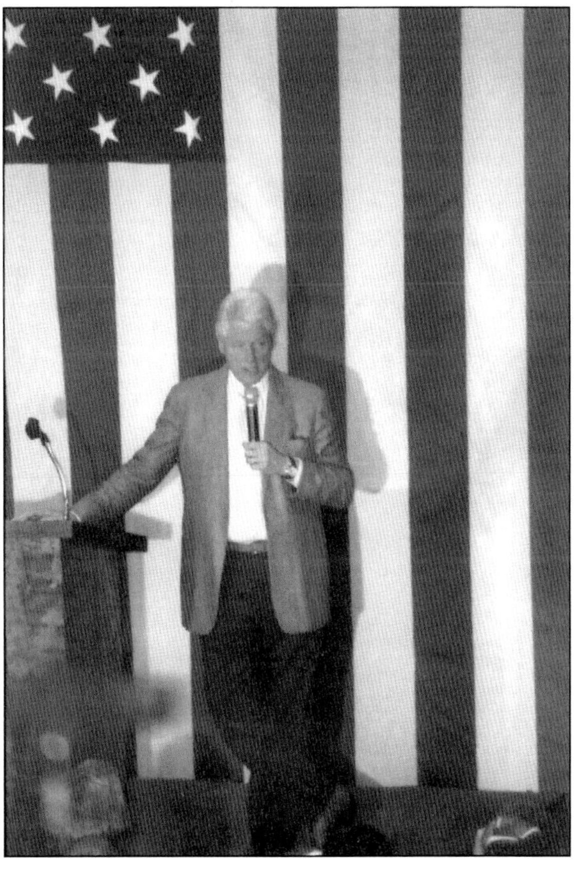

Havre has hosted three U.S. presidents: Franklin Delano Roosevelt on August 7, 1934; Harry S. Truman on May 12, 1950, and September 30, 1952; and William Jefferson "Bill" Clinton on April 1, 2008. Presidents Roosevelt and Truman greeted people at the train station. President Clinton gave a speech at the Armory Gym on MSU-Northern's campus. People drove for hours just to attend this event, and people from all walks of life and political affiliations were there. (Photograph by Emily Mayer.)

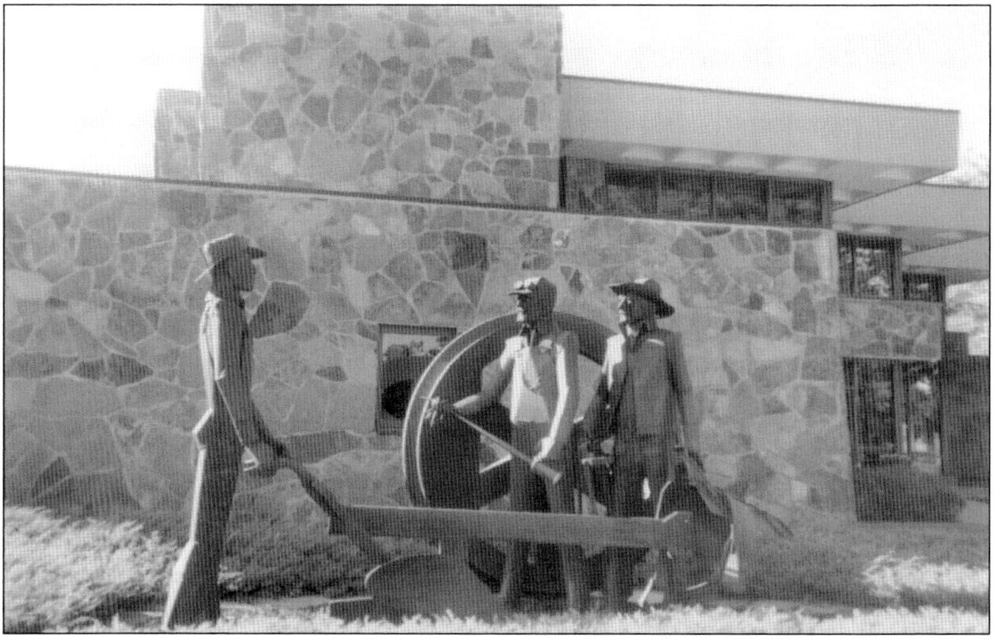

In 1976, Lyndon Fayne Pomeroy, one of Havre's most prolific sculptors, created this familiar statue honoring the three major economies in Havre, featuring a farmer, a railroader, and a rancher. It was placed next to the then Havre Federal Savings and Loan, now Stockman Bank. This sculpture has been featured in books, on postcards, and even on the local Elks Lodge pin. (Photograph by Emily Mayer.)

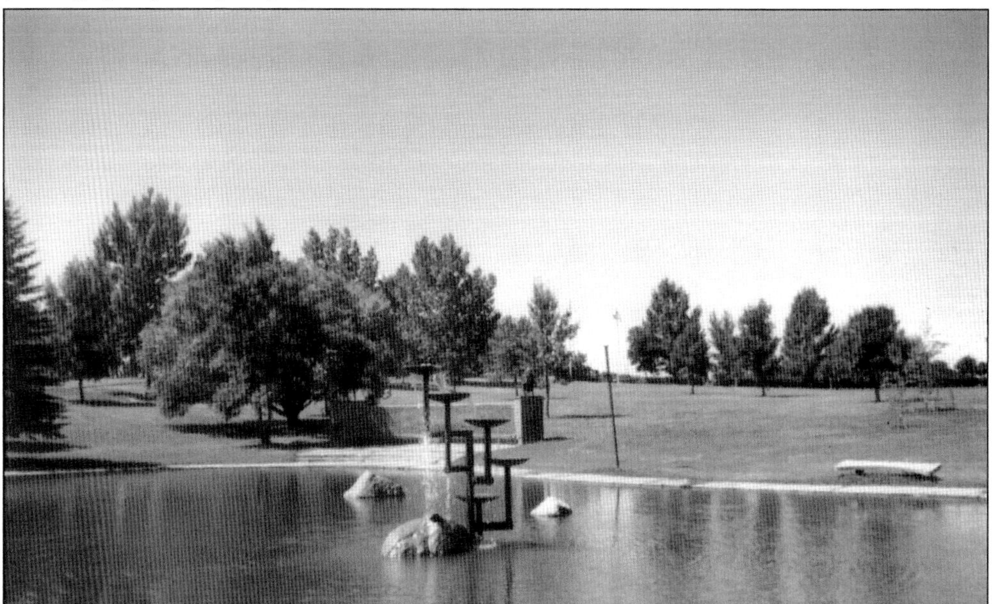

Kuhr Park, on the campus of MSU-Northern, was dedicated in honor of Max Kuhr, a local lawyer and longtime supporter of Northern Montana College. Lyndon Pomeroy designed the modernistic fountain and two sculptures atop a wall of brick salvaged from Fort Assinniboine, which can be seen behind the fountain. (Photograph by Emily Mayer.)

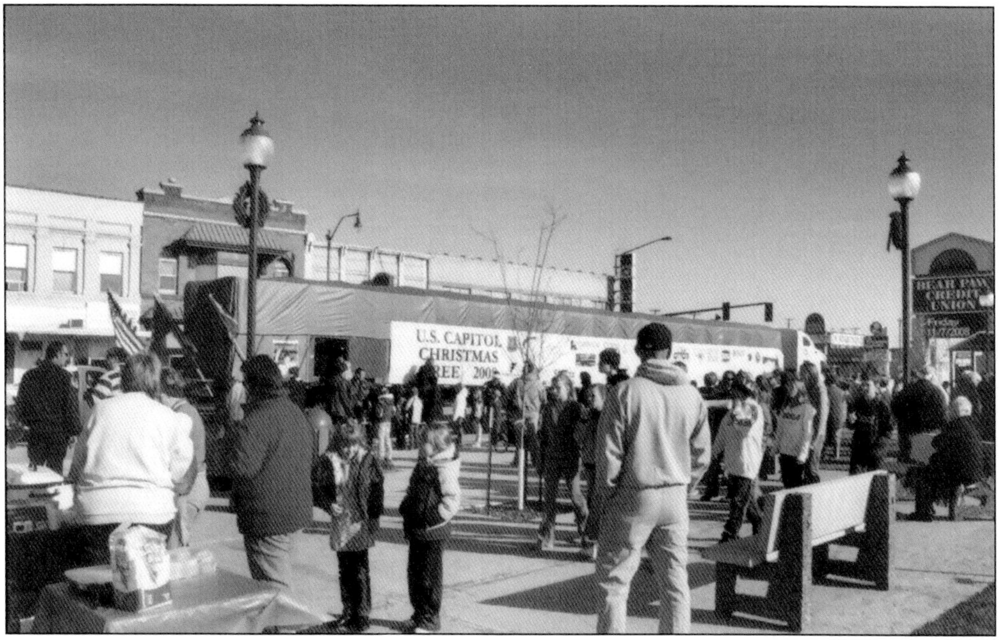

On November 7, 2008, the Capitol Christmas Tree stopped in Havre on its journey to Washington, D.C., to be placed in front of the U.S. Capitol Building. Local 4-H member Chris Gabrielsen from Havre went to Washington to help light the tree. The tree came from the Sapphire Mountains near Hamilton. The last time Montana had hosted a Capitol Christmas Tree was in 1989. (Photograph by Emily Mayer.)

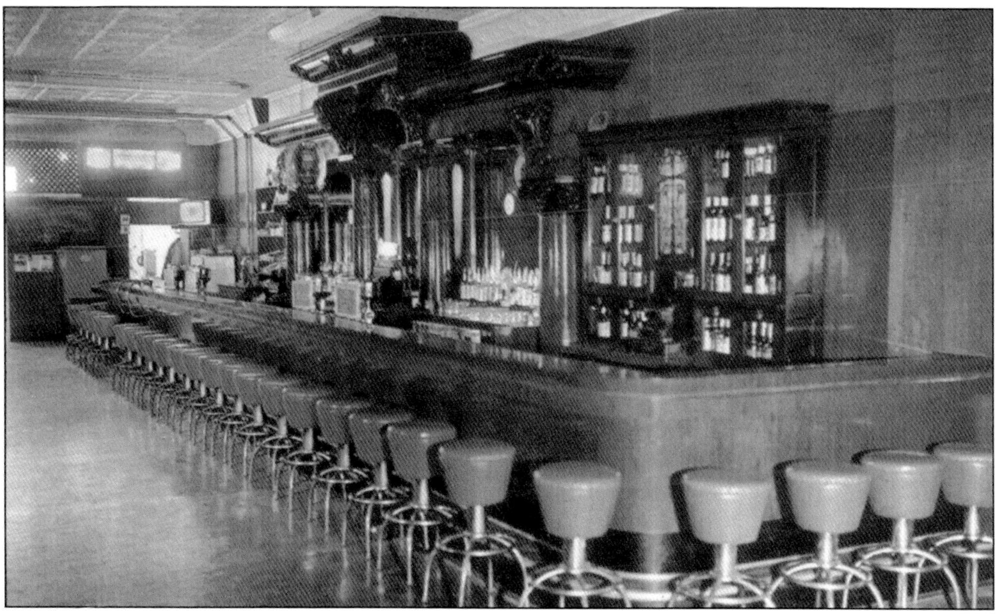

The Palace Bar in Downtown Havre can lay claim to the oldest known back bar in Montana. Made in St. Louis in 1883, it was brought up to Chinook via river boat and wagons and stayed there throughout Prohibition. The Weyh brothers moved it to the Palace Bar in 1933 after Prohibition was lifted. It still retains its original finish, carvings, and stained-glass window. (Courtesy of the Palace Bar/Jupe Compton.)

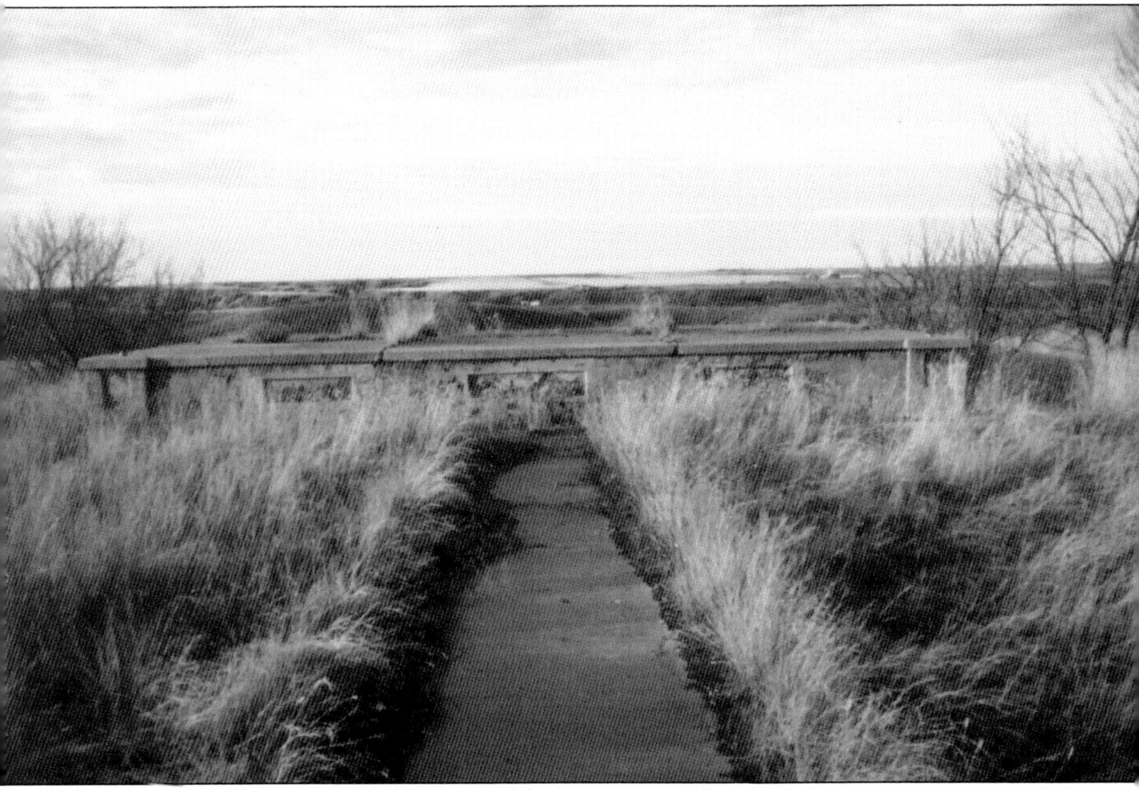

The concrete slab across the old entries of the Calvary and Highland Cemeteries is all that is left of the Veteran's Memorial. The idea was started in 1945 by Clint Clark. It was constructed in 1946, and patriotic ceremonies were conducted here until the early 1950s, when the events were moved to the Hill County Courthouse lawn. (Photograph by Emily Mayer.)

Sunset Memorial Gardens was a private cemetery located west of Havre. Five white stone sculptures occupied the site, each on a stone base with various Bible verses carved into the base. In 2000, efforts began to remove the beautiful sculptures from the defunct private cemetery to the Calvary and Highland Cemeteries in Havre, where they are now located. (Photograph by Emily Mayer.)

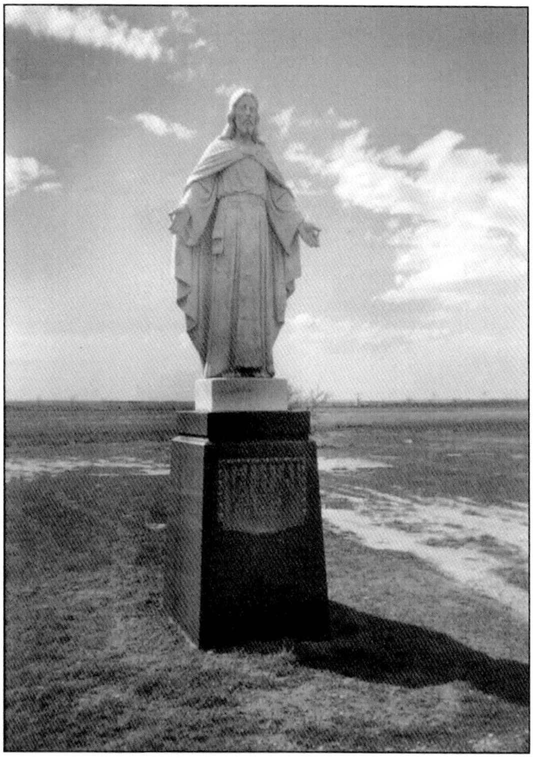

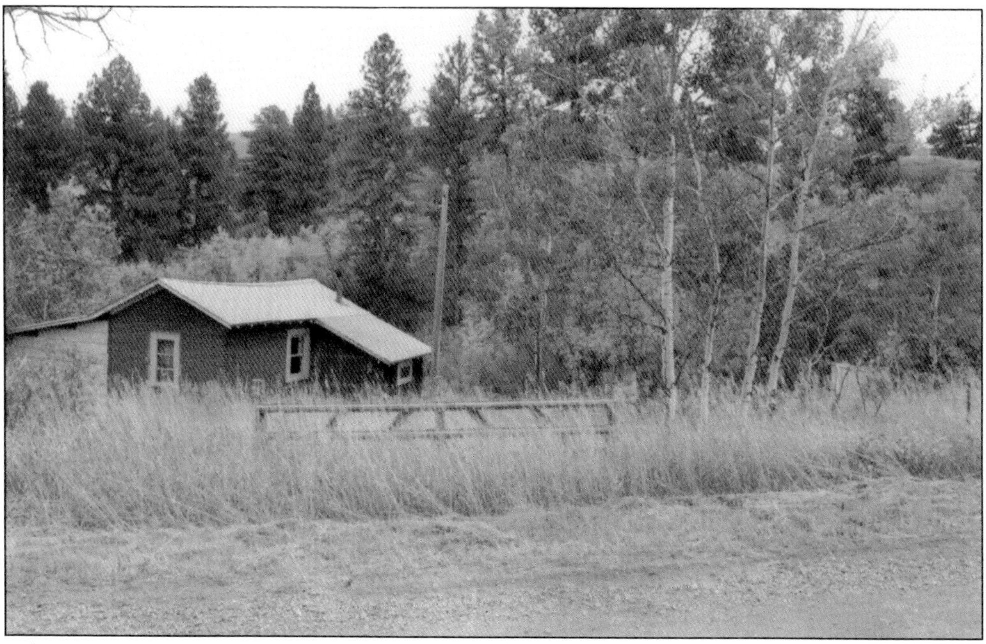

What is now referred to as the Dow cabin was originally Havre Distributors. It was a combination warehouse and office and as a consequence was well insulated and has 6-inch-thick walls. Percy and Clair Dow owned Havre Distributors. Arnie Kronebush gave the Dows permission to move the building onto his ranch after a new concrete building was constructed. Dr. G. A. Jestrab and his family used the cabin after the Dows built a new cabin at Essex. (Photograph by Emily Mayer.)

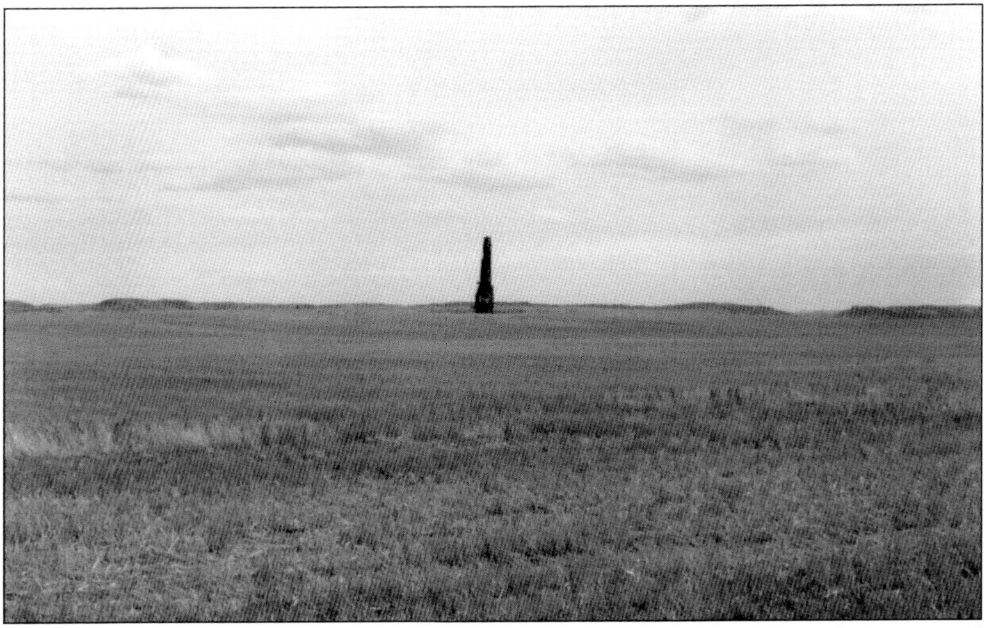

A longtime Hill County icon, the Christler Chimney is a familiar landmark on the way to and from the Bear Paw Mountains. It is all that is left of Hillcrest Farm, owned by the Reverend Leonard Christler and his wife, Anna. In October 1922, Reverend Christler was murdered, and his killer, Margaret Carleton, committed suicide shortly thereafter. The house was never finished or lived in and burned around January 1932. (Photograph by Emily Mayer.)

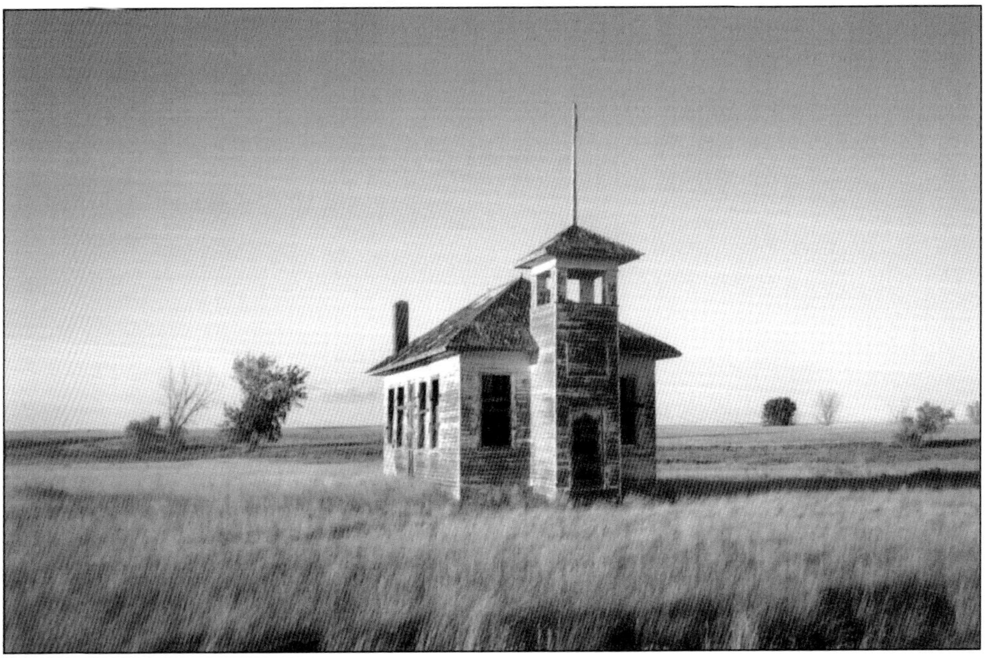

The Burnham School is located west of Havre along Highway 2 and just north of the railroad tracks. In 1915, the one-room school's teacher was Anna Nodsletten. Burnham was a small town located west of Havre and had a post office whose postmaster was Martha Moss. It operated from 1914 to 1916, when the mail was delivered to Fresno a few miles west. (Photograph by Emily Mayer.)

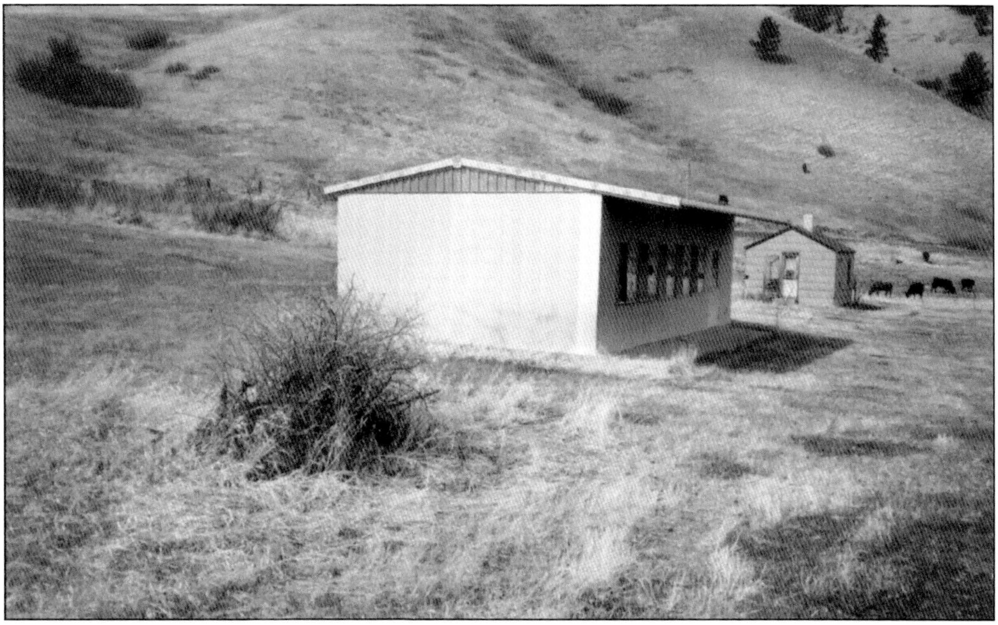

The 1950s Faber schoolhouse and Schoolteacher's House in the Bear Paw Mountains are shown here. When the school closed, schoolchildren were bussed to Havre to attend classes. The school remained as it had been left: desks, books, maps, even a piano were there for many years as testament to days gone by. Unfortunately, those less caring vandalized the building, which has resulted in it being boarded up. (Photograph by Emily Mayer.)

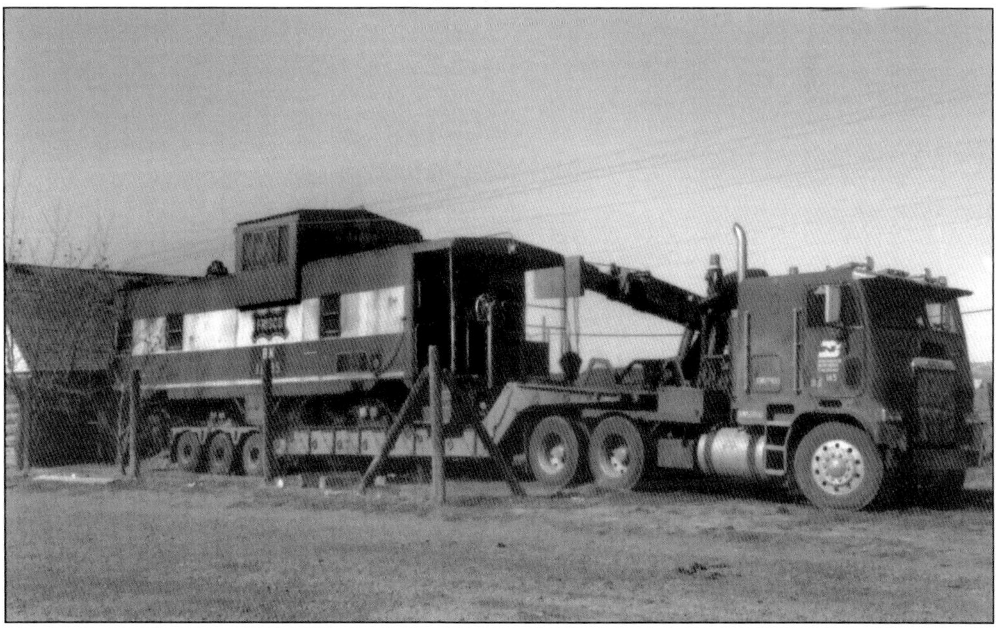

The Frisco caboose was added to the Clack Museum collection in the 1970s. This picture shows it being moved to its first location in Havre. It was later moved behind the Heritage Center after the Clack Museum moved into the old post office. After the City of Havre sold the historic Heritage Center to a private party, it was moved for a third time, near its first location. (Courtesy of Elinor Clack.)

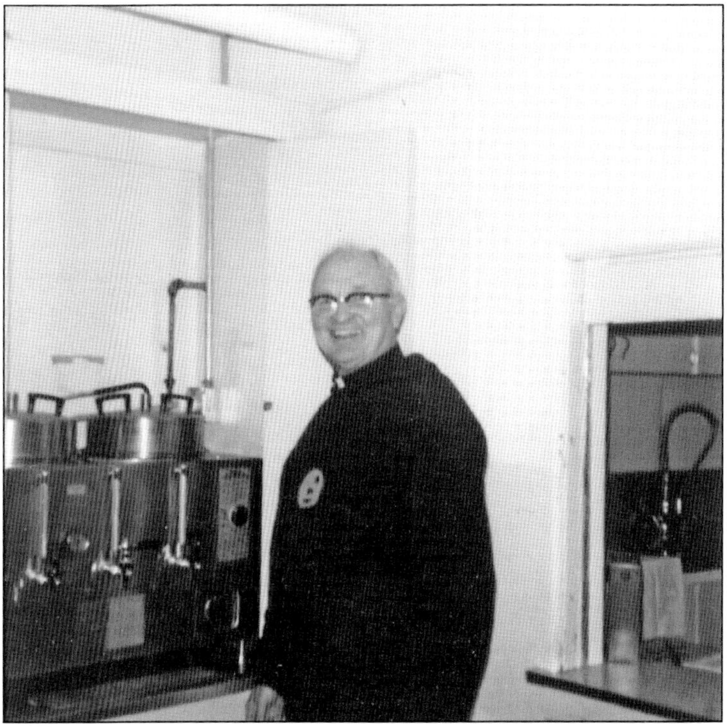

Fr. Michael McHugh, S.J., was a well-respected and beloved priest at St. Jude Catholic Church. Born in 1921, he lived in the Seattle area and entered the Oregon Province of the Society of Jesus in 1938. He was ordained to the priesthood on June 15, 1951. Soon after, he was stricken with polio. With the support of fellow Jesuits, he recovered. He moved to Havre in 1974 and remained until 1985. Father McHugh passed away on May 1, 2007. (Photograph by Emily Mayer.)

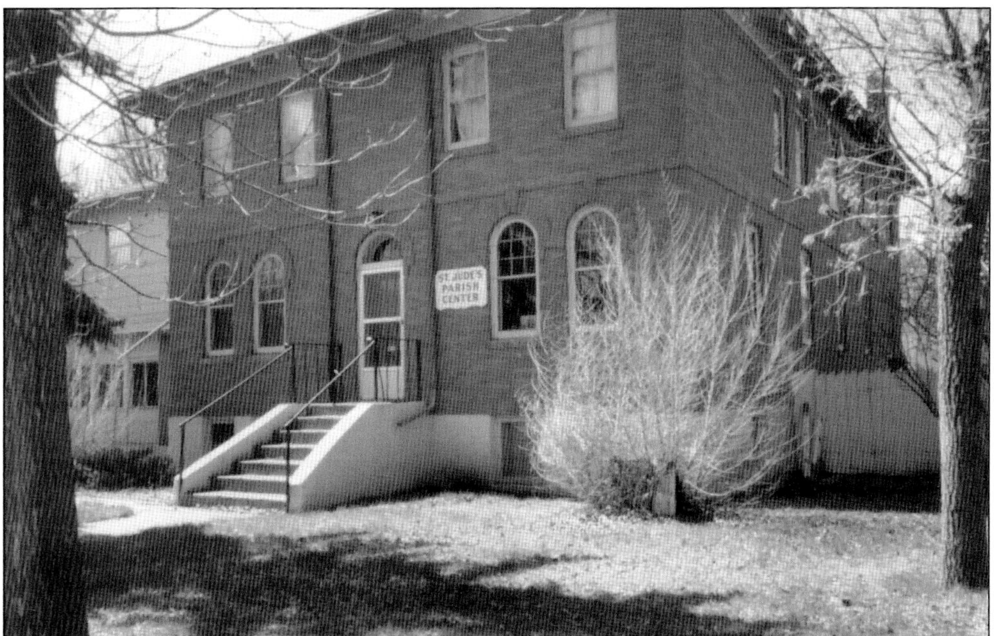

St. Jude Parish Center, also known as the Emmaus House, was originally housing for the Catholic nuns who served at the church, the school, and the Sacred Heart Hospital. An addition to the south of the building was constructed in 1952. After the nuns left, the building became the parish center. Seeing a need for a larger and more modern structure, it was demolished in 1999 and the new parish center was built. (Photograph by Emily Mayer.)

Faith Lutheran Church served the spiritual needs of Box Elder residents for many years. It saw many weddings, confirmations, funerals, and sermons before closing its doors in October 2005. The church was moved to a settlement near Billings the following year, where it is still serving its original purpose. (Photograph by Emily Mayer.)

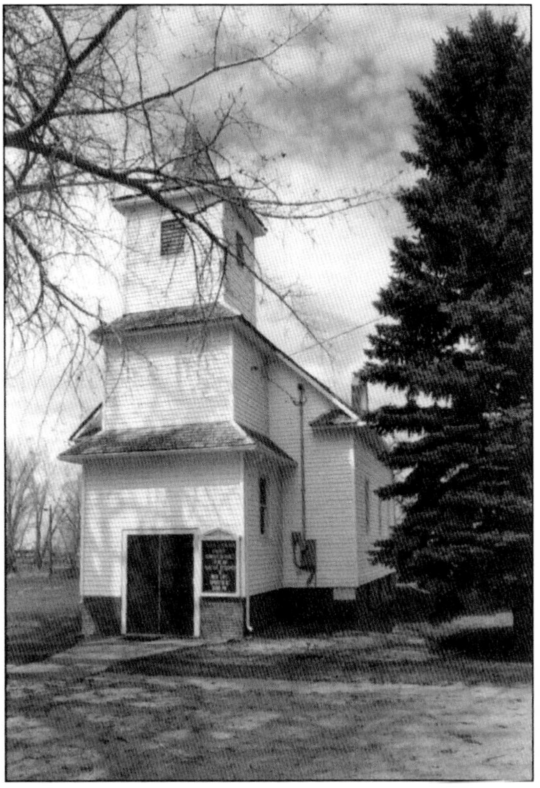

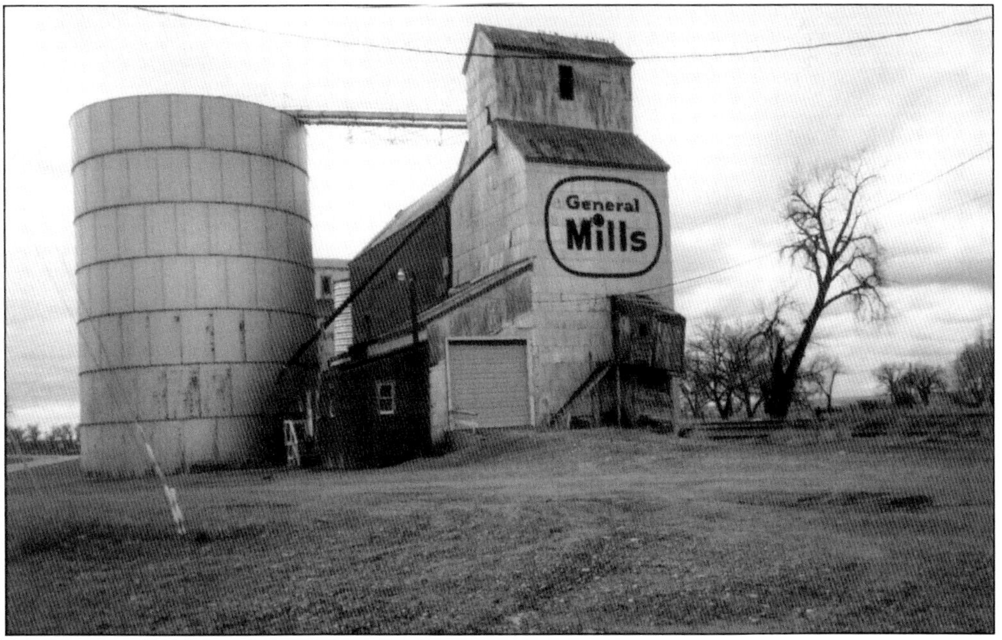

In addition to storing grain to later be put on a train and shipped elsewhere, grain elevators were also an indication of prosperity and hope for the future. The General Mills and Cowan and Son grain elevators stood in Box Elder for many years; however, they were razed in 1998. (Photograph by Emily Mayer.)

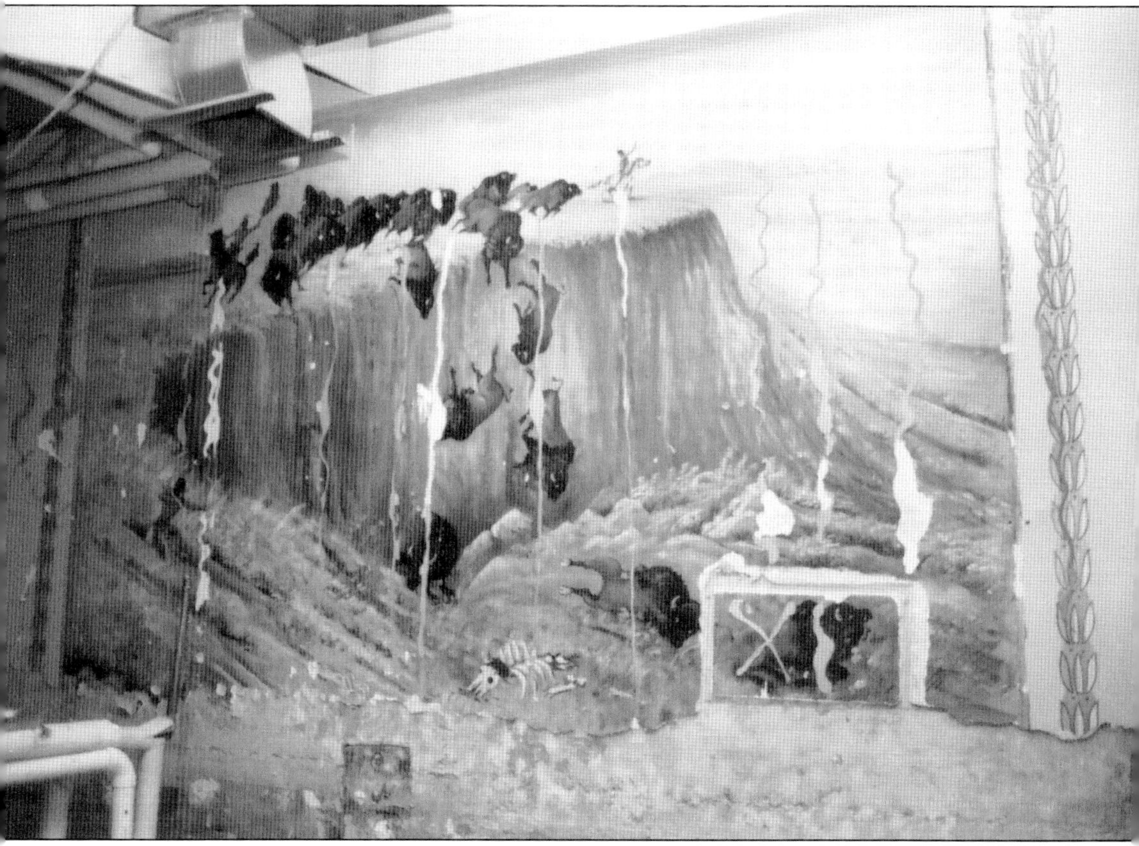

In 1964, Arvid Kristoffersen was asked by the Hill County commissioners to paint murals and various borders throughout the courthouse, replacing most of the old murals that were there. The final mural he painted was a buffalo jump located in the basement of the courthouse. A 1977 renovation of the courthouse covered over the mural, which was rediscovered in 2007. (Photograph by Emily Mayer.)

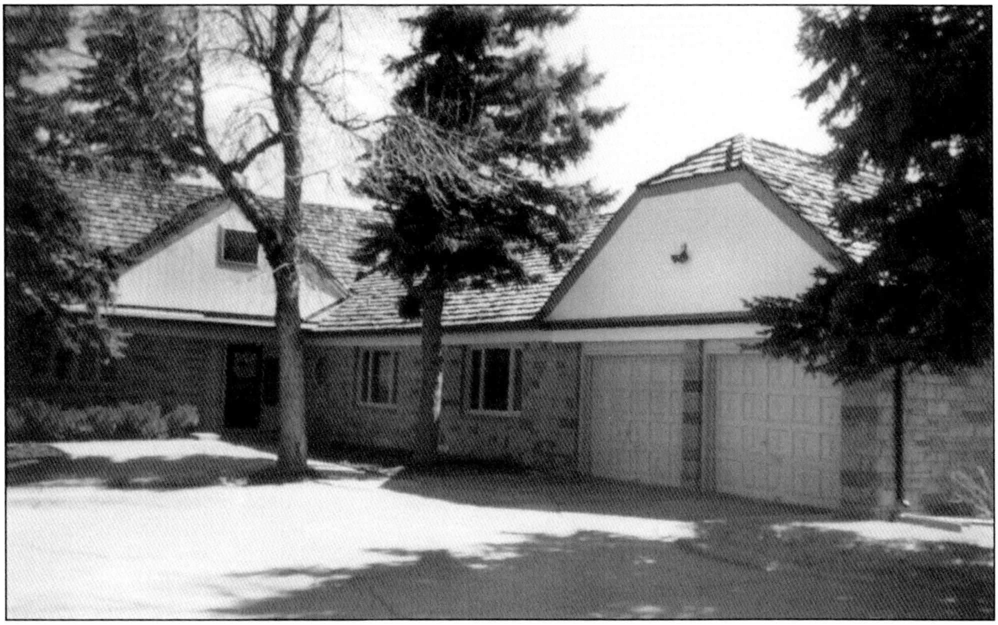

The Dr. G. A. and Mrs. Jestrab Home was located in an area called "Pill Hill" for the number of doctors living there. In honor of his profession, the snake-and-staff symbol was incorporated into the panels of the garage door. The home was completed in 1952 and in the 1970s became the home for the president of Northern Montana College. In 2000, the building sustained structural damage resulting from a water break. It was later demolished. (Photograph by Emily Mayer.)

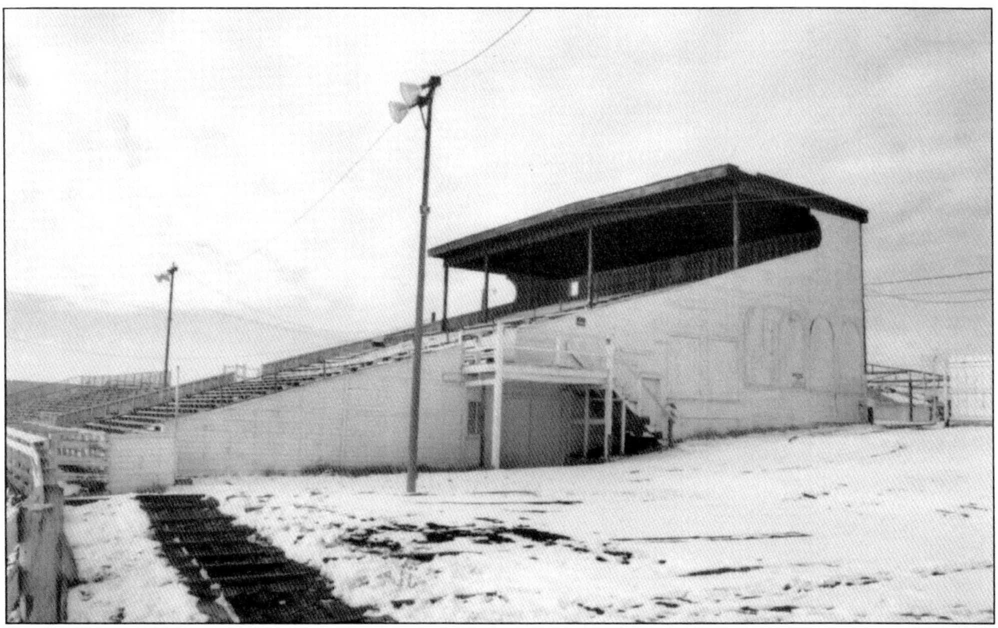

The Grandstand at the Great Northern Fairgrounds held spectators for rodeos, demolition derbies, horse races, circuses, concerts, and other popular activities for many years. It was constructed of wood, and an area below the bleachers was last used to exhibit school projects submitted for the fair. It fell into disrepair, and due to concerns over safety, it was razed on February 26, 2005. (Photograph by Emily Mayer.)

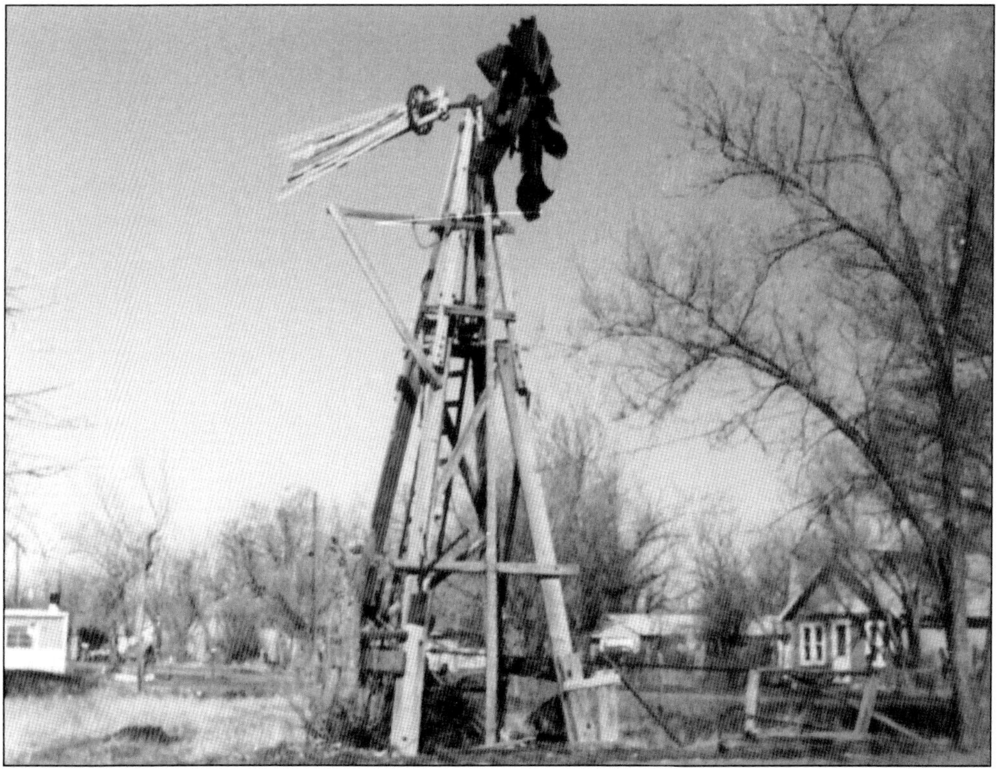

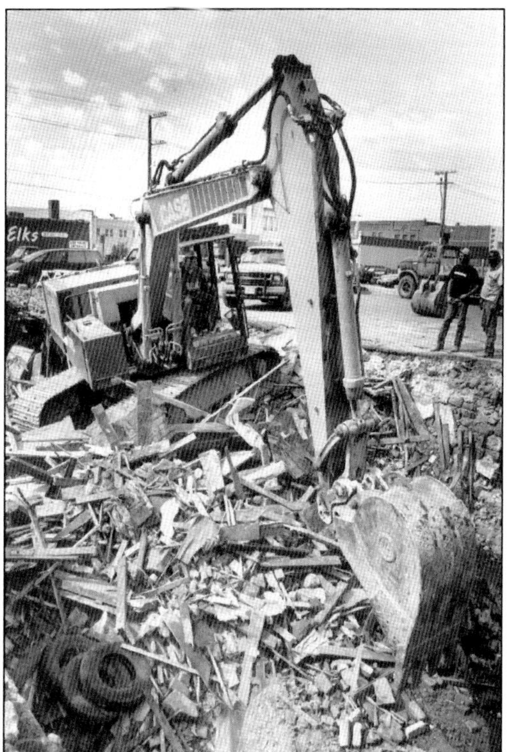

The north side of Havre between the railroad tracks and the Milk River is home to some of the area's hardest working people. They are also resourceful. Paul Erickson built this windmill out of an old Model T Ford. The windmill stood for many years on Fourth Street North. One recent Halloween was very windy—so much so that the old windmill couldn't take the strength of the wind and came crashing down. (Courtesy of Paula Kase.)

On September 23, 1994, the old Mansfield Hotel collapsed from structural failure. While there were no injuries, some cars parked next to the building sustained significant damage. Issues developed over who was going to clean up the site. Due to safety concerns to the public, the City of Havre cleaned up the site and assessed the cost on the property. The amount owed was later forgiven by the city council for the downtown park. (Courtesy of *Havre Daily News*.)

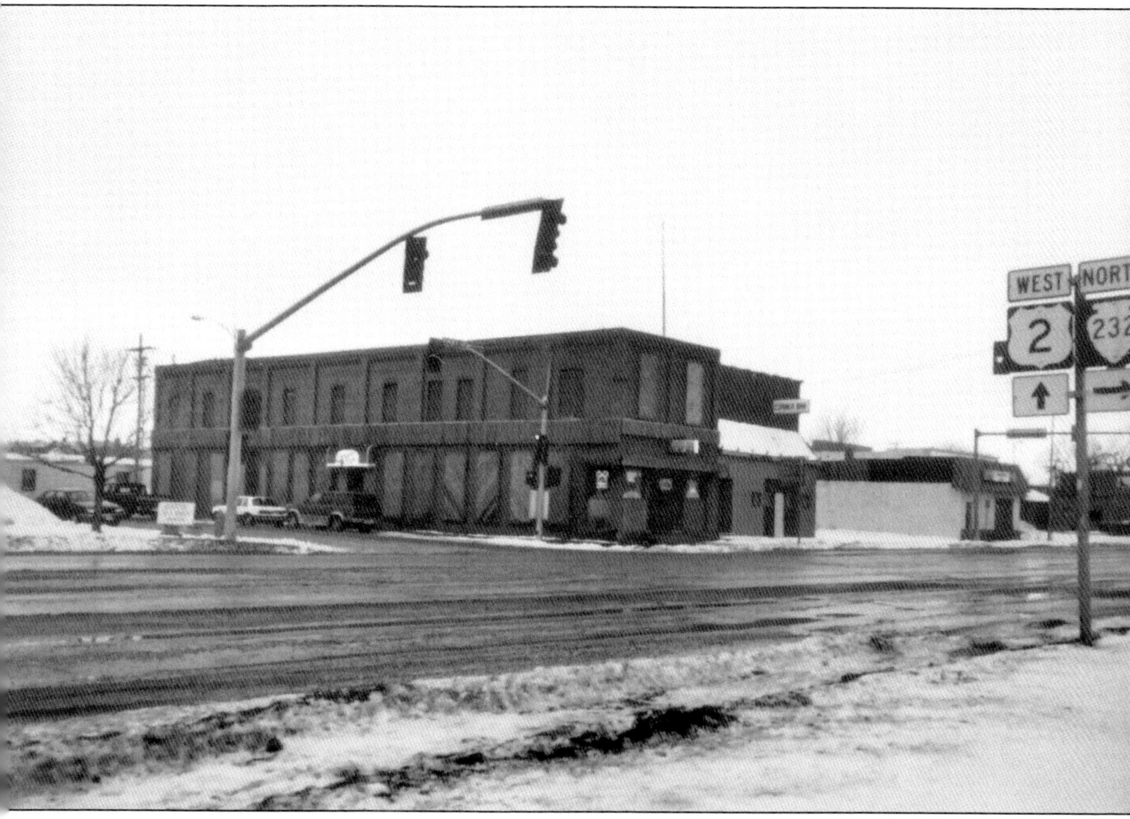

The Corner Bar, once an icon on First Street, was originally the First and Last Chance Saloons, owned by Louie and Frankie Granier, respectively. Constructed of brick in 1913, the building saw many uses over the years. The Arlyss Apartments were located on the second floor. The Corner Bar was one of Havre's most lively establishments before it closed, and the building subsequently was razed in 2006. (Photograph by Emily Mayer.)

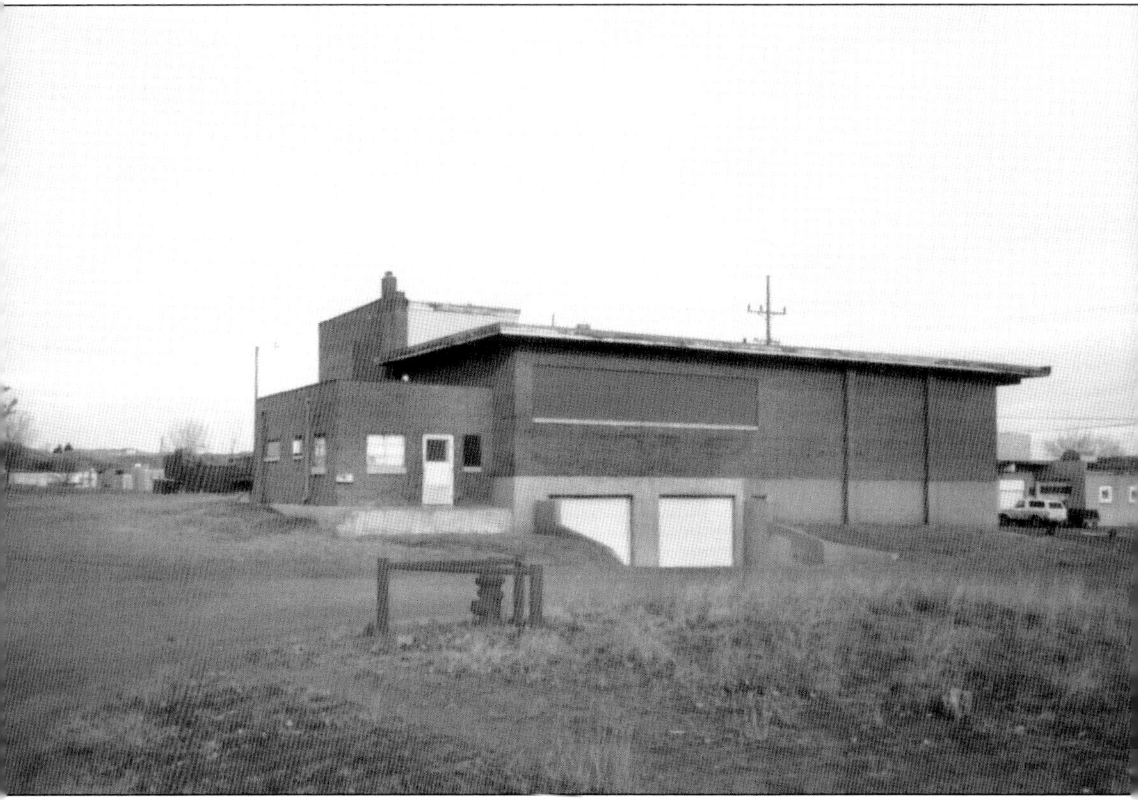

Rocky Mountain Packing Company encompassed an entire city block and was most famous for its Rocky Mountain hot dogs, a popular local treat. There was a slaughterhouse, a meat cutting area, and a wholesale room, later to include retail sales within the complex. It was razed in 2007. (Photograph by Emily Mayer.)

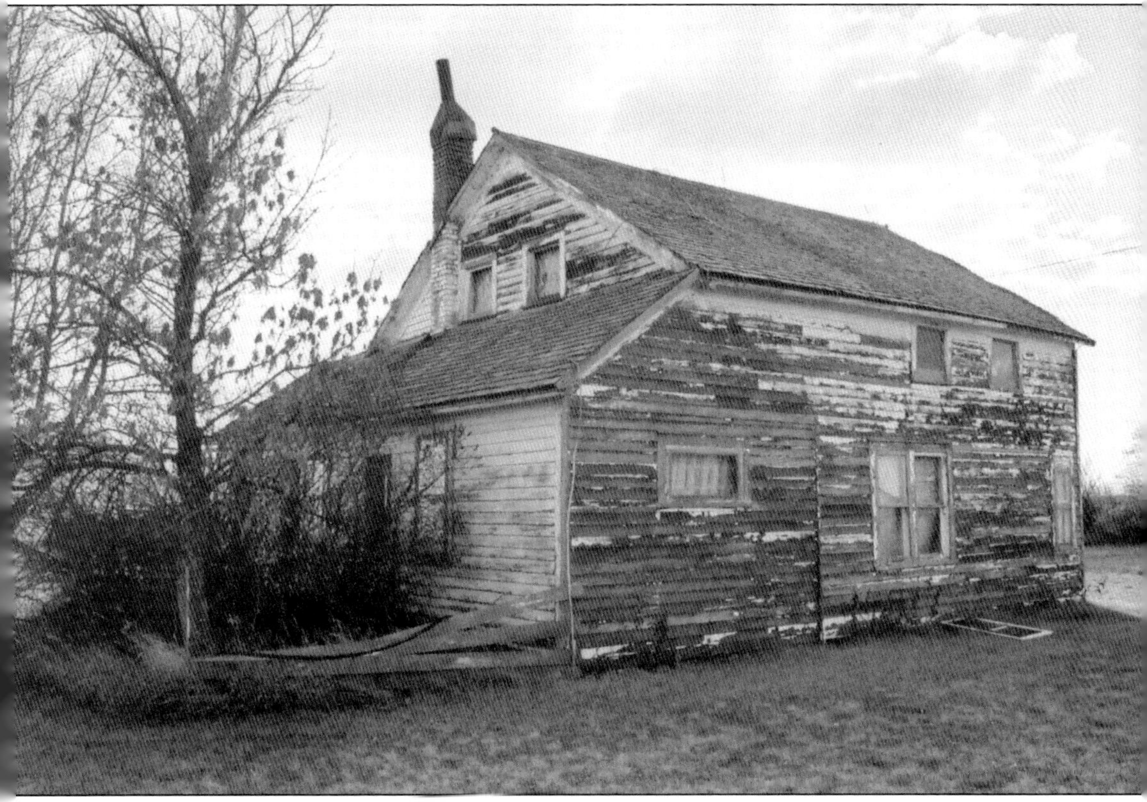

The Cady homestead, located between Kremlin and Gildford on the south side of Highway 2, is a good example of homesteader ingenuity. The original homestead was to the front of the home and over the years was added on to, including incorporating the former Xenia school into the structure. It was razed in 2006. (Photograph by Emily Mayer.)

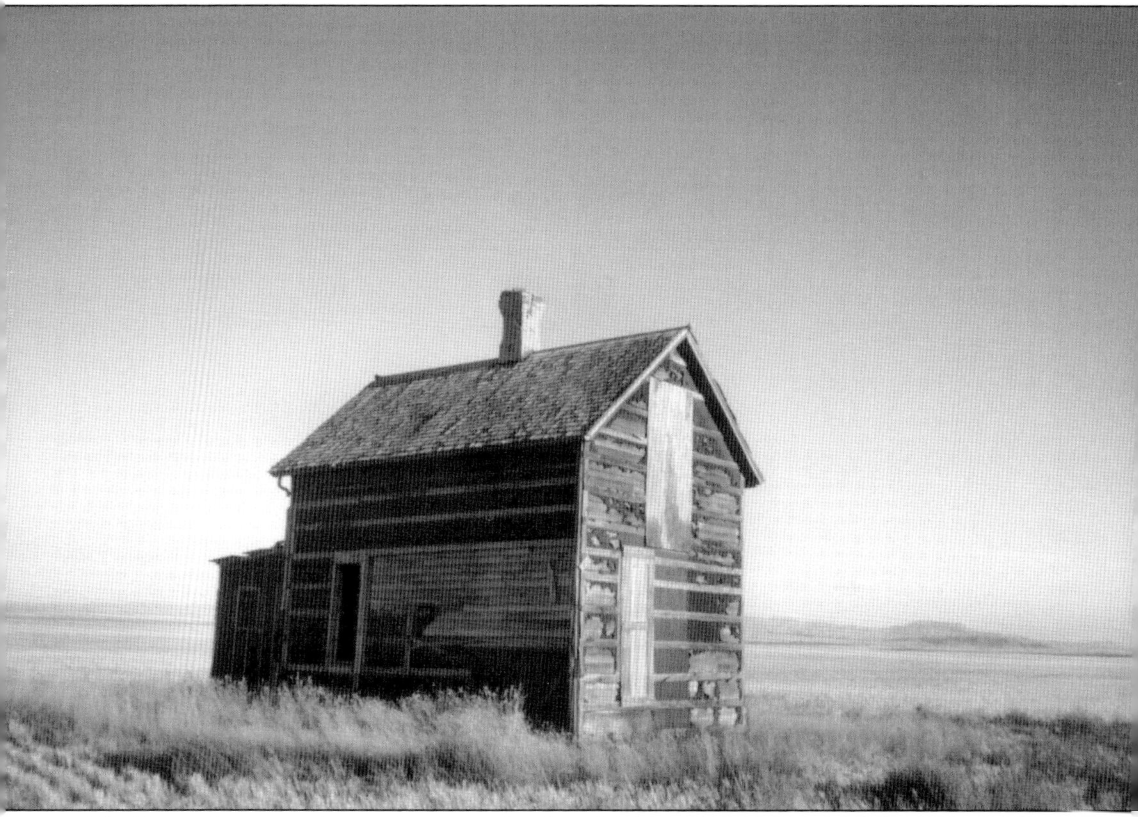

The Fenton homestead was a familiar sight along Highway 2 near Kremlin. The two-story home indicates the homesteader had a little more financial means than those who constructed the usual 16-by-16-foot structure needed in order to "prove up" on the property. It was burned in 2006. (Photograph by Emily Mayer.)

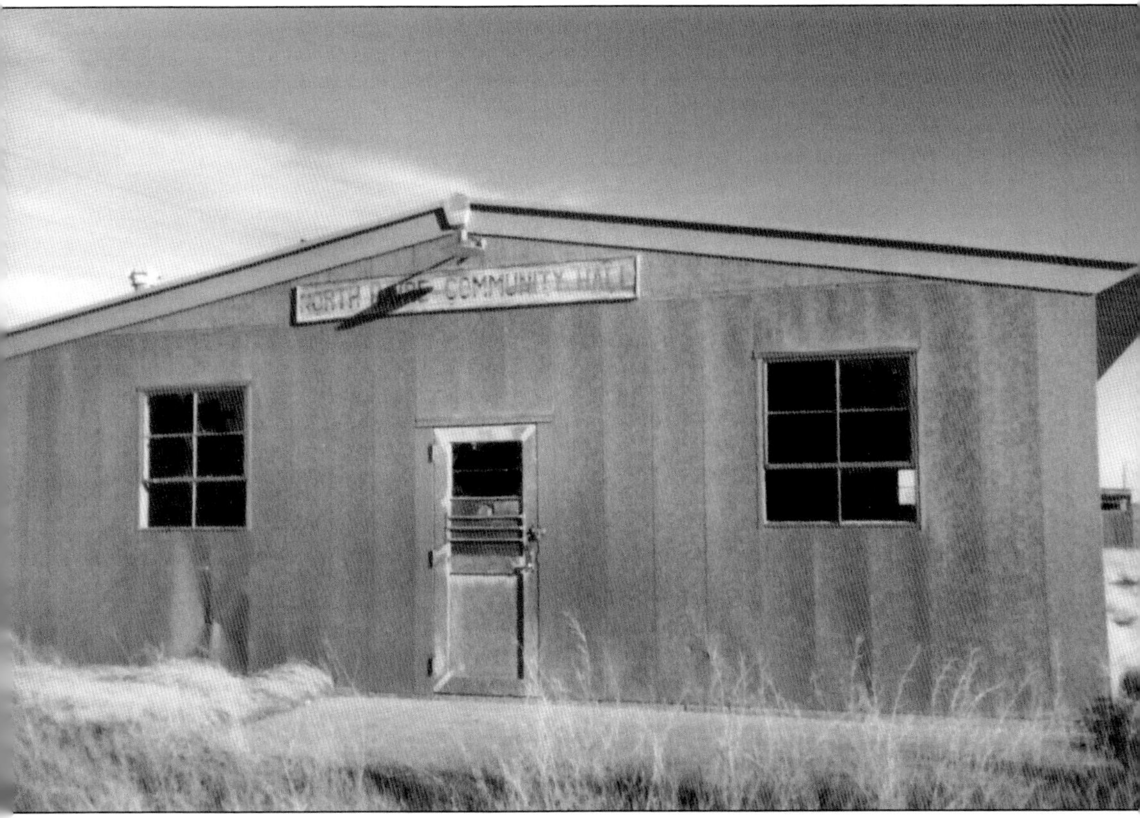

The North Havre Community Hall was located on the St. Joe Road and was a popular gathering place for those living in the area. Dances, music, food, and neighbors all gathered for what is best described as "good, clean family fun." As the population of the area dwindled, the building was no longer used and sat vacant for many years. It was moved near Chinook, Montana. (Photograph by Emily Mayer.)

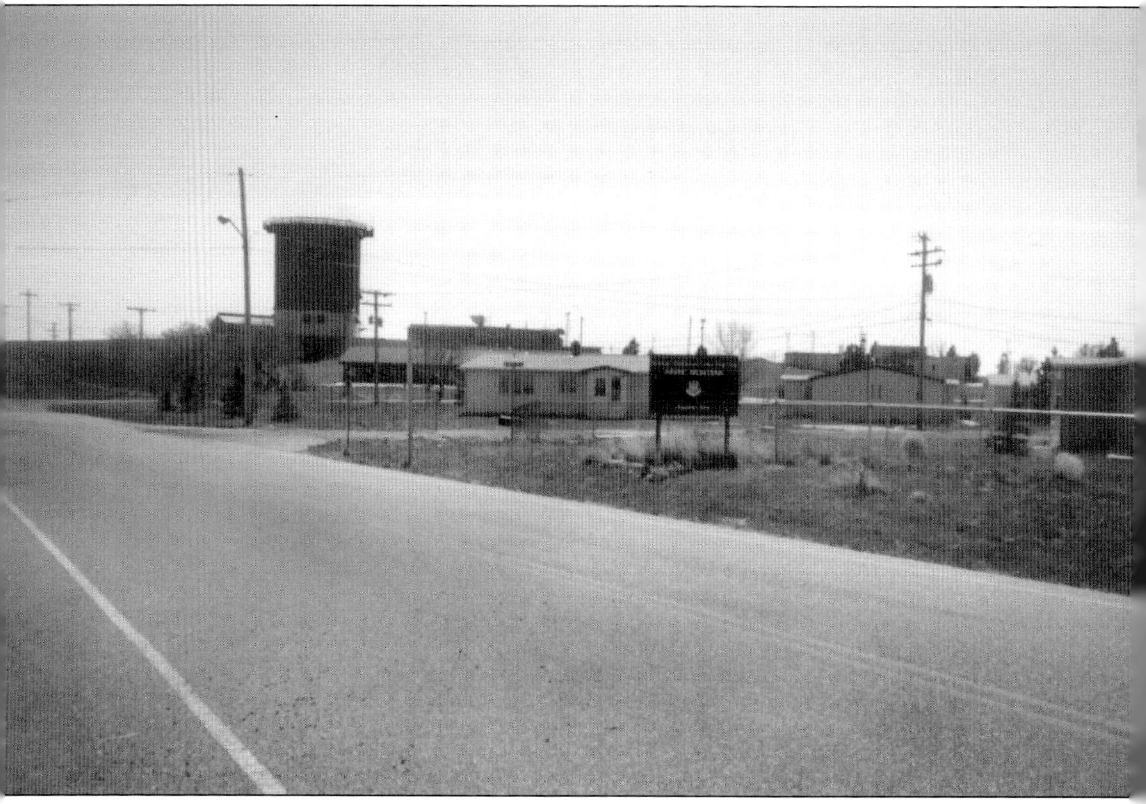

The Havre Air Base, located north of Havre close to the Canadian border, served as a radar station looking for enemy aircraft. During a phase of military downsizing, the Havre Air Base was decommissioned and several uses were proposed for the site. Many of the homes were moved to other places, such as Rocky Boy, Box Elder, Fort Belknap, and Havre. The Anchor Academy for Boys occupied the site for a few years. (Photograph by Emily Mayer.)

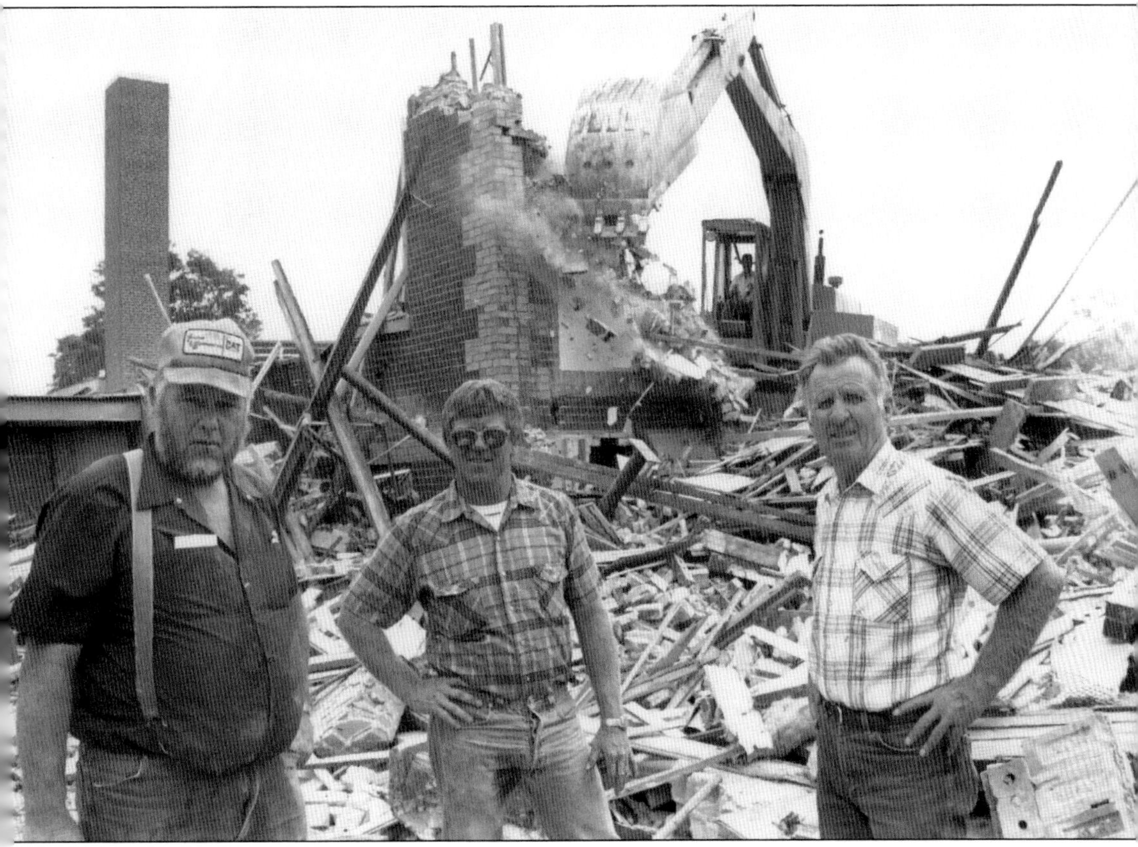

Devlin School was constructed in 1912 because of the increasing number of students in Havre. It was named after L. K. Devlin, a longtime supporter of public schools in Havre. In 1995, the Havre School Board decided to demolish the 1912 Devlin School and keep the 1954 addition. Assisting in the demolition are, from left to right, Richard Smith, Bill Henry, and Bill Baltrusch. (Courtesy of *Havre Daily News*.)

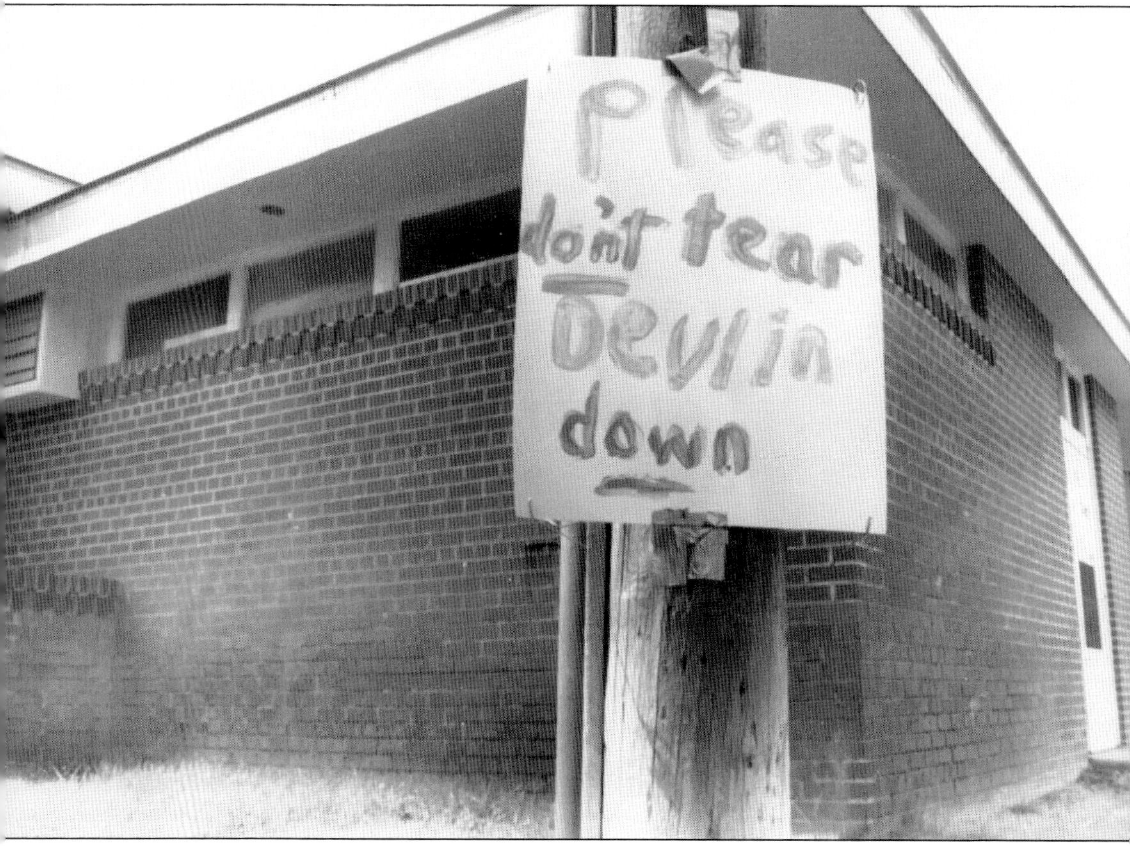

The decision to demolish Devlin School was not without controversy. Concerned citizens wrote letters to the editor, requested the school board to reverse their decision, and circulated petitions, and Pete Kuhr filed a petition with the district court to delay demolition. The intent was to allow for further study of the structure and its cost effectiveness. The board refused to reconsider, and it was demolished in July 1995. (Courtesy of *Havre Daily News.*)

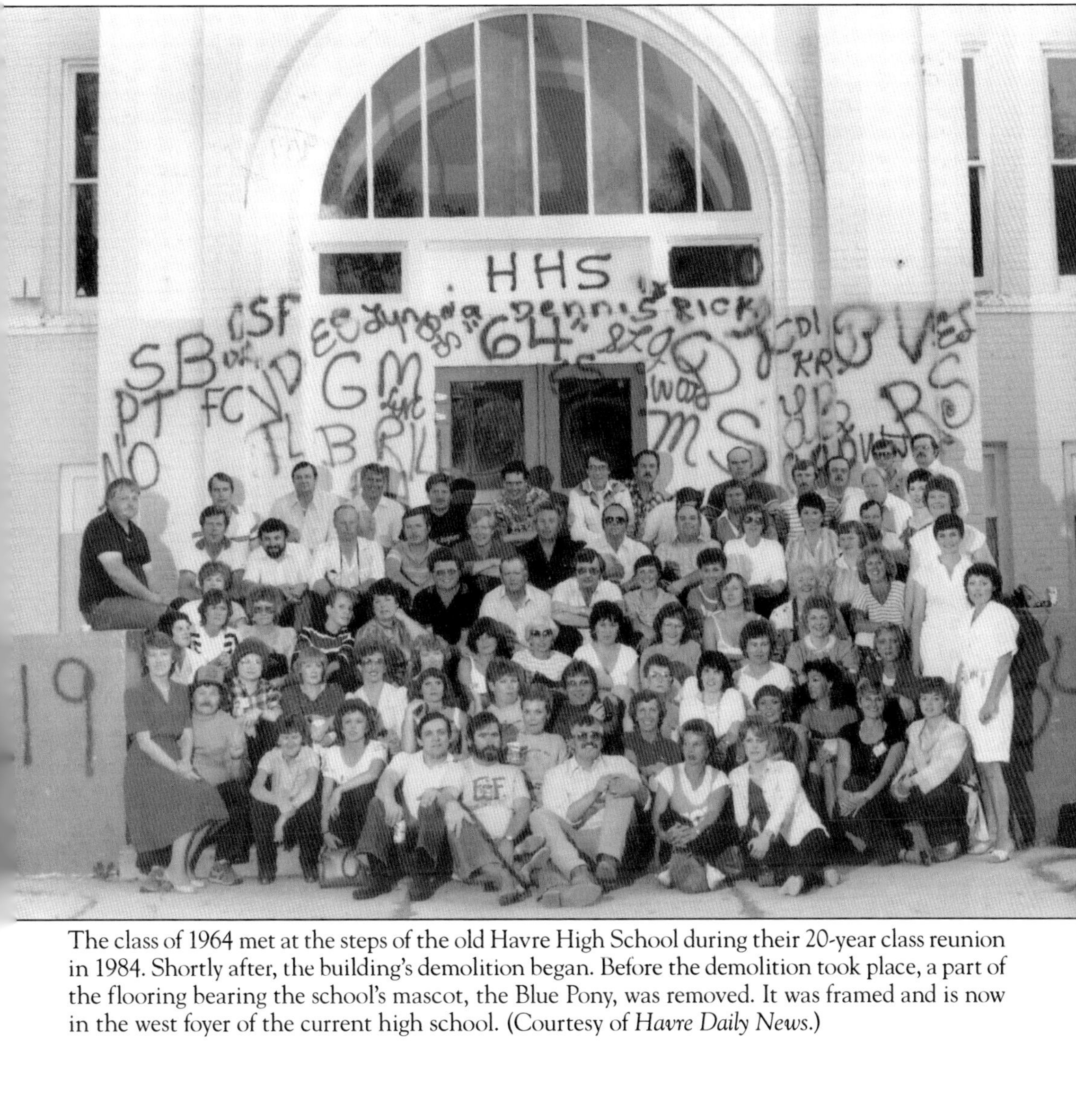

The class of 1964 met at the steps of the old Havre High School during their 20-year class reunion in 1984. Shortly after, the building's demolition began. Before the demolition took place, a part of the flooring bearing the school's mascot, the Blue Pony, was removed. It was framed and is now in the west foyer of the current high school. (Courtesy of *Havre Daily News*.)